Doing Qualitative Research in Psychology

Doing Qualitative Research in Psychology

A Practical Guide

Edited by
Michael Forrester

Los Angeles | London | New Delhi
Singapore | Washington DC

SAGE Publications Ltd
1 Oliver's Yard
55 City Road
London EC1Y 1SP

SAGE Publications Inc.
2455 Teller Road
Thousand Oaks, California 91320

SAGE Publications India Pvt Ltd
B 1/I 1 Mohan Cooperative Industrial Area
Mathura Road
New Delhi 110 044

SAGE Publications Asia-Pacific Pte Ltd
3 Church Street
#10-04 Samsung Hub
Singapore 049483

Library of Congress Control Number: 2009934722

British Library Cataloguing in Publication data

A catalogue record for this book is available from the British Library

ISBN 978-1-84787-910-3
ISBN 978-1-84787-911-0 (pbk)

Typeset by Glyph International Pvt Ltd., Bangalore, India
Printed and bound by CPI Group (UK) Ltd, Croydon, CR0 4YY
Printed on paper from sustainable resources

FSC
www.fsc.org
MIX
Paper from
responsible sources
FSC® C013604

Contents

Chapter Overview

Chapter 1: This Book and How to Use It

Introduction
    Background to qualitative methods in psychology
How is the book structured and why?
How might I read this book and why?
Chapter learning hints, aids and guidelines
Concluding comment

Chapter 2: Theory and Method in Qualitative Research

Introduction
Psychology, science and philosophy
    Psychology and scientific method
    Where does philosophy come into all this?
Approaches to building a body of knowledge
    Positivism
    Relativist social constructionism
    Attempts to move beyond the relativism–realism debate
    Summary
Theoretical issues
    The relationship between language, reality and thought
    Experience and how we can explore it
    Summary
Summary points

Chapter 3: Conducting Literature Reviews

Introduction
    Why conduct a literature review?
    What does conducting a literature review involve?
Searching the evidence base
    Refining your research question and identifying keywords
    Writing and refining your search strategy
    Screening search results for relevance
    Obtaining full-text articles
    What about Google and Google Scholar?
    Critically evaluating the evidence
    Why is quality important?
    What criteria are used to assess quality?

Constructing your literature review
   Structuring your review
   Building a rationale and presenting your research question
Summary points

Chapter 4: Approaches to Data Collection in Qualitative Research

Introduction
What is data?
How do I collect data?
   Focus groups
   Naturalistic data
   Media data
   Internet data
Visual data
Summary points

Chapter 5: The Interview in Qualitative Research

Introduction
Types of interviewing
Understanding interviews: Some conceptual points
Interviews as excavation
Interviews as co-constructed
Doing interviews: The starting point
Recruiting for interviews
Preparing questions
Conducting the interview
Summary points

Chapter 6: Research Ethics in Qualitative Research

Introduction
What do we mean by research ethics?
Research ethics in psychology
   Informed consent
   Confidentiality
   Right to withdraw
   Assessing risk of harm
   Researcher safety
   Deception
   Debriefing
   Limitations to the researcher's role
   Use of incentives
   Honesty and integrity in the research process

Chapter 7: Introducing the Data Set

Chapter 8: QM1: Discourse Analysis

Chapter 9: QM2: Grounded Theory

Introduction
Background
  Defining grounded theory
Sample analysis extract
Analysis
  Memo writing
  Early in the analysis phase
  Analysis through the project
  Wrapping things up
Coding
  Open coding
  Axial coding
  Generating theory
Writing up the analysis
Summary points

Chapter 10: QM3: Interpretative Phenomenological Analysis

Introduction
Background
  Understanding human experience
  Double hermeneutic
  Case study approach
  Sample analysis extract
Analysis
  Initial thoughts on reflection and quality
  Familiarising yourself with the data
  Identifying initial themes
  Writing descriptive summaries
  Making initial interpretations
  Clustering themes
  Establishing the final themes
  Continuing with other cases
Writing up the analysis
Summary points

Chapter 11: QM4: Conversation Analysis

Introduction
  Sample analysis extract
Background
  Taking turns in conversation: How people use a 'locally managed system'
  Sequence in conversation
  Structures in conversation

Figures and Tables

Figures

Tables

Contributors

Colm Crowley is a senior lecturer in the Department of Psychology and Counselling at the University of Greenwich

Michael Forrester is a senior lecturer in the School of Psychology at the University of Kent.

Stephen Gibson is a senior lecturer in the Faculty of Health and Life Sciences, York St John University

Alasdair Gordon-Finlayson is a postgraduate researcher and tutor in the School of Psychology, Liverpool John Moore's University

Siobhan Hugh-Jones is a lecturer in developmental psychology at the Institute of Psychological Sciences, University of Leeds

Nigel King is professor in applied psychology, human and health sciences, at the University of Huddersfield

Rachel Shaw is a lecturer in psychology in the School of Life and Health Sciences, Aston University

Cath Sullivan is a senior lecturer in Psychology in the School of Psychology at the University of Central Lancashire

Sarah Riley is a lecturer in the Department of Psychology, University of Bath

Sally Wiggins is a lecturer in the Department of Psychology at the University of Strathclyde

Preface

There is a good chance that if you are reading these words, then you are probably a psychology student who wants to learn about qualitative methods and how to use them. This book will make sure you can, but it's not just another research methods book – it is much more akin to a 'how to do it' manual – a book linked with a specifically designed set of digitised video-recordings, transcripts and online resources to make learning about these methods as easy as possible.

Well, you might ask, what are these resources and why are they relevant or even useful?

The primary resources are a set of video-recorded interviews produced by the authors and designed to support your learning. From the beginning, as lecturers and teachers in psychology, we understood that it can be quite challenging for students to grasp, in an accessible way, why psychologists use qualitative methods and what exactly might be done with them. To help explain things, we designed and produced a set of student-focused interviews that form a baseline data set, or data resource, so that readers can see quite quickly how a particular method is used and the kind of analysis that can be done. We didn't, however, simply produce a set of online, downloadable video-recordings, useful as these are for using this book. Alongside the recordings, which are interviews with students who are discussing friendship and what friends mean to them, we created a full set of transcripts of the actual conversations. Transcripts form the major component of analysis for the qualitative methods you will learn about in this book. And in order to show how different methods call for distinct kinds of transcripts, we have produced two alternative sets for each of the online video recordings. You will find examining the transcripts invaluable when using the book.

To access the resources go to: http://www.psychology.heacademy.ac.uk/ Webdocs_not_nof/tqrmul/dataset/ and you will be able to view the videos directly on the Web or download them for saving on your own computer. You will also find audio-only versions of the interviews, again for downloading or listening online, and the full transcripts for each interview.

These resources are central to the book because they serve as exemplar material typical of the sort of research that a qualitative researcher might do, that is, conducting everyday informal interviews and asking people how they understand this or that particular issue. This is important, because in our experience undergraduate courses in psychology rarely provide the opportunity for extensive data collection using qualitative methods. Doing laboratory-based work and practical demonstrations in psychology classes often means that it is difficult to find the time and resources to conduct full-length interviews, record them and make full transcripts. Again, we understood that if an easily accessible set of such interviews could be made available to the student beginning qualitative methods, then class activities could focus on understanding how different approaches, with their associated forms of analysis, would examine on the material.

This of course does not mean that data collection is not central to qualitative methods, only that in some circumstances it is difficult to achieve in the short term. The book and the data resources can be used in at least three contexts familiar to undergraduate psychology students:

(a) As a foundational element of a first- or second-year research methods course with the specific aim of learning to use at least one qualitative method in detail (e.g., doing a practical class focused on a qualitative method). We recognise that qualitative methods are often taught within a general research methods course, with a typical class or study involving learning how to employ one qualitative method during a half-semester period (around six weeks). This book can be used very successfully by students working within such contexts.

(b) As the main text on a first- or second-year qualitative methods course, whereby students can be introduced to, and gain experience in conducting, a number of qualitative methods. It would be an ideal text and resource set for an accompanying series of lectures in a qualitative methods course.

(c) As a primary data resource for a more detailed final-year project or dissertation. Here, the online resources could form an initial data source for a final-year project in the area of friendship, social relations or social interaction. Alternatively, it can be seen as supplementing a range of possible topics in social psychology, discourse analysis, pragmatics and sociolinguistic areas of the discipline (e.g., communication research). Final-year students carrying out interview-based projects will find examining in detail the interviews, and the example analyses, invaluable for their own research.

The book and online resources can also be used as a supplementary element of qualitative methods courses in sociology, social anthropology and social sciences. It is important, however, to recognise that this book is designed as a practical guide in learning how to *do* qualitative research in psychology – it is not meant to be a comprehensive qualitative analysis of the interview-based data set itself. Nor does it attempt to provide a comprehensive view of *all* qualitative methods to be found in the discipline. The focus is very much on those that are most commonly used in contemporary undergraduate and postgraduate (masters level) psychology teaching. The book is also *not* designed to examine in depth many of the theories and ideas forming the background to qualitative research and qualitative methods. There are numerous other books in psychology which provide such detail, and these are referred to throughout the present book.

As the focus is on practice and 'doing', a major element of the book aims to show you how different methods are used, and the forms of analysis they involve. You will see that although the different methods we describe are being used with the same data set, the research questions that might be asked are different, the forms of analysis distinct to the method employed, and, needless to say, the kinds of answers emerging from the analysis particular to the questions being posed.

In both qualitative and quantitative research, the nature of the question being asked will in part determine the kind of method you will use in order to answer that question. This should never be forgotten.

The student-friendship interview data set also serves as the backbone theme through the various chapters of the book. Needless to say, qualitative research involves many stages, and again, it is often rather difficult to recognise each of these stages and how they relate together. Here, we examine all those key parts of doing qualitative research, such as how to conduct interviews, understand relevant ethical issues, search for relevant literature or write up a qualitative report. And again, what is unique about this book is that in each of the chapters, wherever ideas or issues might be further explained through examples, then extracts drawn from the data set are used. You can go online to see such extracts for yourself, or download them, and see exactly what is being referred to. There is nothing quite like viewing dynamic interaction 'as it happened' to help you recognise a particular point that a qualitative researcher might be making. If you have never used a qualitative method before, or wish to learn about a method you are unfamiliar with, then you need look no further. Simply read on.

Michael Forrester
Cantebury, Kent
December, 2009

1

This Book and How to Use It

Michael Forrester

Introduction

This book is all about qualitative methods in psychology and how these methods can be applied to help answer research questions. The first thing to note about the title of the book, of course, is the focus on 'doing', that is, learning how to conduct research studies that use qualitative methods. There are numerous other books that focus on qualitative approaches in psychology; however, they tend to focus on theory rather than practice. The second thing to note is that we are concerned with doing qualitative research 'in psychology'; so our aim is to provide a text for psychologists, psychology students and anyone else interested in understanding how qualitative research methods are used within psychology. This introductory chapter is best seen as a brief introduction to qualitative methods in psychology followed by a guide on how to get the best out of the various sections of the book.

Divided into four parts – formulating research questions; conducting qualitative research; qualitative analysis; and writing up qualitative reports – the chapters that make up this text reflect the logic, procedures and practices surrounding the whole process of doing qualitative research in psychology. You can see, with a quick glance through the part and chapter headings, that every stage of the whole process is given due consideration. Certainly, by paying considered attention to all sections of the book you will be in an excellent position to understand exactly what to do to conduct a study employing qualitative methods. The most significant feature of this book, however, is the specifically designed accompanying data set produced to enhance your understanding of what can be achieved through the use of the various different methods. The teaching and learning ethos we adopted for this book reflected our recognition that it is often difficult – particularly for students of psychology, where quantitative methods tend to predominate – to see precisely what one or other specific qualitative method might accomplish when trying to answer or address a research question.

Our response to this problem was to produce a set of video-recordings of informal interviews, with accompanying full transcriptions, on an everyday topic – friendship – and make these available in an accessible format (online). Then, through a detailed outline and description of four qualitative methods, we highlight the nature of the different approaches, the procedures they use, the theoretical perspectives they adopt and the distinct forms of analysis they employ. Thus a major feature of this text is the four chapters in Part 3 where the same data set (the interviews on friendship) is analysed using each of the four qualitative methods: Discourse Analysis; Grounded Theory; Interpretative Phenomenological Analysis; and Conversation Analysis.

Needless to say, of course, carrying out a small portion of the analysis on a set of interviews would not constitute a full or complete qualitative research project. So, it is important to begin to see the links between each section of the book and recognise that an appropriately conducted qualitative research project or study will contain elements from all of the chapters. Before outlining some important links between the various parts and chapters, we provide an overview and some background to qualitative methods in psychology.

Background to qualitative methods in psychology

Although the use of qualitative methods in psychology has increased dramatically in recent years, there is in fact a long history of such methods being employed in the discipline. In clinical psychology, for example, we find the clinical case-study, the important place of supervision practices as well as examples of observational and participant-observational studies. Likewise, in developmental psychology there is a long history of diary studies, observational methods, single-case studies of children and research looking at children in naturalistic surroundings (e.g., playgrounds). Other examples are to be found in the discipline: in personality research we have personal construct methods such as repertory grid analysis; in applied psychology, verbal protocol and related forms of content analysis; and in ergonomics, qualitatively based methods such as usability analysis.

However, apart from the clinical case-study, which some indeed have described as a form of narrative analysis (Schafer, 1981), the application and use of the methods described above (e.g., observational methods using time-sampling procedures) lent themselves to quantitative summary analysis – that is, counting, comparing and drawing statistically defensible inferences from these procedures. In other words, these are all methods that psychologists recognise as similar procedures within the same methodological enterprise – one that emphasised the empirical foundations of social science. Since the early behaviourists, psychology had been somewhat sceptical, or even scathing, of any scientific method or procedure that might suggest an over-reliance on interpretation or subjectivity (e.g., introspection). This has been the case within the discipline since the early twentieth century. However, the situation has gradually changed, especially since the early 1980s, with the emergence and predominance of discursive or language-focused qualitative methods – the ones described and used in this book.

There are a number of reasons behind the gradual introduction and use of qualitative methods that have language or discourse as the main focus, and that bring to the fore forms of analysis which are both interpretative and empirically grounded. These can be summarised as:

(i) indications of a 'turn-to-language' in psychology;
(ii) the critique from within social psychology of the epistemological foundations of social–cognitive perspectives and the emergence of discursive psychology;
(iii) criticisms from within cognitive psychology regarding the limits of the experimental laboratory (e.g., ecological validity); and
(iv) the influence of other social science disciplines where interpretative qualitative methods are more common (e.g., sociology, social anthropology).

Let us consider each of these factors that have influenced the emergence of qualitative methods in psychology.

(i) The 'turn-to-language' in psychology. Within psychology, the study of language had traditionally been dominated by the early work of Noam Chomsky on grammar, the emergence of an experimentally focused psycholinguistics, and the view that language should be considered very much as an individualistic, formal, object-like entity, simply serving cognitively based thought processes during communication. However, within the social sciences and the humanities and in disciplines such as English, social anthropology, sociology and linguistics, this view of language had been supplanted by an approach – or one should say a variety of different perspectives – which focused very much on language as an organic social practice. This 'turn-to-language' placed centre-stage the study of collective discursive practices and represented the philosophical questioning and critique of modernism found in the writings of Derrida, Wittgenstein, Foucault, Merle-Ponty, Husserl and others. For the most, part psychology appeared unaffected by such developments outside the discipline but gradually – and particularly from within social psychology – researchers began to consider the implications of this approach to language (Billig, 1990; Edwards & Potter, 1993). Social psychology itself (in Europe) began to differentiate into experimental social psychology and discursive social psychology.

The important point to recognise is that this 'turn-to-language' is not meant to describe the interest within cognitive psychology and cognitive science with language as a formal object, but instead the increasing focus on understanding all those social practices which make up discourse as action – one could say, with the function and meaning of discourse as language use in everyday life.

(ii) Critique of social cognition and the emergence of discursive psychology. A second theme, which has had a bearing on the kinds of qualitative methods now found in psychology, was the emergence of discursive psychology. Dissatisfied with the pre-theoretical assumptions of information processing psychology, a number of notable criticisms of the dominant cognitive orientation of the discipline began to appear

(Potter & Wetherell, 1987; Edwards, 1997). Emphasising the socially constructed nature of theory, methods and research in psychology, these writers outlined an approach to science and scientific research, which highlighted the fact that the whole enterprise is always a set of interdependent contextualised social practices. They argued that psychological research should focus on what people actually say and do – *not* with trying to discover whatever might lie 'behind' people's actions and interactions. Studying people in context, and recording and analysing in detail how they make sense of, construct and describe their social worlds, became the primary research focus.

(iii) Real-world relevance and ecological validity. Alongside the developments taking place in social psychology, within cognitive psychology in the 1970s and 1980s there was growing disquiet over the extent to which results from relatively artificial experimental situations could be generalised to what happens in the real world. Ulrich Neisser coined the term 'ecological validity' to draw attention to the fact that all too often it was very hard to tell if what happened under controlled experimental conditions necessarily approximated to other situations. As he put it,

> the concept of ecological validity has become familiar to psychologists. It reminds them that the artificial situation created for an experiment may differ from the everyday world in crucial ways. When this is so, the results may be irrelevant to the phenomena that one would really like to explain. (Neisser, 1976, p. 33)

Although the debate over whether experimental studies should develop procedures whereby the correspondence between what happens in the laboratory and outside of it could be formally established began to dissipate by the late 1990s, the metaphor of ecological validity had gained credibility in the discipline. Increasingly, people – particularly those in applied branches such as occupational, clinical and health psychology – began to move away from an over-reliance on experimental design and associated procedures as necessarily being the most appropriate way to answer a particular question.

(iv) The influence of other social science and humanities disciplines. Also important was the influence that came from those disciplines closest to psychology in the social sciences. Within sociology, qualitative methods have had a long and distinguished history where many now-common procedures first originated (e.g., participant observation studies and narrative analysis). The qualitatively focused work of sociologists such as Ervin Goffman and Harold Garfinkel have had considerable influence, not least through the work of the ethnomethodologists responsible for some of the earliest studies employing conversation analysis. Likewise, in sociolinguistics, the work of the critical discourse analysts has influenced contemporary research in discursive psychology, and field-study and ethnographic work from within social anthropology has also proved influential. Arguably, the lesson that has been learned from seeing how, when and why these disciplines have employed qualitative methods is that psychologists began to recognise how procedures sensitive to the task of detailing, describing and analysing people's sense-making practices

could be employed in realisably formal ways. And most importantly, the strategies and procedures that made up these methods could be employed in the service of producing research findings that were logical, defensible and accountable.

All the above factors have together influenced the emergence of qualitative methods in psychology. Alongside quantitative approaches, qualitative methods are now an essential part of the research methods that psychologists employ. The aim of this book is to help you learn how to use them successfully so as to answer the kinds of questions psychologists often ask, as well as highlight the possibility that the practice of qualitative research can encourage in asking novel types of research questions.

How is the book structured and why?

The book is divided into sections reflecting four questions asked by many students (Figure 1.1).

Part 1 focuses on the whole business of formulating research questions, particularly on qualitative research in psychology, the theoretical underpinnings of the methods used and the topics, themes and issues addressed. In **Part 2**, we move to the pragmatics of actually doing qualitative research: what is involved in collecting data of many different kinds; how interviews are conducted; and the significance of thinking through ethical issues which warrant careful and considered attention when using these particular methods. The next section of the book, **Part 3**, describes four qualitative methods in detail and shows you how analysis will differ not only because of the questions you might be asking, but also because of the specific analytic focus the approach has. Finally, in **Part 4** we highlight how you would write up a qualitative method report in psychology, one that summarises the research you have carried out according to conventions and formats appropriate to the discipline.

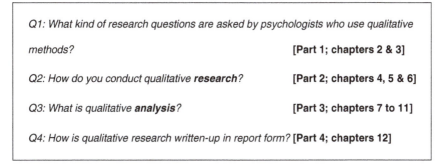

Q1: What kind of research questions are asked by psychologists who use qualitative

methods?   [Part 1; chapters 2 & 3]

Q2: How do you conduct qualitative **research**?   [Part 2; chapters 4, 5 & 6]

Q3: What is qualitative **analysis**?   [Part 3; chapters 7 to 11]

Q4: How is qualitative research written-up in report form? [Part 4; chapters 12]

Figure 1.1   Questions students ask.

How might I read this book and why?

First of all, before you make a start on Part 1, it makes a lot of sense to know what you are doing; that is, what kind of theory and perspective have you adopted simply by just thinking up a possible question? Cath Sullivan sets the scene for you in Chapter 2 by sketching out the background assumptions that underscore psychological inquiry in the social and natural sciences. In other words, when you want to understand something and research a relevant topic it can help a great deal if you recognise what 'knowing' something entails (epistemology). All too often, researchers simply rush into doing something without taking a little time to be clear about what they are doing. Here you will learn how the ideas underlying research in psychology have particular implications for the kind of methodologies that are typically used. In this chapter, you will see how background philosophical views inform different theoretical perspectives in psychology and how this impacts on the research focus that is developed and the types of questions that are asked. Once you recognise the kind of theory and outlook you have adopted, the next stage is to find out much more about the topic.

In Chapter 3, we find Rachel Shaw describing how you go about finding things – what is already known about something, who might have researched it and what sorts of methods did they use? Most importantly, you want to be sure that the question you want to ask is worthwhile, will contribute to our growing knowledge of a topic, and needless to say, not be a question that somebody else has already answered. Of course, doing a literature search is something you would carry out no matter what methodology you were using; however, there are specific issues relevant for qualitative work which are key to understanding how to make sure your research is appropriately focused. In this chapter, we learn how to recognise high-quality work in a particular area, how to develop strategies for searching out relevant findings as well as seeing what is involved in carrying out a review of a relevant area. Without going through these very essential steps, it is very difficult to know whether what you set out to do is really the most appropriate and relevant research question you might want to ask.

This brings us logically to Part 2 of the text and three chapters focusing on how you conduct qualitative research – what is involved in data collection; what kinds of data might you wish to obtain; how do interviews work and how might you go about conducting some; what particular ethical issues and challenges are there in doing qualitative research; and what sort of steps would you take to ensure the highest level of respectful engagement when working with participants doing qualitative research? Beginning with consideration of data collection in Chapter 4, Stephen Gibson and Sarah Riley provide a succinct overview of the numerous sources available to you when seeking to collect data for a research topic using a qualitative method. From the start they ask you to think carefully about what exactly 'data' is, and what typical forms of data do we find in qualitative research. There is indeed a wide range: from interviewing to focus-group work, from data you might collect from the Internet to studies involving visual data, from recording everyday naturalistic contexts to a whole range of data that come from research in the mass media. Chapter 4 not only provides many insightful examples of data contexts you might not at first think amenable to a qualitative analysis (e.g., photo-elicitation studies), but it also draws attention to when, where and under what conditions you would decide that one form of data is more relevant for your research question than another.

One context frequently used for collecting data is the informal interview. As Siobhan Hugh-Jones reminds us in Chapter 5, one of the best ways to find out things about people is to talk to them! Here you will learn about different types of interviews, how to think through preparing to conduct one, what is involved in using different types of questions and many other key elements involved in using this procedure for qualitative research. Often, of course, it is quite difficult to recognise what is involved in running a successful interview – successful in the sense that you are able to elicit from the interviewee rich and detailed information regarding he/she they understands and perceives the specific topic you might be interested in. So, whilst recognising that there is never anything quite as good as interview practice for learning what might work, Chapter 3 provides numerous very insightful pointers about how to proceed as well as what you should try avoid doing. Furthermore, Siobhan Hugh-Jones has been able to utilise the opportunities afforded by the data set produced for this book – using extracts from the recorded and transcribed interviews – thus highlighting some of the best, as well as the occasionally less good, examples of question strategies adopted by interviewers.

Conducting any kind of research in psychology will inevitably involve a close consideration of ethics: ethical issues which arise given the very nature of doing research with fellow-human participants and ethical procedures, that is, thinking through all that is involved in trying to ensure that the research practices minimise any potential harm or discomfort for all participants, researchers included. It is always important to recognise that the emphasis should be on 'potential' discomfort, as a researcher cannot second-guess exactly what that might mean for any participant. Simply going through an ethics 'check-list' doesn't somehow absolve a researcher from thinking through how procedures might be improved. Research involving human beings will always present distinct and challenging ethical issues and dilemmas. Given the nature of continually changing – and one would hope developing – cultural attitudes concerning research practices and procedures, ethical guidelines and protocols should be seen as procedures that can always be improved.

Ethical practices, procedures and protocols surrounding the conduct of research using qualitative methods have their own particular challenges. In Chapter 6 Nigel King provides a comprehensive overview of the various ethical procedures and protocols you would go through in practice – including some insightful examples of ethics application forms, participant information sheets, feedback forms and guidelines about how to consider potential ethical issues in qualitative research. Whilst many such guidelines and issues apply equally to quantitative studies in psychology, Nigel points out the particular ethical dimensions associated with qualitative research. For example, there is often more personal engagement in terms of time spent with participants, there can be specific issues with personal information and confidentiality and the nature of the data collection methods might preclude specifying all procedures in advance of actually doing the research. There are also different sorts of risks and challenges for both participants and researchers doing qualitative research. Through reading this chapter it becomes clear why engaging with ethical practices and procedures is not simply a case of ticking the right boxes, but rather, thinking through all the issues involved in a careful and considered way.

The next and main section of the book, Part 3, turns to the question of qualitative analysis and here the provision of a specifically designed data corpus comes into focus. As noted earlier, the contributors to this volume wanted to make sure that readers unfamiliar with qualitative methods could, through the provision of readily available interview data, begin to see very clearly how each methodology formulates a distinct type of qualitative analysis. We recognise that not only is it difficult to collect high-quality interview material suitable for detailed analysis, but it can also be rather hard to recognise precisely how, and why, different methodologies approach data analysis in the manner they do. Thus, Part 3 begins first with a detailed outline of the interview bases data set produced for the book, followed by each of four chapters (8 to 11) where the selected methodologies describe the forms of analysis that would typically be conducted on such data. Given that within psychology there are a relatively large number of different qualitative methods, the rationale for choosing the ones described in this book was based on a survey of the UK Department of Psychology teaching practices, which identified the most commonly used approaches (Forrester & Koutsopoulou, 2008). These approaches are Discourse Analysis (DA), Grounded Theory (GT), Interpretative Phenomenological Analysis (IPA) and Conversation Analysis (CA).

Using a common data set in this way, you will see that each method has a particular theoretical orientation to the data, asks distinct types of questions and provides forms of analysis unique to the methodology used. In each chapter, and in order to get an overview idea of the distinct type of analysis and transcription each methodology employs, a short extract from the data corpus has been selected, with contributors highlighting the focus of their chosen methodology. This is really valuable to the beginning student who initially may find it rather difficult to grasp how each methodology has a distinctive approach to data analysis. One thing that will quickly become clear is that qualitative analysis cannot somehow be forced or rushed – there is no 'quick fix' involved in doing any of these forms of analysis – and taking time over the analysis is very important. At the same time, qualitative analysis is also extremely interesting and very rewarding to do.

The first chapter in Part 3 provides the background detail to the data set produced for the book and available online through the Psychology Network (see the website address in the Preface). This data set represents five semi-structured interviews of student interviewees discussing friendship with different interviewers, and talking through what they understand by the term friendship and what it means to them. The data set is produced as digital video files (in Quicktime.mov format), split into segments of approximately 15 minutes each, alongside accompanying audio files and full transcriptions. Produced as a teaching and learning resource by the TQRMUL Network group, this corpus provides the data extracts, which are then analysed in the subsequent chapters.

Here you will benefit from recognising the specific challenges and issues in collecting this data set, for example, by comparing some of the suggestions and issues regarding interviewing and data collection in Chapters 5 and 6 with how we actually collected the data. The typical steps one goes through are spelt out or indicated. It will also be helpful for you to look carefully at the details regarding the participants, the interview schedule and the forms of transcription employed. This would help your own data collection procedures or, alternatively, provide background detail were you to be using the data set as a primary data resource for your study.

Turning, then, to Chapter 8, the first of the analysis chapters, Sally Wiggins and Sarah Riley introduce you to discourse analysis (DA), and to two distinct approaches within that field: Foucauldian discourse analysis (FDA) and a discursive psychological approach. At some risk of oversimplification, in discursive psychology the focus is on what is being said, and with understanding the way in which people's accounts are constructed in and through the talk they produce. Here the steps taken in a DA-based analysis are spelt out: collecting and transcribing data; coding for themes; analysing patterns of such themes; and using example extracts for analysis. Complementing this approach to some extent, for FDA, talk is understood as bringing into being the nature of what we are talking about, talk constructs the objects/subjects that we 'know', giving us a place from which to understand ourselves and our world. The FDA analysis indicates how people position themselves in their own identities, drawing our attention to the modernist perspective of the self that Foucault articulated, drawing attention to the fact that talk does things, and we produce ourselves in and through talk. It will become clear that doing the analysis and writing it up are very closely interrelated.

Moving from a discursive methodology to one sometimes described as interpretative, Chapter 9 outlines the main ideas of grounded theory (GT) through a considered analysis of selected extracts. As the approach indicates, what is central to this methodology is that a 'theory' we might have about a topic or issue should be 'grounded' in the data we collect from people, primarily when they are being interviewed about whatever the topic is. One sense of this is that a GT approach wouldn't necessarily begin with a review of existing literature, but instead through collecting data at the outset. You will also see that a carefully considered cyclical procedure is employed in GT with the examination of data transcripts, the production of memo-writing, analysis and reflexive consideration of interpretation 'cycling' through stage-by-stage. Normally conducted on a 'case-by-case' basis, Alasdair Gordon-Finlayson takes the reader through a typical analysis, where throughout there is a constant sense of enquiry and engagement with the material. This chapter provides a lucid and engaging description of how you would go about using the GT approach for your analysis.

Our third approach, interpretative pheneomenological analysis (IPA), makes up Chapter 10, where Rachel Shaw first reminds us of the phenomenological background to IPA – emphasising that the focus of the method is on how people make sense of their experiences. IPA is essentially an idiographic approach, which focuses on the individual level of a person's experience – in other words, it is very much concerned with the fine detail of an individual's meaning-making, and how we can study this. This in-depth approach to the study of an individual is becoming an increasingly popular qualitative methodology in psychology, sometimes used to complement associated quantitative work. Here you will learn that in doing an IPA analysis there is a close interdependence between processes of description and interpretation, keeping a reflective diary, and the production of an audit trail documenting the analysis process. Rachel Shaw, in taking us carefully through the steps involved in doing such analysis, points out that IPA involves what is known as a 'double hermeneutic' – in other words, the analyst is seeking to *make sense out of* how participants *make sense out of* their experiences. As with all the chapters, the reader can see very quickly through an examination of the common sample extract how this particular method differs from the others.

The fourth method of analysis in Part 3 takes you through how a conversation analyst might approach the understanding of an element or aspect of the interview data set. Conversation Analysis (CA) is sometimes described as being 'ethnomethodolgically' inspired; in other words CA is one of a number of examples of the ethnomethodological perspective. Essentially what this means is that the analysis is centred on how people themselves produce 'sense-making methods' in and through their everyday interactions – thus the term 'ethno-method'. Here you will see that a conversation analyst cannot simply say: oh, look, this is what this person is doing/feeling/thinking here. Instead, whatever suggestions or arguments the analyst makes will be based on a careful 'line-by-line' sequential examination of how participants themselves treat 'what happens next'. This is part of the reason why you will immediately see that the orthography used when producing a CA-based transcription will include not just what people say, but many different aspects of the 'talk-in-interaction' – any action might be potentially significant for the participants themselves. In this chapter the CA focus is on how people manage the business of ending a conversation, looking at the conversational structures they use and examining how they produce their own understandings of what an interview is for them.

This brings us, finally, to Part 4 of this book and to Chapter 12, which is focused on what is involved in writing up a qualitative methodology practical or laboratory (lab) report. Colm Crowley begins by reminding you that for the most part the final report you would write looks very similar to that which you have produced for quantitative reports (experiments or questionnaire-based studies). The major difference with qualitative reports is with what would traditionally be called the results section of a report. This is now described as a 'findings and discussion' or 'analysis and discussion' section, where you would detail your analysis, and at the same time discuss what it means for the question(s) you asked. There are a number of other differences, for example: occasional changes in writing style; comprehensive use of the appendix; details about reflexivity and the form of analysis you used. Students writing up qualitative methodology reports in psychology often find it rather difficult to see how the formats they find in qualitative research journals, which can vary depending on the methodology being reported, translate into an undergraduate research report structure. In this chapter you are taken through everything you need to do in order to write a comprehensive high-quality report within the conventions found in psychology (e.g., word length, abstract format, referencing).

Chapter learning hints, aids and guidelines

Throughout the text, contributors have sought to ensure that guidance and hints are included so as to help you get the most from each chapter. In Part 3, for example, all four qualitative analysis chapters (8 to 11) adopt a similar five-part format of '*Introduction - Background - Analysis - Writing up the analysis - Summary points*', so as to highlight the focus of each analysis and how it is done. In addition, each analysis chapter considers a sample extract, again to draw your attention to some essential differences across the methods. Throughout these, and where appropriate in other chapters, a number of other aids have been employed. These include:

- *Procedure highlight boxes.* These summarise or list specific steps, processes or procedures unique to one or other qualitative method, as well as relevant steps in the interviewing and write-up chapters. So, in the case of CA there is a procedure highlight box outlining what 'participant orientation' means in practice – when you are carrying out the analysis. In contrast, in the IPA chapter your attention is drawn to the importance of writing descriptive summaries during the analysis.
- *Definitions boxes.* We recognise that there are many theoretical and technical terms that will be unfamiliar to you, and so will find definition boxes throughout the text. We adopted the view that we must be very careful to make sure we define as many things as we can, given your possible unfamiliarity with qualitative methods.
- *'Where are we now?' boxes.* There may be occasions, although few we hope, where a reader might be unsure as to the stage they have reached in their reading or analysis. Thus we thought these boxes would be useful, reminding the reader where they are, and what has been covered up to that point.
- *'Want to know more?' boxes.* At different points in each chapter you will find indications of where you might want to do further reading. These boxes indicate to the reader where they should go for further information.
- *Critical issues boxes.* At times, throughout the book your attention is drawn to one or other critical questions or issues relevant to the topic being discussed. So, for example, in Chapter 5 you are asked to consider what status 'subjective' experience has in psychology, or in Chapter 4 to critically consider issues surrounding what kind of data is 'naturalistic' or not. These boxes can be helpful for highlighting questions or issues that continue to present challenges for qualitative researchers.
- *Summary points.* This listing provides a brief reminder of what has been covered in each chapter.

Concluding comment

This book is very much about *doing* qualitative research in psychology, particularly in contexts where not much prior knowledge can be assumed. Throughout, there is a close interdependence between chapters and the specially produced data set – the friendship interviews – accompanying the book. The book can used either as a guide for doing qualitative research and analysis in conjunction with the data set or as the basis for work where you collect your own data. We are confident you will find it very useful in learning how to do qualitative research.

Part 1
Formulating Research Questions

2

Theory and Method in Qualitative Research

Cath Sullivan

Introduction

This chapter deals with how theoretical and philosophical assumptions about science, knowledge, truth and evidence relate to the everyday practice of doing research. I consider different theoretical and philosophical schools of thought, such as positivism and social constructionism, and examine the methodological implications they have for psychology. For example, consideration will be given to the differences researchers from alternative viewpoints have regarding the status of participants' own accounts of their experiences and perspectives. In what follows, I will ask you to consider what psychological research is and what kinds of tasks it involves, and introduce you to two types of questions that have a bearing upon the way research – including the work you do yourselves as students – is conceptualised and conducted. These two types of questions are:

- Philosophical questions such as, 'what counts as good evidence', or 'can research give us ways of understanding what might be true and what false'?
- Theoretical questions such as, 'what roles does language have in psychology', or 'what is the nature of people's subjective experience'?

By addressing these types of questions you will have a better understanding of the processes and practices of research and find it easier to make sense of and conduct psychological studies.

Psychology, science and philosophy

Psychology and scientific method

Doing psychology, including the psychology that you do as a student, involves a number of things (although not all psychologists do all of these things). These include:

- examining how people think, feel and behave;
- finding out what influences how people think, feel and behave;
- exploring people's perspectives and the meanings they attach to things;
- examining how ideas, events and things are represented in language and made sense of; and
- determining the consequences of how people think, feel and behave

In order to do these tasks, psychologists carry out research and this involves various activities, including:

- Asking questions or making predictions about how things work.
    - These are called 'research questions' and 'hypotheses', respectively. When we do research we are usually working with an idea of what we expect to find – or at least an idea of what we are asking about.
    - Such questions help us to develop explanations of what is going on (these are called theories).
    - Because particular kinds of research methods are best suited to giving answers to particular kinds of research questions, the kind of question you have will guide the kinds of methods that you use.
- Gathering evidence in the form of data.
    - This could be numerical, quantitative data; for example, data which is often obtained during an experiment (e.g., people's reaction times measured in seconds), or from scores on a set of items in a questionnaire (e.g., a score from a questionnaire that measures a person's attitudes towards capital punishment or the extent to which they describe themselves as sociable).
    - Alternatively, this could be qualitative data, which tends not to be numeric; for example, a set of field notes that a researcher writes to describe what they see whilst they are doing an observational study of children in a playground, or a verbatim (word-for word) record of what was said in an interview or a naturally occurring conversation (known as a transcript).
- Generating and evaluating explanations of how things work. An important part of research is to generate and test various possible explanations, which are often referred to as theoretical accounts. This is also often what you are doing when you do practical/laboratory work as an undergraduate.

When trying to understand the relationship between theories, research questions and data, try to think of it like this:

- Data are the evidence we gather to help us answer research questions.
- Hypotheses are predictions that we make about the possible answers to research questions.

- Theories give us a reason to ask certain questions and are the reasons why we sometimes predict particular answers.
- Theories are explanations of the thing that we are researching. We can test theories against the evidence produced when we gather data and use it to test research questions and hypotheses. We can also generate theories on the basis of data.

Activity suggestion **2.1**

Use a journal article that you have been asked to read for one of your modules and try to analyse it in terms of the above ideas. Can you identify the theory being tested or proposed? Is it clear what the research questions are? Do they relate easily to the theory? How does that data in particular help to address the research questions? Thinking through these kinds of ideas – and possibly identifying flaws in these areas – is one of the ways in which you can critically evaluate research evidence, which is something that will help you get good marks.

There has been a long-standing tradition within psychology to view these research-related activities that we do as 'science'. However, not all psychologists agree about this, or about the best way to go about gathering evidence or generating and evaluating explanations, and there are differences of opinion about how research projects should actually be conducted in psychology. One of the things that influences research practice is philosophy, or to be precise, the philosophical approach that underpins both theory and method.

Where does philosophy come into all this?

Two branches of philosophy are especially relevant to a discussion of science (Ladyman, 2002). These are epistemology and ontology.

Definitions **2.2** !

Epistemology. This branch of philosophy asks questions about knowledge, beliefs and truth. For example, how do we determine what differentiates knowledge from beliefs? How do we recognise knowledge when we see it? How can we determine what a fact is? What is truth and how do we know when we've got it?

Ontology. This branch of philosophy asks questions about what things there are in the world. It is about defining and cataloguing the things that exist – so, in psychology, it might involve questions about whether personality or intelligence exists.

When you read about methodology and philosophy you will probably encounter these terms – especially the terms 'epistemology' and 'epistemological'. For example, people may talk about the epistemological assumptions that a particular method rests upon. What this refers to is the fact that researchers' standpoints in relation to epistemological questions (e.g., how do we recognise knowledge, what counts as evidence, what is truth and how do we recognise it) will determine how they do research and how they evaluate research done by other people. Ultimately, it influences our decisions about what counts as good, defensible, reasonable knowledge – and good psychology.

If we return to thinking about some of the things that psychology is trying to do – examining how people think, feel and behave; finding out what influences how people think, feel and behave; exploring people's perspectives and the meanings they attach to things; examining how things are represented in language and made sense of; determining the consequences of how people think, feel and behave – the importance of understanding some of the underlying assumptions should be clear.

So, the central point here is that there are some key philosophical issues, which are reflected in particular approaches to doing research and building a body of knowledge, and which have direct relevance to research and to questions about science. Let us look at these in more detail.

2.3 Where are we now?

So far, we've seen that there are some key philosophical issues, which are reflected in the ways that we can approach the task of building a body of knowledge through research activities. Next, we will look at some of these approaches to gathering knowledge in more detail and think about their methodological implications.

Approaches to building a body of knowledge

Psychologists have particular views on what it means for psychology to be a science, and the kinds of methods, procedures and approaches to finding things out that should be used. There are a number of philosophical issues that impact upon this, and upon the everyday practice of doing research. In the paragraphs that follow I explore some of these issues in terms of how they might influence how research is actually conducted.

> ## Activity suggestion **2.4** 《《
>
> Spend a few moments considering your opinion on some of the following questions. You may feel that you don't have the answers, and these are not easy questions, but try and think for a while and record your ideas, thoughts and questions in relation to each one.
>
> * What counts as good evidence?
> * What is truth?
> * How do we evaluate truth-claims?
> * Is it possible for us to recognise 'truth' when we see it?
> * Is it possible for research to be totally objective?

These kinds of questions are what epistemology is all about and most psychologists will have views on these kinds of questions, especially if they sit down and consciously try to think about them, as you have just done. Even if researchers do not explicitly express opinions on these matters, the way in which they conduct their research will always involve taking on board certain philosophical assumptions concerning these questions. Similarly, the methodological strategies that you use in your undergraduate practical work will reflect certain kinds of assumptions (both your own and those of the people who developed the methods you are using).

Many researchers' views will be roughly in line with one of two schools of thought that have been common in psychology for some time now: 'positivism' and 'social constructionism'. Until relatively recently, modern psychological research was heavily influenced by the ideas of positivism and it is only now that other approaches can be found in psychology.

Positivism

Positivism was traditionally the dominant view of science within the natural sciences and within psychology. The following ideas (adapted from Robson, 2002)are key features of positivism:

* Objective knowledge (facts) can only be gained from direct experience or observation. There is no place in science for things (theories, concepts) that are hypothetical or simply speculative.
* Science (if done properly) is a value-free and objective process.
* Science is based on the analysis of numerical (quantitative) data that are gathered through a strictly defined set of procedures. These procedures are different from those used to gather 'common sense' or lay knowledge.

- The propositions made within science are based on fact. Hypotheses are tested to determine whether the facts are in line with the propositions (theories) that have been put forward.
- The main purpose of science, according to positivism, is to create universal causal laws – that is, overarching explanations of what things directly cause other things. This is based on the search for empirical regularities whereby two things invariably occur together (this is sometimes known as 'constant conjunction'). So, for example, if our observations of the world (from systematic experimentation) show that cheese is always followed by nightmares then we can generalise a 'law' from this that cheese causes nightmares.
- According to positivism, cause is nothing more than constant conjunction – and all that we need to demonstrate a causal relationship is to observe (reliably and often – not just once) constant conjunction.
- We don't need anything other than these types of general laws to explain the world.
- Psychologists can simply transfer the methods and assumptions of the natural sciences to our discipline.

Positivism, in this form, has come under some criticism in recent years – in psychology and in other disciplines. However, these general principles remain popular and the associated methods have developed as the norm within psychology. To return to the question of what philosophical issues have to do with research, it is useful to consider what methodological implications the key ideas of positivism might have for the way in which we conduct research (i.e., for methodology). Here are some examples of implications of a positivistic approach.

Methodological Implication 1: Positivist assumptions mean that researchers should be sceptical of using participants' accounts and self-reports as useful data because this is not the same as directly observing the phenomena under study.

Methodological Implication 2: According to positivistic approaches, the key to being value-free and objective is the use of objective tools and methods. Therefore, the correct use of method is something that is central to doing good science in all disciplines that use science to accumulate knowledge. Doing science according to tried and tested methods is seen as key. Many of the processes by which scientific activity comes about (e.g., applications for research funding, gaining ethical approval, publishing research findings through peer-reviewed journals – where it is scrutinised for methodological rigour by other researchers) involve strict scrutiny of the way the research will be, or has been, carried out.

Methodological Implication 3: Quantitative data and analysis tend to be seen as superior to qualitative data from a positivistic research perspective. Traditionally, psychologists saw less room for qualitative research in the discipline, as they tended to be more suspicious of non-numerical interpretation. Qualitative research has become more common in psychology partly because of shifting attitudes towards these issues and a decrease in the dominance of traditional positivistic views.

Methodological Implication 4: Experimentation is the most important method, from a positivistic point of view, because it allows the necessary control and manipulation of variables in order to establish whether things are constantly conjoined.

Methodological Implication 5: Replication is seen as important because it helps to build a pattern of constant conjunction and therefore helps us to build causal laws (which, if we're being positivistic, is the main aim of doing science in the first place).

Where are we now?   2.5 ?

The previous section of the chapter summarised some of the key ideas of positivism (some of which are likely to have been familiar to you from the teaching on your course) and looked at some implications of these ideas for the way in which research is done and evaluated. Next, I will look at some of the criticisms of, and challenges to, this approach.

Challenges for positivistic approaches

Realism and psychology

Positivistic approaches to psychology are underpinned by epistemological realism, which is one way of conceptualising the relationship between the entities in the world and our representations of them. In order to understand this, first it is important to grasp that we can divide the world up into the actual things that are in it (the 'entities') and our representations or ways of understanding these things. So, entities include anything that we consider to exist in the world and could include things that we can physically see and touch (like people, places, brains, schools), and things that we consider to exist although we might not directly see and touch them (like personality, memory, intelligence, social conformity). Entities can be straightforward things (like a book, a pen, a person) or fairly complex things (like education, the criminal justice system, or sport). Representations include our ways of conceptualising and describing the entities that exist in the world. This includes our mental representations of things (i.e., the products of our system of visual perception and cognitive representations) and our ways of describing things in words or images (our talk, what we write and draw).

The 'realist ideology of representation' asserts that entities pre-exist and give rise to their surface representations (documents, behaviour, language, knowledge, thoughts). For the realist, science aims to establish links between surface representations (knowledge) and underlying entities (reality). Our attempts to explain what is going on in the world – that is, our attempts to use data as evidence to evaluate our theories and propositions – are seen by realists as a way of comparing different representations with reality in order to judge which of those representations seems to be correct. Realists think that we can meaningfully distinguish between entities and our representations of these entities, and therefore judge whether representations are accurate. This is an idea that is taken for granted in many areas of psychology, and in much of our everyday thinking, so it can be very difficult to recognise that this way of thinking rests on various assumptions (see above).

2.6 Definitions

Realism is the view that our representations of the things in the world are relatively straightforward reflections of the way those things actually are. This is also known as the 'realist ideology of representation'.

Some people argue that a realist approach is one of the most problematic things about positivism – especially if we try to apply positivism to psychological entities (like memory, personality, conformity and intelligence). Instead, they argue that attempting to link surface representations with underlying reality is impossible – and opt instead for a 'constitutive' or 'relativist' view of the link between objects and representations. They argue that our knowledge of the world is not a simple reflection of the way the world actually is, but is created and sustained through social processes – particularly through language (Burr, 2003).

Let's take emotion as an example of this idea and think for a moment about how we might think and talk about our own emotional states. Initially, let's assume (as a traditional approach within psychology would) that there are two things of interest here. First, there are the actual emotional states that we experience. Second, there are our representations of our emotional states. These representations might consist of our private thoughts about our emotions and also of the words that we use to articulate these thoughts to others. If I wake up in the morning and feel a particular way, I will probably create a mental representation of that feeling. In simple terms, I might have the thought 'I feel happy'. If somebody were to ask me how I feel, I might say 'I feel happy this morning'. If we think (as a realist would) in terms of 'entities' and 'representations', the first of these three things is the 'entity' (i.e., my actual emotional state) and the second two things are 'representations' of that entity. We could say, then, that the actual emotional state is the 'reality' and the thoughts and words are 'representations'. The 'realist ideology of representation' would imply that one can examine the entity (my emotional state) in order to determine whether the representations (thoughts and words) are accurate reflections of it or not. But how do we access 'reality' in order to check that what I think I'm feeling, and what I say I'm feeling are accurate representations? Is it possible to directly access my emotional state, or is it only possible to access it through what I say? How can I, or anyone else, tell the difference between what I really feel and what I think I feel?

As you can see, when we try meaningfully to separate out our representations (mental conceptualisations of emotions) from the reality of what they represent (the emotion itself) things become difficult, to say the least. Relativists would use this as evidence that we cannot meaningfully access psychological reality – we can only really access representations of it.

Definitions **2.7** **!**

Relativism is the view that our representations of the things in the world are socially constructed and can't be seen as simple reflections of how those things actually are.

It is most useful to think of relativism and realism as part of a continuum, rather than as two separate camps. Often, researchers' views on this matter will fall somewhere along a line that has extreme relativism at one end and extreme realism at the other (as in Figure 2.1).

Objectivity and the socio-political context of research

Another major component of a positivistic approach is the idea that if science is done properly, then knowledge rests upon objective facts. Many have argued that science, and the knowledge it produces, is actually far from being completely objective. Rather, science, like any other social activity, is done within historical, political and social contexts and all these have an impact upon the way that science conducts itself – the questions it asks, the methods it uses and the way findings are interpreted and used. For example, it would be very unlikely for researchers to conduct a project investigating the most effective way to use physical punishment to encourage learning in children because in our current climate of social norms and morals, such behaviour would not be considered legitimate.

This does not necessarily mean that objectivity is a pointless aim, but that it is dangerous to assume that it is an automatic outcome of employing research methods. Research methods are used by human beings and are interpreted by human beings, and some feel that this means they can never be sufficiently detached from people's values and biases to be truly objective. According to this view, it is important for researchers to be reflexive – that is, to reflect upon how their own views, attitudes and experiences may impact upon the research that they do. It also encourages researchers to consider the social and political context, and the possible consequences, of the research they do.

Figure 2.1   A theory continuum in psychology.

2.8 Activity suggestion

Go back to the journal article that you used for your previous activity in this chapter, or pick a new one if you prefer. Then, make a list of all the potential things that might have influenced the objectivity of that research project. When you do this try and think of the project as beginning with an idea, being designed, carried out, written up, published, read by other people and then perhaps used in some applied context. These could include things like the researcher's personal beliefs, the previous experiences of the participants, the political climate in the country where they live, the political views of journal editors or reviewers and the aims and motivations of the people who might use the research findings to justify some course of action.

Now try and think through what might actually be done about these threats to objectivity. Do you think that they can be removed? How? What does this mean for the status of the project's findings? Can we trust them?

Experimentation and ecological validity

Another criticism of positivism is that it focuses too much on the use of experimental methods. The concern is whether the artificiality and level of control exerted in an experimental situation make the results irrelevant to the real world. The question of how well we can generalise the results from research to situations in the real world is known as 'ecological validity'. A common criticism of experimentation is that it sacrifices ecological validity in order to gain the high level of experimental control that is one of its defining principles. Some would argue that if all we have learnt has come from experiments, maybe we know a lot about how people behave in experiments but not much about how they behave in the real world.

2.9 Definitions

'For a research study to possess **ecological validity**, the methods, materials and setting of the study must approximate the real-life situation that is under investigation.' (Brewer, 2000)

To illustrate this, imagine we set up an experiment to investigate the effects of caffeine on memory and, in doing so, create an artificial situation where we have control over the amount of caffeine a person has had, and where we have removed from the experimental situation as many other potential influences on memory as we can. For example, we might try to control for age and ensure that none of the participants are taking any kind of medication or have drunk alcohol recently. In doing this, we establish experimental control and this helps us to be sure that any changes we notice in memory are due to our manipulation of caffeine levels. However, in the real world, this high level of control does not exist. In the real, world people do take drugs (prescription and otherwise) that affect their memory. So, how can we be sure that the results we have obtained in our experimental situation can really be generalised to other situations in real life?

So, for some critics, there is a need to replace, or at least add to, positivism with an approach to science that employs more 'naturalistic' methods – that is, such methods that allow us to investigate psychological phenomena in naturally occurring or realistic settings and aim to specifically explore the role of context.

Different views of causality: The importance of meaning

Some psychologists have argued that positivism may be appropriate for some scientific disciplines but that it is particularly inappropriate for psychology because of the nature of our subject material. This argument is particularly relevant to areas of psychology that concern themselves with social behaviour. The positivistic idea that if we identify 'constant conjunctions' between variables in experiments we can determine causality rests partially upon the idea that causality happens because one particular variable has causal properties that have some kind of direct action upon the other variable. However, it is often argued that when we study psychology we actually need to think about causation in a slightly different way – that is, we need to think about the significance of 'meaning' in order to understand how causality works.

John Hughes uses an example of traffic behaviour from Hart (1961, cited in Hughes, 1990) to support his argument that '*the regularities we discover by studying society are only the external appearances of what the members of a society understand*' (Hughes, 1990, p. 95). He argues that social reality cannot be understood without reference to shared social meanings rather than the regularities or 'constant conjunctions' that we might observe in quantitative data. In the 'traffic light example' we are asked to imagine that we are trying to study drivers' behaviour at traffic lights in order to understand and explain it – that is, we need to describe it and then try to create an account of why cars and drivers behave as they do. At lights, the traffic displays regularity and to try and arrive at a causal explanation for these patterns, a positivist would aim to specify the conditions that produce certain patterns and formulate and test a theory that postulates the causal link between the lights and the movement of the traffic. What we would notice from our data is that there is a strong association between red lights and traffic stopping. Is it then safe to deduce that traffic lights have causal properties that cause cars to stop moving? Can we be said to have explained why cars stop moving at this stage? Hughes argues that we cannot because traffic lights do not have causal properties that cause cars to stop – there is no force field! Simply observing the association between red lights and stopping doesn't give us the explanation. We may know that red lights are important in stopping traffic, but we haven't truly explained how they have this effect. To get the explanation, we need to talk to people in order to understand the meaning and significance of the traffic lights within that particular social context. What causes cars (generally) to stop at red lights is that the traffic lights represent rules within society. To provide an explanation rather than merely a description of what is going on here, we need to make reference to how people learnt the rules and what they mean to them.

So, for some, the problem with positivism is that it does not allow for the significance of meaning in explanation and it has, as its core methods, techniques which are not very good at helping us to understand meaning. Qualitative methods are generally regarded as being particularly good at giving access to what things mean, and so people who share these concerns about positivism are often attracted to qualitative methods.

? 2.10 Where are we now?

We can see that positivism is not without its criticisms and challenges. These include objections to extreme realism, problems with the notion of objectivity, threats to ecological validity and the question of whether positivism offers psychology methods that allow full causal explanations. Next, I will discuss an alternative way of approaching the question of how best to build a body of knowledge.

Relativist social constructionism

This is a school of thought that has its roots in other disciplines, such as sociology, and began to emerge in social psychology in the 1970s. It is very different from positivism and has been a major influence on the growth of qualitative research methods within psychology. Relativist social constructionism includes the following general ideas (adapted from Robson, 2002):

- Scientific accounts (theories, knowledge) should not be given a privileged position. Science is seen as simply one way of looking at the world and there are held to be other ways of looking at the world that are equally valid.
- Relativist social constructionism asserts that it is not possible to generate rational procedures to determine truth, or to decide which forms of knowledge are 'better' than others in a truly objective way. Culture, morals, values, political beliefs etc. always get in the way of this.
- Even if there is a reality external to our understanding of it, according to relativist social constructionists there is no point trying to find ways of getting a true picture of this reality. Our perceptions and understandings of reality are all we actually have access to, so reality does not meaningfully exist as something separate from our ways of understanding it (which, in turn, are not separate from values, morals and ideology).
- Language is seen as the most important means for representing and understanding the world and should therefore be the main focus of our research. If we cannot get

at the truth of what the world is really like because it only meaningfully exists in the form of our representations of it, then we should study these representations (and that means studying language).

- To try and understand people, relativist social constructionists argue that we must understand context and meaning in its full complexity.
- Research is seen as giving us working hunches about the world that are inevitably shifting and imperfect, rather than as giving us immutable facts.
- Qualitative methodologies are more likely to be used because contemporary forms of these methods focus on language and on meaning.

Again, it is particularly important to try and tease out what the methodological implications of these views might be. If we adopt a more relativist social constructionist viewpoint, how does this shape the ways in which we might go about doing research in psychology?

Methodological Implication 1: Academic attempts to explain what is going on in the world can't really be objectively evaluated with regard to how 'true' they are. Proponents of this approach would argue that we can only ever examine academic explanations in terms of whether they are plausible and compelling. This doesn't necessarily mean that it isn't possible to evaluate knowledge, but that we might evaluate it according to different criteria. So, we might ask whether it helps to provide us with a useful solution to some problem or helps to bring us closer to some kind of outcome that is desirable. Imagine we were interested in finding out about the perspectives of patients who are attending medical screening. From this perspective, we might focus more on whether the understanding we gain helps us to create a screening process that is evaluated more positively by patients, or has better attendance rates, than on whether what we have found out about patients' perspectives is the 'truth'.

Methodological Implication 2: The purpose of psychology is not to discover (pre-existing) truth. So, for example, the consequences of believing certain things to be true and others not true, or the implications of talking about things in particular ways, are seen as more pertinent than whether the things are **actually** true or not. For example, if as a society we think of alcoholism as an illness we will treat it; if we think of it as a moral failing, we might be more inclined the punish it. Relativistic research would be interested in identifying and exploring the consequences of how alcoholism is regarded, rather than in trying to work out whether alcoholism really is an illness or a moral failing (as this would be seen as an impossible task). 'Truth' tends to be seen as something that we create and derive through social interaction and through actively trying to make sense of the world around us, rather than as something that is lying around out there waiting for the researcher to come along and somehow trip over it.

Methodological Implication 3: Many social constructionist researchers use research methods that involve the examination of language (e.g., Discourse Analysis).

Methodological implication 4: Research methods that allow us to explore meaning are seen as more useful by social constructions. So, for example, they tend to value the accounts of participants where positivistic psychology found them more problematic.

2.11 Where are we now?

The previous sections of this chapter have given you an outline of relativist social constructionism and drawn out some of the methodological implications of this point of view. Next, I will consider some of the criticisms and challenges of this approach.

Challenges for relativist social constructionism

Truth claims
The relativistic view that all perspectives, accounts or versions of events are potentially equally valid has political consequences. Many social constructionists are unhappy about the more relativistic forms of constructionism because they seem to thwart any attempts to take moral, ethical or political standpoints or to challenge oppression and falsehood. They argue that a logical extension of the relativist argument – that we cannot legitimately compare any truth claims (surface representations) against evidence of what is 'really going on in the world' (reality) – leaves us in a position where no claims can be either supported or refuted.

2.12 Activity suggestion

To illustrate this, think about the following questions and note down your answers:
- How does one counter claims that the murder of millions of people in the Holocaust of World War II did not actually happen without using some kind of evidence (i.e., without comparing this representation with reality to see if the representation is supported)?
- How can we evaluate whether psychological therapies are useful and beneficial without being able to presume that we can take signs of improvement (surface representations) as an indication of actual improvement (reality) following treatment?

For some, the relativist epistemological view is problematic because it leaves us in a state, arguably, where we cannot distinguish beliefs from knowledge. This is problematic for notions of science, which partly rest on the idea that science is different from other human activities because it allows us to work out the difference between knowing something and 'merely' believing it to be the case. In essence, the people who level this criticism at relativist approaches to psychology are uncomfortable with the idea that we cannot evaluate arguments against any form of evidence.

Materiality, embodiment and power

Cromby and Nightingale (1999), amongst others, have argued that wholly relativist constructionism fails to take into account certain key things. For instance, there is a tendency to gloss over the physical aspects of our existence. So, whilst it is useful to consider discursive aspects of health and illness, for example, they argue that we need to do this in ways that take into the account the physical realities of our bodies and the physical processes that we are subject to. Similarly, and more generally, they argue for a social constructionism that takes into account the realities of the material world and of social structure (e.g., the power of governments, armies, institutions, employers).

Some forms of extreme relativism appear to have an exclusive focus on language. Critics ask, which came first, the 'reality' or the language? If we return to the traffic light example again, it might also be important to consider the consequences of crossing a red light at a busy junction. Those who are critical of extreme relativism might point to the fact that if we have a major collision in a vehicle, there is more going on in such a context than just our shared assumptions, or our sense-making. There is, for many, a tangible reality to a car accident that is somehow beyond our ways of conceptualising and representing it. Notice that this is not necessarily saying that the world is not socially constructed but, for some, it is about finding an approach that acknowledges and accommodates both the socially constructed nature of the world and its material 'reality'.

Critical issue: The relativism–realism debate? 2.13

So, we have looked at two common and quite different approaches to the task of building a body of knowledge: 'positivism' and 'relativistic social constructionism'. We have looked at their key ideas, some methodological implications of these ideas and at some criticisms and challenges of these approaches. One of the most important differences between these two approaches is that positivism tends to lean towards extreme realism, whilst relativist social constructionism is, as the name implies, a much more relativistic approach. This debate between 'realism' and 'relativism' is an important one and at times the debate has become very polarised. Some researchers have, however, adopted approaches that have the potential to allow us to overcome this polarised debate (i.e., to move beyond the sticking point of arguing about whether realism or relativism is the more sensible approach to take). I will consider some of these approaches next.

Attempts to move beyond the relativism–realism debate

In philosophical terms, one of the biggest sources of difference between positivism and relativist social constructionism is their tendencies towards, respectively, extreme realist and extreme relativist positions. Increasingly though, as Vivien Burr (2003) notes, psychologists have been attempting to try and move beyond the 'relativism–realism' debate. Other approaches to gathering knowledge may help us to do this. Let us consider two of these next: critical realism and phenomenology.

Critical realism

For some researchers the extreme realism of traditional forms of positivism and the extreme relativism of some forms of social constructionism are equally problematic. This research perspective is identified in the literature as 'critical realism'. So, if we return to the idea of a theoretical continuum, the addition of critical realism produces a picture like that of Figure 2.2.

Although critical realism shares with more relativistic approaches a strong emphasis on social construction and critique of the idea that science is an objective process, it differs from them fundamentally in asserting that *'the phenomena studied in … research are not completely constructions … but correspond to real entities or processes which exist independently of us'* (Lund, 2005, p. 118). Some relatively common features of this approach are:

- Critical realism rejects the 'extreme realism' of traditional positivistic approaches.
- Knowledge is seen as historically and culturally specific. Similarly, research methods can never be truly objective from this point of view and research is seen as a social process that is always conducted in the context of values.
- Language is not only seen as a simple reflection of the 'reality' of the world, but also as having the capacity to shape our thoughts and our conceptions of what is real. Furthermore, it has direct consequences in terms of what courses of action in the world are seen as legitimate or not.
- It is possible to gain (imperfect) access to a reality beyond discourse. So, 'extreme relativism' is also rejected.
- Knowledge of this reality is always distorted to some extent by our perspectives, by power and by culture.
- This means that truth claims can be evaluated against evidence. But, knowledge and truth are still recognised as being, to some extent, socially constructed.

Figure 2.2 Critical realism and psychology.

Research that explicitly adopts a critical realist position is still relatively uncommon in psychology. However, the existence of this approach illustrates a crucial point here: there are ways to avoid getting stuck in the difficult position of trying to decide between the merits of extreme relativism, on the one hand, and extreme realism on the other.

Where are we now? **2.14** **?**

Critical realism is one way in which we can approach the task of building a body of knowledge that avoids both extreme realism and extreme relativism. Next, I will consider another approach that also does this, but in a different way.

Phenomenology

Phenomenology is both a philosophical school of thought and a long-standing, increasingly popular approach to psychological research. In psychological research, its basic aim is to describe and interpret people's perspectives and perceptions and examine how they are related to their experience of the world around them.

The philosopher Edmund Husserl is regarded as the founder of phenomenology and advocated the position, clearly highly pertinent for psychology, that thorough understanding of experience is central to understanding in any discipline (Ashworth, 2008). The phenomenological approach that follows from Husserl's begins with the 'bracketing' of the question of whether people's experiences (and reports of that experience) can be linked to any kind of reality that is separate from those experiences.

Definitions **2.15** **!**

Bracketing is the idea, in phenomenology, that we can leave aside the question of whether people's experiences are separate from reality.

Ashworth (2008) comments that if we accept that the understanding of experience should be central to psychology, it follows that the scientific method, and the examination of variables and their (arguably) causal relations to one another, is an inappropriate method for psychology. If one takes the view that experience is the key place for us to focus our attention, the question of whether that experience corresponds to some reality beyond it also becomes less significant. There are though, some other approaches to phenomenology that take a slightly different view on the debate about experience and its relationship to reality. However, the key point to grasp here is that certain forms of phenomenology, like critical realism, provide a potential way for us to legitimately avoid the choice between extreme relativism and extreme realism.

Summary

So, the way that we conceive of and conduct research, and the way that we make sense of research findings, are shaped by methodological traditions and epistemological standpoints. This can lead to adopting implicit assumptions that researchers are not consciously aware of, and do not spend much time consciously thinking about, but that are nevertheless still present and reflected in the way we do research. It is important to remember, though, that the relationship between epistemology and method is a fairly complex and flexible one.

For example, qualitative methods can be, and are, used within realist or positivistic theoretical frameworks. Also, quantitative researchers sometimes take a relativistic or critical realist standpoint. In spite of this, some texts, particularly older ones, tend to characterise qualitative psychology as inherently relativist or as incompatible with a more realist approach, whilst others (e.g., Ashworth, 2008) choose to place little emphasis on the use of qualitative techniques within realist approaches. Whilst it is probably fair to say that a more relativistic approach tends to lead one naturally towards more qualitative techniques, and a more realist approach towards more quantitative techniques, these are not formulaic rules and sometimes the choice of method simply reflects the particular question that is being asked.

Like these different approaches to building a body of knowledge, there are also different theoretical 'schools of thought' that offer particular ideas and assumptions about the fundaments and basis of psychology. For example, 'behaviourism' is a school of psychological thought that assumes that psychology is best understood with reference to patterns of reinforcement and stimulus–response patterns, rather than with reference to notions of conscious or unconscious states of mind (Harré, 2006).

? **2.16** Where are we now?

We have considered the issue of how research methodology is related to epistemological issues and seen that there are links between certain philosophical questions and the ways in which we do research and the way it is regarded and interpreted. Similarly, the way that we do research and the way that we make sense of its findings are influenced by broad theoretical approaches to psychology. This will be considered in the next part of the chapter.

Considering these schools of thought and their influence is beyond the scope of this book, but their existence demonstrates that our basic ideas and assumptions about certain psychological issues influence the way we do psychology.

Theoretical issues

There are two particular issues where a researcher's theoretical standpoint is highly likely to influence the way that they conceive of and carry out qualitative psychological research. These two issues are (a) the link between language, reality and thought, and (b) the issue of experience and how we can explore it.

The relationship between language, reality and thought

Psychology has tended to see language as something that reflects thought – as a set of symbols that we use to share information about our inner states (thoughts, feelings, emotions, etc.). However, there are some relativists who tend towards the view that language is actually something that pre-exists and shapes our thought – so, the way we see the world can only be through pre-existing linguistic structures and forms. According to this view, we can only think with the concepts that language gives us, and so the concepts that exist in language will shape the way we think.

In trying to understand this viewpoint, consider, for example, the following quotation from Vivien Burr:

> ... *our experience of the world, and perhaps especially of our own internal states, is undifferentiated and intangible without the framework of language to give it structure and meaning. The way that language is structured therefore determines the way that experience and consciousness are structured.* (Burr, 2003, p. 48)

This is how some relativist social constructionists come to the conclusion that there is 'nothing beyond the text' – that is, there is nothing to be gained by trying to 'see the reality beyond' language or trying to use language to give us a picture of reality. For those who subscribe to this theoretical standpoint, language is integral to sense-making and to thought. From this point of view, studying language is vitally important (or, perhaps, the only fruitful endeavour) for psychology.

We can return briefly to the issue of emotions in order to illustrate this idea. In the example on p. 22 , I said that when I wake up in the morning I might have thoughts about my emotional state; I might think 'I am happy'. People who share my use of the English language know what that means and I can convey my emotional state to others by using this word as a label. I have selected the label 'happy' from a range of concepts that are available and meaningful to me and to those around me – that is, as a meaningful shared resource for labelling my emotional experience. We could think of the available emotion labels (and the concepts they represent) as being like tools in a toolbox. We can use a range of labels as tools to define our experience (what we think) and to convey it to others (what we say). Imagine that I had chosen the label 'squibbly' to describe my emotional state. This would not be something that would have meaning, either to me or to others. It does not actually exist as one of the meaningful labels that I have at my disposal (it isn't in my toolbox).

The crucial idea here is that it is not just that I have a limited and pre-defined number of tools with which to describe my emotional state to others. It is also that I only have a number of tools with which to describe my emotional state to myself – that is, for the relativist, the only way I can meaningfully make sense of my emotional state is through the labels that are provided for me by my linguistic culture. Therefore, the very nature of my thought and experience is shaped and constrained by the concepts that are available to me and that pre-exist my thoughts. This has clear implications for the way we regard people's speech and their 'inner states' (thoughts, emotions, perceptions).

2.17 Activity suggestion

Do you suppose you can think without using any language? Is it the case that you somehow need words just to experience emotions or to think about things in an everyday way? Is it possible that there are some mental experiences (like a daydream, perhaps) that can exist in our minds without involving words? Why not try reflecting on this throughout your day and see what happens!

Relativist qualitative researchers, therefore, would be very sceptical of the idea that participants' accounts can give us a simple window into the 'reality' of their inner state. This is because, for the relativist, the reality of our inner states is not actually distinguishable in any meaningful way from our representations of it (the things we think or say). Relativist researchers would tend to use qualitative methods to analyse people's talk and interaction as a way of examining things like: the way in which particular things or groups of people are made sense of, defined or 'constructed' in talk; and the way in which language might be used in a 'performative' way to achieve certain kinds of things in interaction – for example, to make claims, to lay blame, to defend a position or to negotiate identity. They do not tend to see talk as a realistic way of finding out 'what people really think' about things behind the language. Rather, they are interested in the way that language is used to make sense of the world, to describe and construct the world. For realist qualitative researchers, talk is the medium through which the world becomes 'real'. They do not necessarily deny that there is a reality beyond talk (beyond 'representations'), but they argue that we cannot gain access to it.

This, oddly, gives relativist researchers something in common with more positivistic approaches (although for very different reasons) – that is, the rejection of the notion that participants, accounts give us simple access to their inner states. It also, importantly, sets them apart from those qualitative researchers who believe that they can access people's perspectives, beliefs, experiences and thoughts through listening to their accounts of things. These researchers, who are less relativistic in their outlook, may value participants' accounts as giving us insight into 'meaning'. So, the issue of language is related to another theoretical issue which shapes the way qualitative research is designed, conceptualised, conducted and interpreted. That is, the issue of 'experience'.

Critical issue: What can interview data actually tell us? 2.18

We have seen that the position we adopt about the relationship between language and reality will have a strong influence on the way we regard participants' accounts. A key implication of this is how we regard interview data. For some relativist qualitative researchers, it makes little sense to try and use interviews as a way of getting at what people really think and feel. However, some other qualitative researchers hold epistemological and theoretical positions that, for them, make it perfectly sensible to use interview data to gain access to the experience of others. This is a very good example of the extent to which different forms of qualitative research can vary, and shows us the dangers of thinking that all qualitative research is based on the same ideas and assumptions.

Experience and how we can explore it

At the beginning of this chapter, I outlined some key things that psychology aims to do. Reflecting upon this list, you might notice that some of this involves trying to gain insight into the experiences of others. We would try to do this, for example, in order to meet the goals of:

- Examining how people think, feel and behave
- Exploring people's perspectives and the meanings they attach to things

Whether we can do these things and, if so, how we might best go about it is clearly influenced by our views on what language is. If we are unable to treat people's accounts as a window into their inner states it seems difficult to see how we can somehow address the aim of understanding their experiences and their perceptions of the world. For this reason, one of the key areas of recent debate has been the issue of whether it is possible to create a relativist social constructionism that allows us to gain knowledge about the experiences and perspectives of others. Some researchers have turned to the ideas of psychoanalysis as a way to try and resolve the issue of experience and subjectivity (Burr, 2003).

For others, this is a key reason why a critical realist form of social constructionism seems more attractive and appropriate than a relativist form. Research projects adopting this standpoint are more likely to see their research methods as allowing us to gain insight into the perspectives of others (because they are more likely to see language as giving us some insight into 'inner states') and to tap into their ways of experiencing the world around them.

We also noted that one of the most important theoretical traditions that has approached the subject of experience is phenomenology. Some phenomenological approaches hold that one can transcend the relativism–realism divide by 'bracketing' this question and focusing on experience as the key subject matter of psychology. There are also, arguably, some similarities between phenomenological approaches and the critical realist view discussed above. For example, Smith and Osborn (2008) state that researchers have to *'interpret people's mental and emotional state from what they say'* (p. 54), which suggests that it is possible to access people's perspectives and experiences (their 'inner states') through listening to their talk. The key thing to note is that both of these approaches are viewed, by their advocates, as making it possible for research to serve the purpose of understanding experience.

? **2.19** Where are we now?

Many qualitative researchers are interested in using their research to gain insight into people's perspectives and experiences. The kinds of philosophical and theoretical positions that tend to lead researchers towards this, or that suggest to us that it is a feasible thing to do with qualitative research, include less relativist forms of social constructionism, critical realist approaches, phenomenological approaches and the use of psychoanalytical approaches in combination with social constructionism. Again, the key point that I want you to take from this is that we can see links between our philosophical ideas and theoretical assumptions on the one hand, and on the other hand, the way that we carry out and interpret research.

Summary

With these two examples of language and experience, I have highlighted the connections that occur between our basic theoretical orientations towards psychology and our ways of approaching research. Such orientations influence the way that we view our data. (e.g., what do we think an interview transcript actually *is* – is it insight into people's points of view, or an account constructed in a particular situation and context that should be analysed as just that?) There are many such theoretical debates and issues that permeate psychological research and they have implications for how we think about and conduct research.

Critical issue: Mismatches between theory and method? **2.20**

A common potential problem in qualitative work can arise when there is some kind of mismatch between theoretical concerns and the form of analysis performed or the way that the data are implicitly or explicitly conceptualised within the research. For example, research that is based within a relativist social constructionist approach would not logically *'treat people's talk of experience as a transparent window on their world'* (Braun & Clarke, 2006, p. 95). A fuller understanding of epistemological and theoretical traditions and standpoints can help us avoid these kinds of inconsistencies and difficulties. It will also help you to spot these kinds of inconsistencies should they occur in the literature that you read for your course, which is another way of showing that you can use critical evaluation.

Summary points

1. This chapter describes the complex ways in which epistemological and theoretical issues are related to research.
2. Theoretical issues can influence fundamentally the ways in which we approach research problems and questions, the ways that we design and conduct research, and the ways in which research findings are interpreted and utilised by others.
3. The relationship between theory, research question and method is a complex one, and it is important to remember that not all qualitative approaches share the same epistemological or theoretical assumptions. This is much less likely to be the case with quantitative approaches.
4. Understanding the role of epistemological and theoretical issues in shaping methodological practices and traditions will enhance getting-to-grips with the methods presented in the following chapters.
5. It is good to keep in mind that qualitative research can be very diverse, partly because of the issues surrounding the relationship between theory and method.

2.21 Want to know more?

More on social constructionism, realism and relativism:

Burr, V. (2003) *Social Constructionism*. London: Routledge.
Parker, I. (1998) (Ed.) *Social Constructionism, Discourse and Realism*. London: Sage.

For more discussion about how these ideas relate to methodology:

Braun, V. & Clarke, V. (2006) Using thematic analysis in psychology. *Qualitative Research in Psychology*, **3(2)**, 77–101.
Madill, A., Jordan, A. & Shirley, C. (2000) Objectivity and reliability in qualitative analysis: Realist, contextualist and radical constructionist epistemologies. *British Journal of Psychology*, **91**, 1–20.
Robson, C. (2002) *Real World Research*. Oxford: Blackwell.

3

Conducting Literature Reviews

Rachel Shaw

Introduction

This chapter will outline the general principles of the two main components of conducting a literature review: searching the literature and reviewing what you find. In each section, we guide you through the process, so that you will be able to perform your own literature review in your own area of interest.

Why conduct a literature review?

Conducting a literature review is the usual first step in any research project. The reason we do this is to identify what others have found out about the topic that we are interested in, before we start. Often, when we start a research project we think of a general area of interest – for example, friendship – without really thinking about exactly what we want to know about 'friendship'. Doing a literature review helps us to think about the specific research question that we would like to ask about friendship. Reviewing the literature identifies what research has already been done and what questions have already been answered. At the end of a research project, however, the findings often open as many new questions as they answer. This means that thinking about what evidence already exists in the literature helps us think about what we don't know and therefore what is a useful question. This process is implicit in the word, 're-search'. Research involves searching again (*re*) through what we know in order to establish a novel research question. It is important to have a novel question, because if someone has already answered the question, it makes our project redundant. Conducting a literature review therefore ensures that there is a need for our project, that is, to answer previously unanswered questions, and that the question we ask is appropriate according to what we already know.

What does conducting a literature review involve?

There are two key phases of activity which make up a literature review: (1) searching the evidence base (i.e., what we already know); and (2) critically evaluating the evidence (i.e., establishing whether we can trust what people have found in the past). In phase 1, the objective is to conduct a thorough and focused search of the evidence to ensure that (a) we identify as much as possible that is (b) relevant to our research topic. The objective of phase 2 is to critically evaluate the evidence in terms of methodological quality and trustworthiness. The remainder of the chapter is split into two sections detailing the processes involved in phase 1 – searching the evidence base – and phase 2 – critically evaluating the evidence.

Searching the evidence base

A number of stages are involved in conducting a search of the evidence base. This section of the chapter will outline these stages and provide illustrations using the subject matter used throughout this book, friendship.

Refining your research question and identifying keywords

As mentioned above, a key objective of a literature review is to identify a novel research question. Thinking of a question can be challenging, but searching the literature can help. The first task in conducting a literature search is to identify keywords. An effective way of doing this is to create a mind-map (see Figure 3.3). To do this you need to start with your topic area, in this case, friendship. Next, you need to think of synonyms. You can do this by using a thesaurus, which might identify the following: companionship, acquaintance, comradeship, camaraderie, alliance. You also need to identify related words, for example, friends, mates, buddies, peers. Whilst doing this, be careful to think in terms of both singular and plural, that is, friend and friends, mate and mates, buddy and buddies, peer and peers. Also, remember to think of UK and US spellings and terminology, for example, behaviour/behavior, university/college, secondary school/high school. Include all ideas that come to mind in your mind-map. This can be as messy as you like with as many bubbles as you think are necessary.

You can use the CHIP tool (Figure 3.1) to help develop your mind-map. CHIP helps ensure that your search of the evidence is thorough and covers all aspects of a research project to help identify literature that is relevant to your study. It also helps with writing your research question. A number of research questions about friendship would be feasible, but using the mind-map and CHIP tool helps us to

Context	Friendship groups at university (or college)
How	Qualitative methods
Issues	Meaning of 'friendship'
	Development of friendship groups at university
	Ways friends socialise
Population	Students

Figure 3.1   CHIP analysis of friendship study.

What is the meaning of friendship?

How do friendship groups at university develop?

What do they do to socialise?

Figure 3.2   Research questions for friendship study.

focus our thinking. The CHIP tool has identified the following areas about friendship that we are interested in (see Figure 3.1). The research question to be used in this illustration is shown in Figure 3.2. In qualitative research, questions asked at the outset are often exploratory, with one overarching question and a number of subordinate questions. In this case, the overarching objective is to discover what friendship means to students at university. Alongside this question, we want to know how friendship groups at university develop and what university friends do to socialise. The research questions are shown in Figure 3.2.

Once you have exhausted ideas for your mind-map, done your CHIP analysis and written your research question (Figures 3.3 and 3.4), you can start writing search strategies. This will be covered in the next section.

Activity suggestion **3.1**

Think of a topic that you're interested in and have a go at doing your own mind-map:

(i) Did the mind-map help you think through the range of issues related to your topic?
(ii) Use the CHIP tool to check you have covered all angles of the topic you are interested in.
(iii) Identify your research questions based on the issues raised by doing the mind-map.

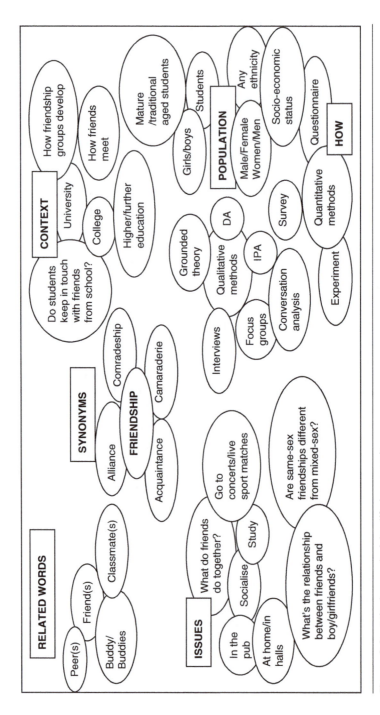

Figure 3.3   Mind-map to identify keywords.

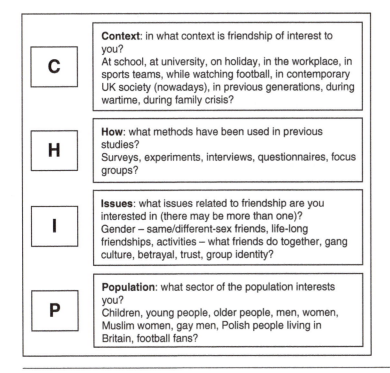

Figure 3.4   The CHIP tool for ensuring comprehensiveness in your literature search.

Writing and refining your search strategy

A search strategy is a list of keywords that you use to search a database. A comprehensive literature search will involve several keywords and may involve several databases. This is an iterative process which means it is very much trial and error.

Despite the technology available to us for searching the evidence base, an element of manual work is still required. Bibliographic databases are an incredible resource and the techniques for searching them are very sophisticated. However, the likelihood of identifying everything that is relevant to us without missing anything is very slim. Typically, when searching the evidence we are compelled to make a trade-off between comprehensiveness (or recall) and specificity (or precision). This means that in our efforts to be comprehensive – that is, not to miss anything – we need to broaden our search, thereby making it less specific. However, if we altered our search to be as specific as possible, it is very likely that this would miss records which are relevant, but which perhaps use different terminology or are categorised in a different way, thereby sacrificing comprehensiveness. The aim, therefore, in a literature search is to find a balance between comprehensiveness

*	Asterisk	Represents any group of characters, including no character
?	Question mark	Represents any single character
$	Dollar sign	Represents zero or one character

Figure 3.5   Wildcards on ISI Web of Knowledge (check the online help if you are using other databases to see which wildcards are available to you).

and specificity – be as comprehensive as possible whilst narrowing the search as much as possible to increase the chances of records being relevant.

What follows is a demonstration using the Institute for Scientific Information (ISI) Web of Knowledge. This is one of the most widely available bibliographic databases, but if you are using a different database, you can use the online help to assist with writing your search strategy.

A good place to start with searching the database is with your initial term, friendship, and the context, in this case, university; for example, see Example Search Strategy 1. We have included friend$ or friendship* to exclude terms like friendly which are likely to retrieve articles about user-friendly programmes or websites which are irrelevant in this case.

Example Search Strategy 1:

Topic = (friend$ OR friendship) AND Topic = (universit*)*

An important aspect of writing search strategies is the use of wild cards and Boolean search operators. Wild cards are used to represent unknown or changeable characters, for example, within the ISI Web of Knowledge: friend* will search for friend, friends and friendship; wom?n will search for woman and women; behavio$r will search for behaviour and behavior.

Boolean search operators – AND, OR, NOT, SAME – help you manage your strategy and are particularly useful in the later stages in order to refine your search.

It is advisable to save your search history whilst you are experimenting with different strategies, so that you can combine them later if you wish. This also makes it possible for you retrieve your search strategies – and the results they retrieve – at a later time. To do this you are usually required to register with a username and password.

Example Search Strategy 2 retrieved 1,259 records.[1] A limitation with the initial search is that some studies may refer to friendship with a different term,

---

[1] Note that all numbers of records were true at the time the search was conducted. Data stored in bibliographic databases are updated regularly as more studies are published and so these numbers should only be used as a guide.

AND	To find records containing **all** terms separated by the operator.
OR	To find records containing **any** of the terms separated by the operator.
SAME	To find records where the terms separated by the operator appear in the **same sentence**. A sentence is defined as: the title of an article, a sentence in the abstract or a single address.
NOT	To **exclude** records including certain words from your search.

Figure 3.6   Boolean search operators on ISI Web of Knowledge (check the online help if you are using other databases to see which wildcards are available to you).

for example, acquaintance or camaraderie. The inclusion of synonyms like these should open up the search making it more comprehensive.

Example Search Strategy 2:

> *Topic=(friend? OR friendship* OR acquaintance OR comradeship OR camaraderie) AND Topic=(universit*)*

This second strategy did indeed retrieve more records, with 1,337 studies identified. Nevertheless, there may still be some studies that this strategy does not identify. For example, in the USA, the term college is used more readily than university. There are also other terms, such as higher education, which may be used in British studies. A third search with further synonyms should make the strategy even more comprehensive, see Example Search Strategy 3.

Example Search Strategy 3:

> *Topic=(friend? OR friendship* OR acquaintance OR comradeship OR camaraderie) AND Topic=(universit* OR college* OR "higher education" OR "further education")*

This strategy retrieved 5,124 studies, indicating that the initial searches did miss some potentially relevant studies. These results illustrate the need to include synonyms to ensure your search strategy is comprehensive. If we are happy with this level of comprehensiveness, we can begin to narrow the strategy by including more keywords from our mind-map. With each trial search strategy, additional keywords are added to incorporate further items from the CHIP analysis, see Example Search Strategy 4.

Example Search Strategy 4:

> *Topic=(friend$ OR friendship* OR acquaintance OR comradeship*
> *OR camaraderie) AND Topic=(universit* OR college* OR "higher*
> *education" OR "further education") AND Topic=(peer$ OR classmate*)*

Example Search Strategy 4 includes synonyms of 'friend' from the mind-map resulting in 632 records. A way of making the search more specific might be to include the methodology of studies you would like to read. As you are concerned with conducting a qualitative project it would be useful to identify some qualitative studies relevant to your own research. As this book illustrates, there are a number of qualitative methods with different names, such as Discourse Analysis and Interpretative Phenomenological Analysis, each of which is associated with different traditions, including social constructionism and phenomenology. However, in the interests of being inclusive (and because the categorisation by qualitative methods is not always as advanced as categorisations of quantitative studies), it is possible to use what is known as a broad-based strategy using just three keywords: findings, interview, qualitative. This strategy for identifying qualitative research has been found to be almost as effective as entering long lists of method-specific keywords (Shaw et al., 2004). When added to Example Search Strategy 4, we can see how many of the 243 records identified are potentially qualitative studies.

Example Search Strategy 5:

> *Topic=(friend$ OR friendship* OR acquaintance OR*
> *comradeship OR camaraderie) AND Topic=(universit* OR college* OR*
> *"higher education" OR "further education") AND Topic=(peer$ OR*
> *classmate*) AND Topic=(findings OR interview* OR qualitative)*

Example Search Strategy 5 retrieved 223 records, which suggests that just about a third of the studies identified used qualitative methods. Remember, at this stage the records retrieved are considered only as *potentially* relevant. This means we cannot yet know for certain whether these studies are about friendship at university or whether they used qualitative methods. To find this out, we need to screen the studies for relevance. Please note that, whilst you are particularly interested in reading those studies which used qualitative methods you also need to review studies which used other methods. This means your review should include studies which used both qualitative and quantitative studies, that is, your pool of potentially relevant literature should include the yield from Strategy 4 as well as those from Strategy 5.

Exploring the use of keywords is helpful when designing a search strategy. The steps taken so far illustrate that starting with broad terms helps ensure the search is comprehensive. Steps can then be taken to narrow the search in order to increase the likelihood that studies retrieved are relevant. Once an effective set of keywords has been identified, a useful exercise is to organise your search according to the different elements of CHIP, as in Example Search Strategy 6.

Example Search Strategy 6:

CONTEXT:	*universit* OR college* OR "higher education"*
	or "further education" (Topic) AND
HOW:	*findings OR interview* OR qualitative (Topic) AND*
ISSUES:	*friendship* OR acquaintance OR comradeship*
	OR camaraderie (Topic) AND
POPULATION:	*friend\$ OR peer\$ OR classmate\$ OR student\$ (Topic)*

Example Search Strategy 6 retrieved 206 results. You now have two options: (1) begin searching through this list of records to identify those which are relevant; or (2) further narrow your search if your research question has become more specific. For example, you may want to focus on how friendship groups affect performance in academic study or whether social groupings affect levels of violence, or whether there is a relationship between friendships during teenage years and success in employment or the development of romantic relationships. Whatever you decide to do, it is recommended that you save the records retrieved to a bibliographic management software package, such as Endnote or Reference Manager, or save them to a file. Make sure you select abstract as a required field in the export so that you have this information available to you in the screening process.

Activity suggestion **3.2** 《《

Have a go at writing your own search strategy for a topic you are interested in:

(i) Remember to do this whilst sat at a computer, so you can test out different search terms in a bibliographic database.
(ii) Once you have built your search strategy, remember to save it.
(iii) Now run your search. Remember to export the search results to some reference manager software.

Screening search results for relevance

Once potentially relevant records are saved – either using reference manager software or in a document – it is necessary to search through them thoroughly by reading the abstracts. This is why it is essential that you include the abstract when exporting records from a bibliographic database.

To help screen the records effectively, you can refer back to your CHIP analysis and ask of each record questions about each aspect of the study (see the example in Figure 3.7). During this stage you need to be working from the full reference of each record which includes the title, journal, publication date and abstract. This should be sufficient information for you to decide whether or not you need to read the full text article. On occasions when you are unsure, it is advisable to code the record as relevant to be on the safe side.

Whilst answering the CHIP questions you need to decide whether the question has inclusion/exclusion power; that is, if the answer to the question is 'no', will the study be excluded from your review? It is unlikely that the 'How' question will function as an exclusion criterion, because although your interest is in finding qualitative literature – to help you think about designing your own study and to find studies which are similar to your own – you also need to consider findings of studies which used quantitative methods. If we take a logical approach to the problem, we can consider guidelines which may help to make the decision of whether a record is relevant. If a study has more 'yes' responses than 'no' responses then it should be included in your review. If there is a full set of 'no' responses, this study is unlikely to be useful to you. Having said all that, it is difficult to be prescriptive,

3.3 Activity suggestion

Go through your own search results using the CHIP questions to decide what is relevant to your research question.

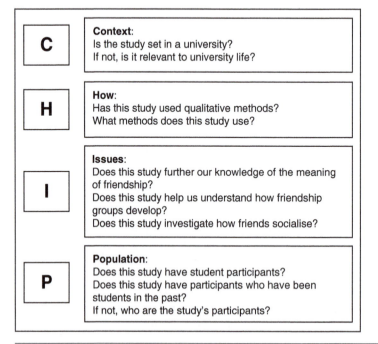

Figure 3.7   Screening questions using CHIP.

especially with qualitative research, which can often be exploratory. These suggestions should be read as guidelines rather than rules to be followed strictly. Whilst you are doing your CHIP analysis to establish relevance, it is useful to keep some brief notes on each abstract to which you can return later when writing up your review (more on this in Chapter 12).

Obtaining full-text articles

Once all records have been screened, it is necessary to obtain the full text articles of all those you have judged as relevant so that you can read them. Most universities now have systems that link directly to electronic bibliographic databases, which means you can click on the record in the database. If the university has a valid subscription to that journal at the time the article was published, you will be able to click straight through to the full text. If not, you will simply need to look up each article in the library or online using your university catalogue or e-library system. If the article is not available at your institution online then check the hard-copy holdings – it might be necessary to search the shelves and photocopy the article, particularly if it was published before about 1997 when publishers began to store electronic copies of articles. On the other hand, if the article is not available at your institution at all, there are a number of ways of obtaining it. You can search the library catalogues for other local university libraries (these are normally available online) and if they have the article you need you may be able to visit that library yourself. Check with your own institution's library for details on how to get access to other libraries. Alternatively, you can submit an Inter-Library Loan request to your own university library which will submit the request to the British Library. There is a fee for this service (via your university library) and often students have a limited annual allocation. Finally, when attempting to obtain a specific article you can search for it on Google Scholar or contact the corresponding author to request a reprint.

A brief note on full-text versus bibliographic databases

Many UK institutions now have access to full-text journal databases. These have been developed by publishers and so are limited to their own journals. For example, PsycARTICLES is a full text database produced by the American Psychological Association (APA) and only includes articles published in APA journals. Other full text databases include ScienceDirect, which includes journals published by Elsevier. The benefit of full text databases is obvious – they take you directly to the full-text article. However, your search is severely limited by the selective coverage offered. Bibliographic databases, such as Web of Knowledge, PubMed, and PsycINFO (a bibliographic database including all available published literature of psychological relevance since the 1800s) provide far greater coverage, often with more sophisticated searching options and therefore give you more likelihood of an adequately comprehensive and systematic literature search. For example, if you are working on a piece of assigned coursework where your lecturer has recommended the use of a couple of journal articles in preparing your work, you may choose to access a full-text database, where you will find a limited number of articles which you can access in full text from your desktop. By contrast, a systematic literature review requires you to have searched across all the literature in your subject area, including those articles that were only published in print and those for which your institution does not have a full-text subscription.

What about Google and Google Scholar?

The Internet has become an integral part of everyday life and even more so in academic work, which means we are all familiar with search engines such as Google and its academic search engine, Google Scholar. Using these search engines offer a 'quick and dirty' way to search the literature. It may be useful in an initial search to stimulate ideas when you are first exploring what area to study. It is also useful for looking up references. Say you remember reading an article, you know in which journal it was published and the title but not the date or the authors. You can put all the information you remember into Google Scholar and the likelihood is it will find the full reference for you. However, it is not a good tool for conducting a literature search proper. In the same way that we choose a bibliographic database over a full-text database in order to be comprehensive and systematic in our literature searching, we must also choose a bibliographic database over Google Scholar. At the time of writing, Google has yet to inform the research community about Scholar's source of data and how frequently it is updated. This means you cannot know what you are searching, which makes a systematic and thorough search impossible.

Searching the literature and identifying studies of relevance are only the first phase of conducting a literature review. The second phase, critically evaluating the evidence, is discussed in the next section.

Critically evaluating the evidence

Once a set of relevant work has been obtained and full-text articles read, it is necessary to assess the quality of literature identified. You can conduct the most thorough and systematic literature search possible, but all that hard work becomes of limited value if you then do not consider the quality of evidence retrieved.

Why is quality important?

Psychology is a science and its pursuits must therefore be judged by scientific standards in order for its findings to be considered a valid contribution to knowledge.

As psychologists in training, therefore, we must not take for granted what we read in journal articles (or what we are told in lectures, for that matter); we must take a critical stance – that is, question everything. This enables us to take a step back from research papers we read, so we can fully consider their quality. Thinking about quality is an inherent part of a literature review – this is evident in its name. Just as a film critic would review a film, so we must review the literature: pick holes in the plot/the appropriateness of the methods to the research question; find fault with the film set/context in which the study took place; criticise the camera work/how the methods were employed; analyse the characters/the roles of the researcher and participants during data collection and analysis; scrutinise the happy ending/claims made in the discussion to ensure they are evidenced by data reported.

Quality is important because as researchers reviewing the evidence base we need to be able to trust the findings of the research reports we retrieve. A central objective of conducting a literature review is to present a rationale for your own study, that is, demonstrate why your study is necessary. To achieve this we need to identify studies that we can trust and those that have limitations. Those of high quality, which we can trust, help support the argument in favour of doing our study. Those with limitations indicate ways in which we can improve our study design; for example, to ask questions that have not been asked previously or to introduce new methodology to a subject area which has been studied from a largely experimental perspective.

What criteria are used to assess quality?

Methodology is very important to psychologists, so when we talk about critically evaluating the literature, a major aspect of this is to review the articles retrieved according to their methodological quality. You will no doubt already be familiar with the terms objectivity, reliability, internal and external validity, and generalisability (see e.g., Robson, 2002 for definitions of these terms). These are the criteria by which the methodological quality of quantitative psychology studies is judged. However, the appropriateness of these constructs for assessing qualitative research is questionable. This is because qualitative research is fundamentally different from quantitative research, both in terms of its objective and its methods. The objective of quantitative research is to make predictions about future behaviour by, for example, observing people's behaviour in a controlled setting, designing a survey based on a particular theory or measuring people's reactions when faced with different stimuli. Qualitative research, on the other hand, aims to explore phenomena that are relevant to people's everyday lives in order to understand some aspect of human experience. This might be achieved, for instance, by conducting interviews with students to understand their friendships and what friendship means to them, or recording a conversation on a telephone helpline to understand the mechanisms at work in the listener's and caller's talk. A different framework is therefore required to assess the quality of qualitative evidence identified during the literature search.

We have already talked briefly about trustworthiness – whether you can trust the findings reported in a journal article (see Robson, 2002 for a discussion of trustworthiness and criteria for assessing qualitative research). This is at the core of establishing research quality. When we are conducting a review of articles published in academic journals, it is the written article that we use to assess quality. This means the transparency of information in the article is paramount; everything the researcher did must be described clearly for us to judge whether it was appropriate and whether it was performed systematically and conscientiously. When we evaluate research evidence, therefore, an adequate level of transparency in the article will enable an informed decision regarding the trustworthiness of its findings and claims made. Hence, when we conduct a literature review that includes qualitative and quantitative research, our measure of quality is designed around these two constructs: trustworthiness and transparency.

The prompts in Figure 3.8 are adapted from Dixon-Woods et al. (2004) and can be used to judge the quality of the science reported in each article. The questions direct your thinking to the design of the research study, whether its methods are appropriate and whether you can understand how the study was conducted. This provides you with 'ammunition' for your review; if you identify problems with the methods or insufficient information is provided to explain how a method was performed, then this lack of transparency makes it difficult for you to trust the findings reported. As a result you will be able to critique the paper based on its poor methodology. Similarly, if the methods seem inappropriate for the question asked you can challenge the evidence on these grounds; if the methods were inappropriate, it is unlikely that the question will have been answered adequately or the question may have been altered in order to fit the methods available. This helps create a rationale for using new or different methods in order to provide a better fit between question and method. When conducting this evaluation, you need to keep notes on each study assessed. Refer back to the CHIP analysis notes you made whilst establishing relevance and add to those the responses to these

- Are the research questions clear?
- Are the following clearly described?
    - Sampling
    - Data collection
    - Analysis
- Are the following appropriate to the research question?
    - Sampling
    - Data collection
    - Analysis
- Are the claims made supported by sufficient evidence?
- Are the data, interpretations, and conclusions clearly integrated?
- Does the paper make a useful contribution?

Figure 3.8 Prompts for assessing quality of studies retrieved.

prompts. You will also find it useful at this stage to summarise the 'take home' message of each research report, that is, what this study achieves and what conclusion it draws. It will also pay off later if you describe any further details of the study, which may form part of the argument made in the write-up of your literature review. For example, the study may offer insight into the significance of gender in the forming of friendships but it was conducted with school-aged children. Whilst its subject matter – the issues it addresses – is relevant, the population is different to that in your own inquiry. This enables you to argue that further work with people of university age is required to fill a gap in our knowledge and therefore justifies the need for your study.

Activity suggestion **3.4** 《《

Find a couple of published journal articles that report studies that have used qualitative research methods. Use the prompts for assessing quality to review those articles and write a brief report and their good and bad points.

Constructing your literature review

Writing up your literature review can be a daunting task. The first challenge is to establish what you are going to say about each article. This doesn't have to be a great deal but should summarise the main point you want to make. The second is to decide the order in which you present the studies. The finished review should be a coherent account of the relevant studies identified, their findings, their failings and what your study will add to them. This will build the rationale for your study.

A literature review is essentially the story of what has happened so far, which sets the scene for your study. Think of it as a prequel to the main event; like *Star Wars – The Phantom Menace* (1999), the first of three prequels to the original (fourth in the series) George Lucas film, *Star Wars* (1977). In providing this background you have two objectives: (1) to inform the reader what we know already; and (2) to demonstrate how your study will fill a gap in current knowledge. To achieve this you need to construct a series of arguments with evidence to back them up.

Structuring your review

The structure of your literature review will depend on the results of your search and your critical evaluation. Return to the notes you made during screening with your CHIP analysis and during the critical evaluation stage using the prompts in Figure 3.8. These will help identify points of significance in each study – what

exactly was the study about, details of the sample population, how it was conducted, the appropriateness of methods used, and whether you can trust the
conclusions drawn. Once you have familiarised yourself with the evidence in this
way you need to organise the studies by theme. Whether you organise by 'context',
'how it was conducted', 'issue', or 'population' depends on the nature of the evidence you are reviewing as well as the focus of your research question. Hence, the
structure of your review very much depends on the nature of your rationale.

Building a rationale and presenting your research question

Alongside presenting the reader with the story so far, a literature review must build
the rationale for your study. The rationale is the justification of your study – why it
is necessary. This comes largely from your critical evaluation. Through highlighting the limitations in existing research you can draw attention to gaps in the
literature that your study will help fill. As you go through each theme in your
review, you need to clearly indicate what is missing and what needs to be done to
address the unanswered questions. Research studies often throw up more new
questions than those it answers. This makes the task of justifying new research relatively simple because there are clearly issues which have not been addressed
previously perhaps because they were considered unimportant or because the
methods to investigate them were not available. In essence, the rationale you provide needs to address each aspect of the CHIP analysis (see Figure 3.9).

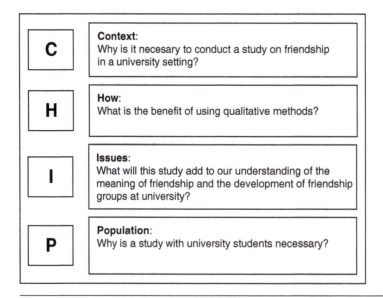

Figure 3.9   Creating a rationale using CHIP analysis.

A literature review should close with a statement of the research question(s) of the current study. In qualitative research we often ask open-ended exploratory questions, such as those in described in Chapters 5 and 7. It is likely, as in our example, that you will have one over-arching question and one or more subsequent questions which are more specific. The reader should almost be able to recognise what the research questions are likely to be from reading your literature review.

Summary points

1. Conducting a literature review is fundamental to the research (re-search) process.
2. We need to establish what is already known before we can decide with any great certainty exactly what questions we want to ask.
3. Searching the evidence is a systematic process which must be followed by the critical evaluation of the literature that is identified.
4. The rationale for your study is developed in part through explaining what is missing and what your project will add.
5. The literature review is the foundation of any research project.

Want to know more? 2.11

Shaw, R. L., Booth, A., Sutton, A. J., Miller, T., Smith, J. A., Young, B. Jones, D. R. & Dixon-Woods, M. (2004) Finding qualitative research: an evaluation of search strategies. *BMC Medical Research Methodology*, 4: article no. 5. Available at: http://www.biomedcentral.com/1471-2288-4-5.

Dixon-Woods, M., Shaw, R. L., Agarwal, S. & Smith, J. A. (2004) The problem of appraising qualitative research. *Quality and Safety in Health Care*, **13**, 223–225.

Part 2
Conducting Qualitative Research

4

Approaches to Data Collection in Qualitative Research

Stephen Gibson and Sarah Riley

Introduction

This chapter introduces a range of different approaches to data collection in qualitative research, and provides practical advice to help you to decide on the most appropriate source(s) of data for your investigation. However, practical issues are frequently difficult to separate from theoretical concerns, and as such we introduce some key considerations regarding the nature of data itself. The chapter is organised into sections outlining different ways of collecting data, and covers many of the most common sources of data used by qualitative researchers in psychology.

What is data?

Typically, psychologists have sought to collect quantitative (numerical) information that can be submitted to statistical analysis. However, increasingly, researchers have begun to collect other forms of data that can be analysed qualitatively – that is,

---

Definitions **4.1** **!**

Although often used in the singular, ***data*** is in fact the plural of *datum*. One of the most useful ways of thinking about the meaning of *datum* is as 'a piece of information' (*Compact Oxford English Dictionary*)

with a view to exploring issues of meaning. For example, a qualitative researcher might be interested in how the meaning of friendship changes as one begins studying at university. Addressing such questions usually requires data in the form of detailed written or verbal descriptions and explanations, such as the interviews used as exemplars in this book. However, it can involve the analysis of visual data, as we will see under 'Visual data' the section. This can be contrasted with quantitative research, which seeks to produce data that can be statistically analysed in order to address questions that typically focus on differences or relationships between groups or contexts. For example, a quantitative researcher might be interested in whether students who have a larger friendship group report better experiences of university, and so might collect data using a questionnaire or structured interview, or may perform a quantitative content analysis of semi-structured interview data (e.g., counting the number of friends a respondent mentions by name).

It will therefore be apparent that the same data (e.g., semi-structured interview data) can be used to support both qualitative and quantitative research. However, even when quantitative researchers start off with similar data, such as interviews about friendship, how they deal with these data will be very different. Thus statistical analyses will require a procedure to convert text into numbers (e.g., content analysis), whereas qualitative researchers will be more interested in studying what people have said. This is not to rule out the possibility of combining some form of quantification with qualitative analysis, but to point to quite a different treatment of data in qualitative research. We should, therefore, think of qualitative research as involving qualitative *analysis* rather than qualitative *data*, since it is both the data that qualitative researchers use and what is done with it that makes a project qualitative.

This is not to say that all qualitative research shares the same assumptions, or makes similar kinds of claims. Rather, qualitative research is an umbrella term that brings together a range of approaches. For example, some qualitative researchers (e.g., those working in Interpretative Phenomenological Analysis), may use semi-structured interview data to draw inferences concerning a participant's experience of, for example, friendship (see Chapter 10). Others, such as discourse analysts (see Chapter 8), would treat the interview talk as a set of accounts, constructed for a particular purpose in a particular context, and would avoid drawing inferences concerning 'experience' or other underlying psychological phenomena. It therefore makes more sense to refer to qualitative research as involving a variety of different approaches, rather than a singular 'qualitative approach'. What these approaches share is an interest in analysing data to explore meaning-making rather than statistical differences or relationships.

How do I collect data?

There are a variety of techniques for data collection in qualitative research. By far the most common of these is interviewing. It is for this reason that the example materials produced to accompany this book use a semi-structured interview, and also why interviewing as a method of data collection is covered separately in

Chapter 5. In this chapter we cover some of the other most commonly used methods of collecting data in qualitative research, namely: focus groups, 'naturalistic' data, media data, visual data and data from the Internet. This is not an exhaustive list – we don't cover, for example, diary techniques or open-ended questions on surveys. Nor should these techniques necessarily be treated as mutually exclusive, as projects may combine techniques in order to address a research question.

Focus groups

Definitions **4.2** !

A **focus group** is 'an informal discussion among selected individuals about specific topics' (Beck, Trombetta & Share, 1986, p. 73).

Focus groups bring together people who have pre-existing ties (e.g., family) or shared characteristics (e.g., university students) that are of interest to the researcher. Typically, a focus group lasts around an hour, consists of four to eight participants and involves a moderator to guide the participants' discussions, which are then recorded (either video or audio) and transcribed prior to analysis. Note that the length of time, number of participants and level of guidance can vary significantly and should reflect the researcher's and the participants' needs.

Current uses

Focus groups are useful in a wide range of research designs, examples of which are given in Table 4.1.

When would you use a focus group?

Focus groups are used when it is an advantage to have interactions between your participants. These interactions can give you access to more naturalistic processes of communication which include 'storytelling, joking, arguing, boasting, teasing, persuasion, challenge and disagreement' (Wilkinson, 2008, p. 187). If you are interested in how people negotiate ideas, or in types of communication styles, then focus groups are useful.

Additionally, focus groups can be particularly useful if you aren't a member of the community you're researching, since participants may present themselves differently to a researcher in a one-to-one interview than when amongst peers (e.g., by using more formal language). Focus groups may help you get data in which participants give detailed or nuanced accounts, as they discuss their perspectives

Table 4.1 Examples of uses for focus groups

Use	Example	Reference
As a precursor to quantitative work	Development of questionnaire on quality of life	Skevington, MacArthur & Somerset (1997)
Assisting analysis of quantitative data	Interpretation of questionnaire responses on magic mushroom use	Riley & Blackman (2008)
Examining interpersonal processes and social understandings in organic or artificial groups	Discursive 'othering' of family members	Billig (1998)
Action research	Facilitating change	Chiu & Knight (1999)
As means to gather in-depth data from a large number of people	Using structured group discussions to identify solutions to communication problems in institutions	Powell, Hunt & Irving (1997)

and experiences with each other. Having more participants than researchers tends to dilute the researcher's influence, since participants can act as facilitators by, for example, asking each other questions or challenging each other's statements.

These interactions between participants can help focus the discussion on topics that are important to them, shifting the direction of your research to interesting areas you may not have thought of. The group dynamics often make focus groups more enjoyable than one-to-one interviews, which can be considered an ethical issue, given that it's important that people are able to feel positive about their participation in research. Note, however, that interactions need to be skillfully managed (see 'how to' section below).

Finally, you might use focus groups as a method of gathering information that requires less resources than do surveys that use one-to-one interviews – although, note that this should not be done as a form of 'quick and dirty' research, but because your research will benefit from having a wider range of voices, and in a context where the interactions between participants might inform the research topic. In comparison to interviews, however, focus groups may be less suitable for research interested in chronological information concerning specific individuals and in some contexts when the topic is particularly sensitive or controversial.

How to collect focus group data

Barbour & Kitzinger (1999) and Krueger & Casey (2000) are excellent resources, which discuss a range of focus group designs and provide detailed guidance on deciding which one is most appropriate for your research. We recommend anyone planning on using focus groups to read these beforehand. To help start your thinking, see Table 4.2.

Table 4.2 Do's and don'ts in focus group research

DO	DON'T
Define the issue in a way that makes sense to the participants. It needs to be a topic that can be discussed in public and phrased in everyday language	Don't use psychological jargon
Think about the kind of equipment needed, for example, whether to use audio or video recorders	Don't forget to test your equipment or rely on one piece of equipment (use at least two to make sure you pick up all the talk in the room)
Consider how to get your participants talking (e.g., with discussion initiators such as asking a general question or asking participants to comment on TV clips)	Don't forget to have a look at the guidelines for interview schedules (see Chapter 3)
Consider group dynamics when recruiting, including the extent to which your groups represent features that are important to the research, and other aspects that may affect interactions (e.g., gender, ethnicity, class, level of involvement in the group, how participants will perceive themselves as different from each other/you)	Don't bring a group of people together without thinking about how their similarities, differences and relationships with each other may create power dynamics that affect what people feel they can say (e.g., bringing teachers and students together)
Choose a topic that is of interest to your participants	Don't recruit participants who are particularly busy (they probably won't find a time when they can all attend)
Plan in advance the number of groups you will need, something that will depend on the kinds of questions you want your research to address. The number of groups may be as many as can be recruited, until you hear no new stories, or enough to get rich data	Don't risk under-sampling by only conducting the number of focus groups you want to be able to analyse. Instead, you should aim to over-collect data, in case one of the groups does not work, has to be cut short, or if participants withdraw their consent
Consider facilitation: how you will manage the meeting (such as explaining to the participants what to expect or where the toilets are); how you will manage interactions (e.g., how to bring in people who are less talkative); and the level of structure you want to impose on the discussions (e.g., allowing participants to talk freely on whatever issue they move on to, or managing their time so that they cover the issues that you are concerned with)	Don't make it up as you go along. Avoid assuming that you will be able to facilitate a focus group without thinking very carefully about how you will manage it first
Be flexible and sensitive when facilitating focus groups	Don't stick rigidly to your plan even when it's not working, or ignore bullying or other negative behaviour.
Run a pilot group to get a sense of how your ideas may work in practice.	Don't pilot test using friends (they will behave differently from 'real' participants)

4.3 Want to know more?

Two useful introductions to focus group work can be found in:
Barbour, R. S. & Kitzinger, J. (Eds) (1999) *Developing focus group research.* London: Sage.
Krueger, R. A. & Casey, M. A. (2000) *Focus groups: A practical guide for applied research.* London: Sage.

Naturalistic data

4.4 Definitions

Naturalistic, or naturally occurring, data 'derive from situations which exist independently of the researcher's intervention' (Silverman, 2006, p. 403).

Naturalistic video or audio recordings are the most commonly found form of data examined in Conversation Analysis (CA) and, increasingly, in a form of Discourse Analysis (DA) known as Discursive Psychology (DP) (see Chapter 8 for the distinction between DA and DP; see also Edwards, 2005). They can also be used in conjunction with a range of other approaches, but CA and DP research is distinctive in that many researchers in these traditions actively express a preference for naturalistic data. Indeed, you will be most likely to see data referred to as naturally occurring or naturalistic in CA or DP work, where it tends to be used to refer primarily to naturally occurring *talk*.

Current uses

Conversation and discourse analysts have recorded naturally occurring talk in a wide variety of settings. CA originally made extensive use of recordings of telephone conversations (Sacks, 1992; for a summary, see Silverman, 1998, pp. 109–114), and these are still one of the major sources of naturalistic data in use today (e.g., Potter & Hepburn, 2003; Kitzinger & Kitzinger, 2007). Other researchers have recorded data from settings as diverse as family mealtimes (Wiggins & Potter, 2003), police interrogations (e.g., Stokoe & Edwards, 2008), psychic consultations (Wooffitt, 2001), doctor–patient interactions (e.g., Heath, 1992), discussions between people with learning disabilities and their carers (e.g., Antaki, Finlay & Walton, 2007), and counselling and psychotherapy sessions (e.g., Peräkylä et al., 2008)

More recently, conversation analysts have begun to analyse new media of communication such as the Internet (e.g., Antaki et al., 2006), mobile phone conversations (Hutchby & Barnett, 2005) and text messaging (Spagnoli & Gamberini, 2007). In addition, naturalistic materials can be collected from the mass media (see section on 'Mass media').

When would you use naturalistic data?

Researchers such as Potter (2004) argue that naturally occurring data are useful if you are interested in how people interact in any particular setting, so that you can see and hear for yourself what is said or done and don't have to rely on people's retrospective accounts of an event. However, there are some important debates surrounding the assumptions underlying the idea of 'naturalistic' data (see Critical Issue box).

Critical issue: The 'dead social scientist test' **4.5**

Potter (2004, p. 612) proposed the 'dead social scientist test' for determining whether data can be considered 'naturalistic'. By this he means that 'if the researcher got run over on the way to the university that morning, would the interaction nevertheless have taken place, and in the way that it did?' (ibid.). So, interviews and focus groups are 'out', whereas recordings of ordinary conversations are 'in'. Potter & Hepburn (2005) have developed this line of argument to suggest that naturalistic data are *preferable to* researcher-provoked or 'got-up' data. They argue that studying interactions which have been set up by a researcher, and in which the researcher participates, only tells us about how people talk in these highly specific social situations. However, other researchers have suggested that data gathering procedures in which the researcher plays an active part actually have some virtues over naturally occurring materials (e.g., Griffin, 2007), and that in some cases a researcher may be compelled to intervene in an interaction for moral and/or political reasons (Guimaraes, 2007)

What do you think? **4.6**

Some researchers have challenged the notion of 'naturalistic' or 'naturally occurring' data itself, arguing that anything that is used as data in social scientific research is inevitably in some part a product of the research process, even if the researcher was not directly involved in the interaction which constituted the data (Billig, 1999; Speer, 2002).

Does this make you think.... How 'natural' is any recorded interaction?

How to collect naturalistic data

In one sense, collecting naturalistic data is quite straightforward – all you really need to do is record some bit of 'real life' and there you have it! However, this apparent simplicity conceals some important decisions which need to be considered first. To begin with, are you going to make audio or video recordings? The former has the advantage of being more portable once the equipment is set up, and of being less intrusive than a video camera. On the other hand, video allows access to important visual features that would be lost with audio. Moreover, it would be mistaken to assume that participants will simply 'forget' about the presence of an audio recording device (Speer & Hutchby, 2003). As Rapley (2007) points out, it is important always to be sensitive to issues of how the presence of recording equipment (and, more generally, of the process of doing research) impacts on the data you collect. Finally, and on a much more practical level, you should ensure (as with all research) that you are familiar with your equipment, and that if your participants are making the recordings that they too know how to use it. For more detail, Rapley (2007, Ch. 4) offers an excellent guide to some of the practical issues involved in recording naturalistic data (see also, Chapter 8 of this book).

4.7 Want to know more?

Some good sources for following up on the question of what's 'natural' are:

Potter, J. (2004) Discourse analysis as a way of analysing naturally occurring talk. In D. Silverman (Ed.), *Qualitative research: Theory, method and practice* (2nd edn) (pp. 200–221). London: Sage.

Rapley, T. (2007) *Doing conversation, discourse and document analysis.* London: Sage.

Silverman, D. (2006) *Interpreting qualitative data* (3rd Edn) Chapter 6: 'Naturally occurring talk'. London: Sage.

Media data

Radio, TV and print media data are interesting because they present particular world views, are naturalistic in the sense that they are not created by researchers, and because they have their own communication styles or formats that differ from everyday conversation. This makes media analysis particularly attractive to conversation analysts and to a range of discourse analysts.

Definitions **4.8** !

Any medium of communication can properly be said to be part of '**the media**', but when psychologists refer to the gathering of data for qualitative analysis from the media, they are generally referring to the **mass media**. Even this concept is actually quite difficult to define (see Giles, 2003, pp. 6–9), but, at the very least, it includes TV, radio, newspapers and magazines. Increasingly, the Internet is becoming an important medium of communication, but this has some unique features which make it worthy of consideration in its own right (hence its inclusion as a separate section below).

Current uses

Typically, qualitative researchers in psychology analyse the media to address one of three issues: (1) representations and constructions of issues or people; (2) the management of identity, accountability and interest; (3) and differences in the way people communicate when using different media. Table 4.3. gives examples of studies in these categories.

When would you use media data?

As will be apparent from Table 4.3, the approaches most commonly used in analyses of media data tend to be DA and CA. Figueroa (2008) provides advice on the use of Grounded Theory (GT) to analyse mass media texts (see also, Burgoyne, 1997), but such data would be less well suited to IPA, given the focus of this

Table 4.3   Uses of mass media data

Issue	Examples
Representations and constructions of issues and people	Discourse Analysis of media representations of asylum seekers (Lynn & Lea, 2003); men's health (Gough, 2006); acculturation (Bowskill et al., 2007); place and national identity (Wallwork & Dixon, 2004).
Management of identity, accountability, stake and interest	Identity construction in TV interviews (Abell & Stokoe, 2001); the management of stake and accountability (Edwards & Potter, 1992); the social production of nationalism (Billig, 1995)
Differences in communication styles in different media	Conversation Analysis of radio talk (Hutchby, 1996) and television talk (Clayman & Heritage, 2002; Ohara & Saft, 2003)

approach on understanding idiographic experience (see Chapter 10). Perhaps most obviously, you would use media data when you are interested not in what ordinary people feel, think or say about something, but when you want to understand how a particular discourse functions within the media. A DA or GT approach would be well suited to the first type of research question, whereas CA, and some variants of DA (particularly DP; Edwards & Potter, 1992), would be better suited to the second kind of question.

How to collect media data

Regardless of your media of interest, you will need to make various decisions regarding the selection of materials for analysis. For instance, are you interested in exploring particular types of newspaper articles (e.g., editorials, features, news stories), radio or television shows (e.g., discussion/talk shows, phone-ins, news interviews)? Are you interested in a particular topic (e.g., the representation of the single European currency), or are you interested in exploring the communication styles employed in a particular medium (e.g., how news interviewers maintain the impression of neutrality)? Radio or televisual material will need to be recorded using appropriate equipment and transcribed. If analysing newspapers and magazines it is always advisable to make photocopies on which you can write notes, keeping the unblemished originals safe to refer to at a later date or from which to make further copies.

You might also need to think critically about the precise claims you want to be able to make from your data. For instance, avoid assuming that a sample of 'national' newspapers purchased in, say, London, represents the 'national' newspapers being consumed by readers in, say, Glasgow, as there are frequent geographical variations, even in what is ostensibly the same newspaper (MacInnes et al., 2007). Equally, beware treating media texts as being able to tell us about popular consciousness – although it may be tempting to assume that people who read a particular newspaper or listen to a certain radio station may 'believe' or agree with what they are reading or listening to, this should be treated as an empirical question in itself.

4.9 Want to know more?

For more information on media, see:
Giles, D. (2003) *Media psychology*. Mahwah, NJ: Lawrence Erlbaum.
Hutchby, I. (2005) Conversation analysis and the study of broadcast talk. In K. L. Fitch & R. E. Sanders (Eds), *Handbook of language and social interaction* (pp. 437–460). Mahwah, NJ: Lawrence Erlbaum.

Internet data

It is important to point out that these two types of internet data need not be thought of as an 'either/or' option, as it is perfectly possible to draw on both approaches to collecting data from the Internet. For example, Murray (2005) reports a study of the meanings of artificial limb use that employed IPA to analyse e-mail interviews, postings on a discussion forum, and face-to-face interviews.

It is also worth pointing out that although these techniques represent the most common uses of the Internet as a means of data collection at present, the potential for the Internet to be used for a much wider range of data collection activities will increase.

Current uses

Researchers employing most of the techniques commonly used in qualitative research in psychology have used the Internet as a means of generating data for analysis (Table 4.4).

When would you use internet data?

e-mail interviewing is particularly useful for accessing participants who may be otherwise difficult to get hold of, either because they are located some distance from the researcher, or because they may feel more comfortable discussing certain issues electronically rather than face-to-face. For example, James & Busher (2006) point out that e-mail interviewing was particularly advantageous in one of their studies in which some participants were located in different time zones, which meant that face-to-face interviews were impractical and too costly, and telephone interviews would potentially have to occur at inconvenient times. Pre-existing internet material is particularly useful if you want to analyse the way in which people communicate and make sense of their world via the Internet, but it also allows access to a variety of data – such as media reports, political speeches and images – all of which are viable objects for qualitative analysis.

Table 4.4   Examples of recent uses of internet data

Approach	Topic	Reference
Interpretative Phenomenological Analysis	E-mail interviews with people with dementia	Clare et al. (2008)
	Messages posted on a pro-anorexia website	Mulveen & Hepworth (2006)
Grounded Theory	Online gaming addiction	Chappell et al. (2006)
	Parental perspectives on caring for children with autism	Fleischmann (2005) Huws et al. (2001)
	'Consumer' accounts of electroconvulsive therapy	Rose et al. 2004
Discourse Analysis	Identity construction by people with eating disorders	Giles (2006)
	Far-right websites	Billig (2001) Wood & Finlay (2008)
	Social networking websites	Goodings et al. (2007)
	Welfare reform discourse	Gibson (in press)
Conversation Analysis	Online discussions	Antaki et al. (2006) Sneijder & Te Molder (2004)

Continuing advances in computing technologies are making the Internet increasingly useful as a source of non-textual data. For example, interviews may be conducted via webcams (Matthews & Cramer, 2008) and researchers are increasingly making their audio and video data available for download via the Internet (as in Chapter 7). Conversation analysts in particular have pioneered this approach to data sharing, and though it raises important ethical issues, these are not insurmountable. Indeed, many conversation analysts argue that it serves as an extra reliability check on their interpretations – other researchers can access their data and challenge and/or confirm their analysis if they wish to do so. As a result, there is a steadily growing archive of pre-collected interactional data available via the Internet (for particularly good examples, see the Talkbank database [http://talkbank.org] and Emanuel A. Schegloff's website [http://www.sscnet.ucla.edu/soc/faculty/schegloff/sound-clips.html]).

How to collect internet data

How you go about collecting data using the Internet depends upon whether you are using the Internet as a means to conduct interviews/focus groups, or exploring pre-existing material.

There are several useful sources for conducting e-mail interviews and online focus groups. Bampton & Cowton (2002) provide practical advice on e-mail interviewing, and Holge-Hazelton (2002) offers a reflection on her experiences of conducting research using e-mail interviewing to study the experiences of young people with diabetes. Similarly, Murray & Sixsmith (2003) discuss some of the advantages and disadvantages of e-mail interviewing, and James & Busher (2006) usefully include examples of the information provided to their participants in order to obtain informed consent. Finally, Evans, Elford & Wiggins (2008) provide a discussion of the use of the Internet for qualitative research in psychology, which is primarily focused around conducting online interviews. Online focus groups can be conducted using specialist software, or by simply making use of existing chat and discussion facilities (see e.g., Mann & Stewart, 2000; O'Connor & Madge, 2003; Stewart & Williams, 2005).

One major advantage with all forms of textual data on the Internet is that it does not require time-consuming transcription. However, there are a number of practical issues specific to the use of pre-existing internet material as data (see Robinson, 2001, for a useful discussion), including how to reduce your data set if you have more material than is manageable. For example, you can employ a variety of sampling procedures, such as random selection, choosing threads that are most relevant to your research interest, or choosing topics that have received the most responses or endorsements from other internet users (e.g., Gibson, 2009). The procedure you use should be based on the kind of analysis you employ, your research questions, or the kinds of claims you want to be able to make about your findings (e.g., whether they can be extrapolated to wider populations). The sources cited in the 'current uses' section above are good places to start thinking about the ways in which different analytic approaches might influence the collection of pre-existing online data. Additionally, if you are seeking to use this sort of material to draw inferences about a particular population, you will need to bear in mind the biases inherent in the Internet, particularly those around access to computing facilities (Martin & Robinson, 2007).

Finally, the use of the Internet as a means of data collection raises a number of ethical issues (see Brownlow & O'Dell, 2002). For example, it can often be difficult to determine what constitutes public domain material, which is usable without the need to obtain informed consent, and material that writers may assume will reach only a limited audience (Robinson, 2001). The British Psychological Society

---

Want to know more? **2.11**

For more information about internet data, see:

Bampton, R. & Cowton, C. J. (2002) The e-interview. *Forum: Qualitative Social Research*, **3**. Accessed online 18th June 2008 from http://217.160.35.246/fqs-texte/2-02/2-02bamptoncowton-e.htm

Evans, A., Elford, J. & Wiggins, D. (2008) Using the internet for qualitative research. In C. Willig & W. Stainton-Rogers (Eds), *The Sage handbook of qualitative research in psychology* (pp. 315–333). London: Sage.

James, N. & Busher, H. (2006) Credibility, authenticity and voice: dilemmas in online interviewing. *Qualitative Research*, **6**, 403–420.

Robinson, K. M. (2001) Unsolicited narratives from the internet: A rich source of qualitative data. *Qualitative Health Research*, **11**, 706–714.

(2007) has published a set of guidelines for the use of the Internet in psychological research, which addresses this and many other issues.

Visual data

When people talk about qualitative research they are usually referring to research which involves the collection and analysis of textual material. As Reavey & Johnson (2008) point out, this is perhaps a result of the so-called 'linguistic turn' or 'discursive turn' in the social sciences in the 1970s and 1980s, which came to place increasing importance on the role of language in social life. However, there is a rich tradition of analysis of visual material – particularly in anthropology (Banks, 2007) – and in recent years, many researchers have sought to address psychological questions through the qualitative analysis of visual materials.

!

4.12 Definitions

Visual analysis typically involves the analysis of images, as distinct from the analysis of text. This definition requires a certain amount of qualification, as some researchers have argued for the definition of 'text' itself to be sufficiently broad to allow for a whole range of apparently non-textual representations to be treated as 'text' which can be 'read'. For example, Nightingale (1999) has explored the possibility of treating the body as a text. However, for present purposes the idea of visual data involving images rather than (or as well as) text is more than adequate.

Visual data can be developed by the researcher or by participants. For example, in some studies participants might be provided with a camera with which to take photographs, whereas in other studies researchers might use photography themselves to record visual phenomena. Further distinctions can also be made. For example, Temple & McVittie (2005) outline three types of visual data: first, there are pre-existing data that are not specifically created for the research project; second, there are data that are collected for the project, but which cease to exist following the end of the project (e.g., observational data or performance pieces); and third, there are data that are created specifically for the project, but which continue to exist beyond the end of the project. It is also important to recognise that researchers often combine different forms of data collection and studies often benefit from an analysis of both visual and textual material. For example, a researcher might analyse photographs in conjunction with interviews in which participants talk about what the photographs mean to them (e.g., Radley, Hodgetts & Cullen, 2005).

Table 4.5   Examples of types of visual data used in recent research

Data	Reference
Paintings	Gillies et al. (2005)
Video recordings	Sparrman (2005)
	Toerien & Kitzinger (2007)
Graffiti	Lynn & Lea (2005a, b)
Murals	Finn (1997)
Photographs	Mitchell et al. (2005)
	Radley et al. (2005)
	Radley & Taylor (2003a, b)
Images used in psychology textbooks	Hansen et al. (2003)

Current uses

Researchers have analysed a wide variety of visual material (Table 4 5). To begin to get a sense of the diversity of uses to which visual data can be put, it is worth considering two studies in a bit more detail.

Radley et al. (2005) used a technique known as photo-elicitation (see Definitions box below) to investigate experiences of homelessness. They asked a sample of 12 homeless people to take photos that represented what it was like for them to be homeless, and then used these photos as a basis for interview discussion. This process allowed the researchers to explore the different identities that their participants drew on. For example, one woman strongly identified with the homeless community (as evidenced in how she talked about the many images she took of other homeless people), whereas another woman's interview and photographs showed how she attempted to fit into the everyday life of the city in which she lived.

A quite different use of visual data can be found in studies that apply Conversation Analysis (CA) to video recordings of everyday interactions. For example, Toerien & Kitzinger (2007) discuss the emotional labour involved in the service industry using video-recorded interactions in a beauty salon. Their analysis focused on how beauty therapists did more than just apply a treatment, but co-ordinated their talk and actions with their clients to maintain positive social interactions. This would not have been possible with audio recordings alone.

Definitions **4.13** !

Photo-elicitation is a research method that involves the use of photographs as a basis for interview or focus group discussion, and frequently involves asking participants to take photographs themselves. It is gaining

(Continued)

> # 4.13 Continued
>
> popularity amongst some qualitative researchers who perceive it as a method with several advantages including:
> - It gives the researcher access to areas to which she/he might not otherwise have access.
> - It provides a way to do more participatory research, since participants are given the opportunity to produce the analytic materials themselves.
> - It is easier and more enjoyable for participants to do: researchers are able to draw on a cultural familiarity with the act of taking a photograph that may not be the case when one is asking people to participate in interviews, or to produce written accounts.
> - It is also easier to share: this type of research has the potential to produce more accessible and engaging material for dissemination to a wide audience (see e.g., Gleeson et al., 2005)

When would you collect visual data?

Visual data can be used to support a wide range of different research projects. As a general rule, though, whichever analytic approach you are using, visual data is especially useful (indeed, it is essential) when you are interested in questions that cannot be adequately addressed through analysis of textual material alone. It may be useful to draw a distinction between approaches which focus primarily on experience and meaning (as in Radley et al.'s, 2005, study described above), and those which are concerned with discourse and interaction (such as Toerien & Kitzinger, 2007). These examples show that many different approaches to qualitative analysis are suitable for the analysis of visual data, but the sorts of analyses produced using these different approaches will sometimes be quite different.

How to collect visual data

Given the variety of forms of visual data, and the uses to which they are put, it is impossible to provide a set of guidelines or instructions on how to collect all forms of visual data. If you are interested in using visual data, the best approach is to use the references listed in the further reading at the end of this section, as well as the studies mentioned in Table 4.5 to give you a sense of how they can be used in research.

There are also some unique ethical issues involved in visual research – particularly where photographs are used. For example, Radley & Taylor (2003a) used photo-elicitation to investigate patients' experience of their time in hospital. Due to concerns expressed by hospital managers about the inclusion of people on the photographs, Radley and Taylor asked their participants to refrain from taking pictures of other individuals. This raises an important ethical issue with visual research – namely the fact that individuals present in visual material will most likely be identifiable. It is possible (and relatively straightforward if using digital photography) to disguise people's identities by, for example, pixelating their faces, but it should be remembered that individuals may still be identifiable to people who know them based on factors such as dress, physique or location. Again, these can be digitally obscured but this can lead to difficulties in the presentation of findings if, for example, the way an individual dresses is central to the analysis. Additionally, it is worth noting that one of the most common contexts in which you might typically expect to see people with pixelated faces is in material that forms part of a police investigation. You might therefore need to bear in mind the risk of inadvertently making your participants look as though they were engaged in criminal activity.

Technical issues are also important in photographic research – it is no use taking lots of photographs and then finding out that the images have not been recorded properly. As with all equipment used in any research project, the advice here is simply to ensure that you are familiar with the photographic equipment you are using, and if you are asking participants to take photos, making sure that they too are familiar with it. Even with sufficient preparation, though, it is always likely that things won't go according to plan, so it makes sense to aim to over-collect data initially so that your project won't suffer if, for example, one of your participants accidentally drops the camera and you can't then access the images.

Want to know more? 4.14

For more information on visual data, see:

Banks, M. (2007). *Using visual data in qualitative research*. London: Sage.

Gleeson, K., Archer, L., Riley, S. & Frith, H. (Eds) (2005) Visual methodologies. *Qualitative Research in Psychology*, **2**(3) (Special Issue).

Radley, A., Hodgetts, D. & Cullen, A. (2005). Visualizing homelessness: A study in photography and estrangement. *Journal of Community and Applied Social Psychology*, **15**, 273–295.

Reavey, P. (Ed.) (2009) *Visual psychologies: Using and interpreting images in qualitative research*. London: Routledge.

Summary points

In this chapter, we have discussed some of the key issues involved in some common forms of qualitative data collection.

1. Different approaches to data collection should not be thought of as mutually exclusive. As will be apparent by now, it is possible for example, to collect mass media data using the Internet, or to analyse visual material appearing in the mass media.
2. A research project might make use of two or more sources of data (e.g., Murray, 2005; Radley et al., 2005).
3. Rather than distinguishing between 'types' of data, and thinking that any project should concentrate on only one such 'type', the key questions concern:
   (a) what you want to be able to find out (which may, or may not, be formalised into a specific research question);
   (b) what assumptions you are making about your data; and
   (c) practical concerns regarding issues such as the time and resources available to you.
4. It is worth noting that we have generally avoided dealing with the politics of data collection and focused instead on practical and conceptual issues. However, there is always a danger in neglecting the political dimension of research, or implying that it can be straightforwardly distinguished from other concerns. There has been a tendency in psychology (especially in social psychology) for qualitative research to be associated with explicitly 'critical' approaches (see e.g., Hepburn, 2003).
5. The assumption that one is automatically doing 'critical' or politically radical research by virtue of using qualitative methods is one that should be resisted (Parker, 2005). In fact, qualitative research is used widely by commercial organisations and government agencies, and techniques such as focus groups have long been used in attempts to monitor and govern populations.
6. Whatever method of data collection you employ, it may be worth remembering that these methods have often developed more through motivations of coercion than liberation. For examples of influential discussions of the role of psychology in the maintenance of power structures, see Henriques et al. (1998) and Rose (1999).

5

The Interview in Qualitative Research

Siobhan Hugh-Jones

Introduction

Each of us has a private, personalised and often complex inner life of thoughts and feelings that shape, and are shaped by, everyday experiences. However, as well as having a private self, we also have a social self, and most of us spend a significant proportion of each day interacting with others, primarily through talking. In doing so, we express both something of ourselves (e.g., sharing knowledge, expressing views, remembering, articulating feelings) and learn about others (e.g., their perceptions of things or their wants and needs). So, talking and listening is a part of everyday human experience and is a key way in which we understand our own and others' worlds. Indeed, it is the ways in which we each attribute meaning to our day-to-day experiences that we tend to talk about most, typified in exchanges like 'I wish I had understood what she meant', 'I just felt so nervous' or 'I felt so great when I heard the news'.

The practice of understanding other people by talking with them, and listening to them, is one that is fully embraced by qualitative researchers, given their concern with ways that people experience everyday life (Willig, 2001), and is most commonly seen in the form of a research interview. Indeed, the qualitative research interview is now the most common form of systematic social inquiry across the social sciences, and the verbatim data generated in interviews enjoy a particularly high status (Holliday, 2002). Some qualitative researchers have described the qualitative interview as 'one of the most common and powerful ways in which we try to understand our fellow human beings' (Fontana & Frey, 2000, p. 645).

Definitions 5.1 !

Verbatim means using exactly the same words as were originally used.

Figure 5.1   Images of interviewing in contemporary culture.

Moreover, not only is interviewing a popular research method, it is also an established feature of everyday society, so much so that Atkinson & Silverman (1997) claimed that ours is an 'interview society'. As well as the research interview, there are other types of interviews pervasive in our society: for example, journalistic interviews (including popular media interviews), which seek accounts of people's lives, events or decisions from public figures, and therapeutic interviews, common in the medical profession, which aim to understand patients' experiences. Thus, in Western culture, interviews are familiar, legitimate, and (mostly) respected ways of generating information and understanding of others.

This chapter will help you to understand the different ways that in which we can think about interviews, ways of conducting them and characteristics of a good interview. It identifies important considerations in recruiting participants and in preparing interview questions and guides you through the tricky aspects of actually doing the interview. Remember though that interviewing is a craft and the best way to become a good interviewer is through lots of practice; one's first interview is usually less than brilliant. Finally, the chapter will consider some of the oft-cited criticisms of interviews and interview data.

Types of interviewing

Many types of research interview exist, from highly structured (researcher controlled), through semi-structured to highly unstructured (uncontrolled). Structured interviews involve asking each interviewee the same set of standardised questions and in the same order. They are often used in large-sample surveys and are not typically used by qualitative researchers, who are more concerned with an evocative communication of people's life experiences, activities, emotions and identities. Thus, qualitative researchers tend to employ interviews that are less structured and which offer interviewees opportunity to expand their answers and give complex accounts of their experiences. Such less-structured interviews (typically referred to as either semi-structured or open/unstructured) often have distinct theoretical frameworks underpinning them. This means that they have a theory-informed view of the person and the experiences they are trying to understand, and they typically imply the use of a specific approach to data analysis (Hopf, 2004).

Common across all forms of qualitative interviews, though, is the focus on subjective accounts of individual experience. That they are exploratory means that they do not presume that all of the issues, or ways of experiencing them, are known in advance. The fact that qualitative interviews focus on subjective accounts means that they are not concerned with 'fact-finding' or getting verifiable accounts. Rather, they acknowledge that human experience has diverse qualities and meanings, that the interview can explore these and that they can tell us something important about human behaviour (Holstein & Gubrium, 1995). As Arksey & Knight (1999) state, the qualitative research interview is a valuable research method for exploring 'data on understandings, opinions, what people remember doing, attitudes, feelings and the like, that people have in common' (p. 2).

Critical Issue: Subjectivity in psychology **2.13**

Many qualitative approaches in psychology are interested in people's subjective experiences (i.e., what were things like for them? How did they experience an event/phenomenon?). However, using subjective accounts as research data is sometimes criticised by psychologists. Why do you think this is?

Do you think subjective accounts have a value in psychological research?

(See Chapter 2 on different approaches to generating knowledge).

Interviewing typically involves one researcher interviewing one participant at a time, but there are ways to interview groups (e.g., focus groups), use multiple interviewers, do repeat interviews and conduct electronic interviews (i.e., by instant messaging or e-mail) or telephone interviews. This chapter focuses on the most common form of research interview in psychology – the semi-structured interview. This type of interview involves preparing questions in advance, but with freedom for the interviewee to raise aspects not necessarily anticipated by you. In so doing, the qualitative researcher shows a commitment to understanding what is important to the interviewee rather than driving the interview along a pre-determined route. The interviewers themselves also have freedom to be flexible in their questioning (as in Extract 5.1), and to respond in natural ways in the interaction (see Extract 5.2), as long as they broadly address the research question they set themselves.

> ### Extract 5.1: Freedom in interviewing questions (Int. 5; lines 464–467)
>
> In this extract, Deborah refers to mother and toddler groups, so the interviewer picks up on this and pursues it with another question. This area of questioning was not pre-planned, nor was it touched upon in other interviews. However, it was entirely appropriate for the interviewer to respond with interest, and further questions, to areas brought up by the interviewee.
>
> Interviewer: Yeah. And then did you develop, so when, when you became a mum you mentioned about going to sort of mother and toddler groups.
>
> Deborah: Mother and toddler groups, yeah, yeah.
>
> Interviewer: So did you develop new friendships from becoming a mum?

> ### Extract 5.2: Responding in natural ways (Int. 3; lines 67–70)
>
> Here, the interviewer responds to Louise's sarcasm about enjoying Business Studies. Think how differently the sequence may have gone if the interviewer had ignored Louise's sarcasm; Louise may have been left feeling that her style of humour was misplaced or that the interviewer did not approve. The short response and natural laugh by the interviewer conveys acceptance of Louise's view.
>
> Interviewer: Are you doing the same course?
>
> Louise: No she does business studies, so yeah, she enjoys it.
>
> Interviewer: You sound unconvinced [laughs]
>
> Louise: I know, it's not my type of thing but ....

Understanding interviews: Some conceptual points

Interviewing for research purposes has a long history, dating back to 1886 and Charles Booth's work on the economic and social conditions of life in London. Interviews have also been used by psychologists for many years – think of Freud's (1914) use of clinical interviews to develop his theories, or Piaget's (1959) more relaxed interviews with children. However, as qualitative researchers, our under-standing of what interview data is has undergone a radical change in the last 20 years.

This change has been from seeing interviewing as a data-excavation project to seeing it as social interaction that can constitute data (Kvale, 1996; Kvale & Brinkmann, 2009). These are considered here as conceptual points. Developing a concept of something means drawing together all of its parts, or instances of it, to form an idea of it – what it is like and how it may function. There may be different ways to do this, meaning that there are different conceptual views of it. For example, we can talk about love as a concept and some may conceive of it as an individualised, biologically driven experience, whereas others may prefer the conceptual view of it as a community-based, more spiritual experience. In relation to interviewing, there are many different ways of understanding the process and the outcome. Here we consider the two prominent conceptualisations of interview data that have been dominant in psychology.

Critical issue: Why is it necessary to think about conceptualisations of interviewing? 5.3

Some students ask: 'What is the problem with just going about and asking people the things we want answers to? Why should we have to delve into seemingly remote and philosophical discussions about conceptualisations of interviews?'

The reason why it is important to think about conceptualisations of interviews is that the view you take of them will have a powerful and obvious influence on the way you analyse your data, and what you say in your discussion. Any good researcher needs to consider what his or her conceptual, and possibly theoretical, position is before beginning research.

Want to know more? 5.4

You can read more about how to conceptualise data (or knowledge) in the early sections of Chapter 2. You could also read:

Kvale, S. (1996) *InterViews*. London: Sage.

Lyons, E. & Coyle, A. (2007) *Analysing qualitative data in psychology*. London: Sage.

Interviews as excavation

For a long time, the research interview was thought to be a way of accessing information that resided in the interviewees' head. The information (e.g., attitudes to birth control or experiences of loss) was understood to be pre-existing – rather rigid and unchanging – and fundamentally available for retrieval. The interviewer, through careful questioning, would be able to unlock, or access, that information, with the interviewee being rather passive in the whole process. What was retrieved, namely the interviewees' responses, was thought to be relatively uncontaminated by the research process, and certainly not significantly affected by the interviewer. Indeed, the interviewer was seen as a neutral, if not invisible, entity in the entire endeavour (Fontana & Frey, 2000), and in this sense reflects positivistic notions of science (see Chapter 2). However, this conceptualisation has lost favour with many qualitative researchers who have argued strongly that we cannot ignore the role of the interviewer, nor should we consider the interviewee to be passively handing over personal accounts in a disinterested and direct manner. Thus, the interview process and the data that are available at the end, may be most helpfully understood in ways that recognise the role of the interviewer and the interviewee.

Interviews as co-constructed

A more contemporary understanding among qualitative researchers conceives of the interview as a way of formulating, rather than collecting, data. This conceptualisation focuses on two main features. The first is rather straightforward and relates to the fact that any interview situation, no matter how standardised, relies on the interaction between two people, so saying that one is less involved in the interaction than the other is a mis-representation of the interactional nature of interviewing (Dingwall, 1997). It is after all an 'inter-view' (Kvale & Brinkmann, 2009). Thus, the interviewer plays a role with the interviewee in the co-production of the data, as illustrated in Extract 5.3.

The second feature is slightly more complex and concerns the 'big questions' about the nature of knowledge, or meaning, in our own minds. Essentially, the argument is that one's thoughts, feelings, attitudes, beliefs and memories can be talked about in many different ways – each one of them viable and worthy of attention. Furthermore, *we can choose how we talk about things,* and our talk may be influenced by several factors, not least what we have been asked and why. The Critical Issues box below offers an example of this, illustrating that when people speak, their narrative has both a 'what' component (i.e., what they are talking about) and a 'how' component (i.e., how they are choosing to tell it) (Sarup, 1996). Among qualitative researchers, there are different opinions about how conscious this choice is; some argue that people are entirely aware of the version of things they are presenting, whereas others argue that the 'how' of talk is often unconscious. Each method of qualitative data analysis has its own distinct view on this (see Chapter 2, p. 28–31 and Chapter 8, p. 138–140 for further discussion.

Extract 5.3:   How interview data is co-produced (Int. 3; lines 183–195)

In this extract, the interviewer responds to Louise's account by focusing on friends who have 'fallen by the way side' and how 'fizzling out' of friend-ships happens. The subsequent sequence may have been very different had Louise focused on a different aspect of going to the same school/college, or if the interviewer had picked up on Louise's reference to male friends, or what it means to be 'really close friends'. Thus, both parties are active in co-producing the interview data.

Interviewer:	You all went to the same school and then to the same college, ok.
Louise:	Yeah, so it was really good and there's a couple of people from school like it's a group of lads who we've kept in touch with as well so they're like really close friends, but it goes to show you when you move on who your friends are 'cause they're the people who wanna stay in touch and who make the effort to see you, and you make the effort to see them and it makes you realise, it's like a …
Interviewer:	'Cause I mean there must have been other people who you were friends with who have sort of fallen by the way side.
Louise:	Yeah, but they've just like fizzled, yeah.
Interviewer:	What sort of, what leads to that fizzling?
Louise:	I think it's more a case of people doing different things, and then you don't see each other often so you run out of like a bit of conversation really and then you just never see them, 'cause I'm here, hardly, the people when I go home, the main friends who I spend my time with, 'cause I've not got a lot of time, apart from the weekend or something, it's really …

Critical issue: It's our choice to say what we want, and how we want 5.5

If you were asked about your experience of undergraduate psychology, what you say about it may depend on who is asking (e.g., another student or a tutor), why they are asking (e.g., to see if psychology is worth doing, or to assess why you may not have achieved very high grades) and when they are asking (e.g., 10 years after you've graduated or whilst you're still a student). Your responses may also be strongly influenced by how you want to be seen by the questioner; for example, do you want to be seen as a

(Continued)

5.5 continued

hard-working, dedicated student, or is it important to you to be seen as a fun-loving character with a more *laissez-faire* approach to study. Thus, any speaker has at their disposal, options to speak about things in many different ways.

Student view: What would influence what you say?

If you were asked about your attitude towards ASBOs (Anti-social Behaviour Orders, commonly given to young offenders), what might influence what you say? Would it matter if the person asking had themselves been given an ASBO, or if they had a son or daughter who had one? Would it matter if they were asking you in your capacity as a psychology student, or if they were asking you as a young person who understands youth culture?

Thus, remaining aware that the interview is a form of social interaction, and that the way a person speaks about things depends on so many features of that interactional context, is crucially important in qualitative research. Bearing these things in mind leads to data analysis and interpretation that is not removed from the research context, but can identify how it may be influencing the data produced within it.

Of course, appreciating that people can talk about things in different ways, at different times forces us to ask another question about the data we get. Namely, if it is open to change, and people could tell us any version of events or experiences they wish, then what can we say is real? This question continues to be debated by researchers across the social sciences, and is no way unique to qualitative researchers in psychology. Although there are many approaches to answering this rather philosophical question, we focus here on a widely accepted position in qualitative research, called 'social constructionism'.

The essence of this social constructionist position (see Chapter 2 p. 26) is that whilst people can clearly generate different accounts of events, experiences, attitudes, beliefs, etc. in different interactional contexts, they do not do so in a chaotic and entirely inconsistent manner (unless they want to deliberately lie); rather, there is some consistency to the ways in which people think and feel about things. If we return to the example in the Box 5.5 above, it would be highly unusual in any interactional context to say that your experience of being an undergraduate psychology student was exceptional when you really feel it had been dreadful. Rather, you would want to talk in a way that was consistent with your experience, but that was *sensitive to the interactional context* – who was asking you and why. This sensitivity can be understood as 'double attending'. As Holstein and Gubrium (1995) state, 'meaning is not constantly formulated anew'; there is some underlying constancy in people that is 'crafted to the demands of the occasion' (p. 17). Furthermore, interviewing is a useful resource for inciting the production of meaning, to stimulate interviewees' interpretative capabilties and to apprehend, organise and represent people's reality (Holstein & Gubrium 1995, and Extract 5.4 below). This is why good questioning is so fundamental in qualitative interviewing.

Extract 5.4:   Interviews can stimulate interpretative capabilities (Int. 3; lines 371–378)

Here Louise generates a coherent and accessible description of what support in friendships *means* to her.

Louise	…back as well [Interviewer: yeah], so it's not just like I'm giving, giving, giving, you're getting, you're getting support back as well.
Interviewer:	And you find that with all your friends, it's sort of equally give and take?
Louise:	Yeah definitely, yeah.
Interviewer:	What does it, what does it mean support, like to, to support a friend, what's, I don't know, what's involved with that?
Louise:	It's, it can just be a conversation, or even just like a little bit of affection, and the look they give you that they know something, just saying like 'It's gunna be alright', it's like just affection really, 'cause we are quite close, we do like sit and cuddle and stuff like, which you don't normally see but us girls we're like quite close in that respect so it's easy to see if something's up with someone cause you know them that well, so it is just like affection and just little like expressions that they give you so you know.

What does all this mean for doing qualitative interviews? The *key point* is that it means appreciating that when people give answers to your interview questions they are telling you something important for them in that interaction, and that 'that something' will be largely consistent with their underlying reality and meaning-making processes.

Where are we now?   **5.6**

Interviewing is a form of social interaction, whereby both the interviewee and the interviewer influence the data that is produced. Furthermore, interviewees are free to choose what they say and how they say it, which means that there are multiple ways to answer any one question, and at different times. However, with the necessary sensitivity to the issues of co-production and the impact of the interview context on the data (i.e., what is being asked, by whom and why), analysis of interview data can be extremely effective in answering many different research questions.

Doing interviews: The starting point

Whilst there are no definite 'must-do's' in interviewing, there are things you can do and think about which are more likely to yield good quality research. The first good practice feature that comes once you've decided on your research question (see Chapters 2 and 3), is to consider the best way to find out what you want to know. Although much psychological research employs a single data collection method, there are often many different methods which researchers could use to generate answers to their research questions (e.g., diary methods, observations, examining archived documents, etc.).

For most undergraduate psychology students, and indeed many experienced researchers, time and practical constraints mean that only one method of data collection is possible. Choosing that method is often tricky, but the choice should always be driven by the research question (Willig, 2001). For example, if you wanted to know how the media represent current beauty ideals, then it would make sense to examine those media representations directly rather than, say, interview a magazine editor. However, if you were interested in how professionals in the media make decisions about publishing beauty images, then interviews or focus groups would be appropriate. The *key point* is that you should be able to offer a clear rationale for your choice of data collection method.

Interviewing is often the first choice for psychological researchers interested in the ways in which people experience events, or the ways in which they attribute meaning to those experiences. As Kvale (2009) succinctly comments, 'If you want to know how people understand their world and their lives, why not talk with them?' (p xvii).

Recruiting for interviews

Having decided to do interviews, the next question relates to recruitment. Even if you have been using qualitative methods for many years, the question of how many people, and what kinds of people, to interview is always one that has to be thought through in relation to each individual research question, as there is no 'one-size-fits-all' answer. As with other types of research in psychology, there are different types of sampling procedures, such as random sampling, purposive/ quota, intergenerational, snowball, etc., all of which have implications for the types of analysis and interpretation which are possible from the interviews. For example, if your participants were all recruited via a university society or club, then you would need to consider this when you discuss the implications of your findings. Alternatively, if you recruited people by opportunity sampling, it may be that your participants are particularly motivated to speak about the topic of interest compared to those who did not want to be interviewed.

The next question relates to how many people you should interview. Kvale's (1996) response to this is to interview as many people as you need in order to find

Critical issue: Recruiting for different types of analytic approach **5.7**

Thinking about how, and why, people came to be in your study will be useful when you are attempting to make sense of the data. Most forms of qualitative data analysis (e.g., Interpretative Phenomenological Analysis, Thematic Analysis) will work perfectly well with standard ways of recruiting participants, as long as people's possible motivations to be interviewed are borne in mind. However, if you are going to do a Grounded Theory analysis on your data (see Chapter 9), then there are some alternative recruitment options for you. The founders of Grounded Theory, Strauss & Corbin (1990), suggest a flexible and continual movement between data collection, data analysis, and theorising, and advocate a recruitment strategy called 'theoretical sampling'. This means that, having interviewed some people and analysed their data, you can actively seek to recruit certain types of people, or people with certain experiences, that may help you to expand upon and develop your initial analysis.

Alternatively, if you are interested in conducting Discourse Analysis or Conversation Analysis (Chapters 8 and 10), you may be more interested in what your interviewee considers the interview to be (e.g., are they threatened by the interview or do they have an axe to grind?), rather than how you actually recruited those interviewees in the first place (although this is still important to bear in mind).

---

out what you want to know. Again, we see the centrality of the research question in all of the methodological decisions being made, and again there are multiple ways in which qualitative researchers tackle the 'how many' question; some argue that you should keep on interviewing until you are not encountering any new themes in the data, whilst others would argue for a pragmatic approach to studying experience in-depth, suggesting that 15 ± 10 is appropriate (Kvale, 1996; Lyons & Coyle, 2007).

As well as thinking about how to recruit people, students often ask whether it is acceptable that participants are known to them, or even be close friends, as these are easy to access for undergraduate research. You should consider the following:

- the pressure they might feel to take part;
- how they will feel answering your questions, and how you will feel asking them;
- whether they will feel able to trust you, and your commitment to confidentiality;
- how you will feel knowing something about this person that you are unable to share with anyone else; and
- your ability to maintain your confidentiality agreement, regardless of how mundane their data might be, how many beers you may have had and how much your mates interrogate you.

Preparing questions

Because asking and answering questions is such a fundamental part of daily social interaction, we often think that doing an interview will be easy. And in many ways it is, but it is hard to do well. Interviewing involves many complex processes for the interviewer; he/she has to ask meaningful and answerable questions that the interviewees will be motivated to answer, listen to their accounts and respond appropriately. The interviewer also has to monitor comprehension, seek clarification without being overly directive, be mindful of what the next questions could be and constantly remain sensitive to the interviewee's emotional state (Hoffman, 2007). In qualitative research interviewing, the researcher typically aims to elicit long, detailed extracts of talk from the interviewee, rather than short, clipped answers more typical in journalistic interviews that say little about the person's experiences. However, even though interviewing is complex, good pre-interview planning in developing the *interview schedule* can go a long way to improving the interview, and the data you generate through it.

5.8 Definitions

An **interview schedule** is the term used to describe the list of prepared questions that you anticipate using in the interview. If you are conducting a semi-structured interview, the interview schedule is a guide only, and many other questions may be asked in the course of the interview in efforts to engage in an interaction that is sensitive to each interviewee and the topics that he/she is bringing up.

Spending time preparing your interview questions is one of the best things you can do to promote your chances of generating useful interview data. Underpinning your preparation of questions should be this one fundamental question: *What do I need to ask this participant in order to understand his or her experiences?*

Researchers should also consider whether the types of question asked, and the type of data generated, will be suitable for the anticipated method of analysis. For example, if you are interested in the ways that a student population constructs notions of sexual risk, then Discourse Analysis would be appropriate (see Chapter 8). This approach is concerned with the ways in which people discursively formulate ideas in interaction and examines mundane talk to get at this; so, you might ask the interviewee to describe everyday activities, choices and behaviour. However, a discursive analysis is not focused on people's felt experience or what things *mean* to them. In comparison, Interpretative Phenomenological Analysis is entirely concerned with understanding individual experience, feelings and meaning-making, so there may be more questions in the interview around emotion, values and priorities. Thus, where possible, your interview questions should be sensitive to the anticipated method of analysis.

For many research questions and most methods of analyses, the essence of good interviewing lies in the eliciting of *descriptions* of the interviewees' lived world – what they did, with whom, how things worked out, what they thought then, what they think now, etc. The more participants can tell you about their experiences, however ordinary, the more understanding you will have about their view of the world, themselves and the things that have happened to them. Almost all of the questions put to the interviewees in the friendship interviews were based on descriptions (Figure 5.2 gives examples) and many interviewees' responses to these questions generated insight into meaning-making about friendships (e.g., see Extract 5.5).

What kinds of things do you do with your friend?	[Interview 1, line 41]
How did you find it when you first came to university in terms of making friends?	[Interview 1, line 165]
What was the shift that happened there?	[Interview 1, line 418]
Your other friends, is your relationship with them quite similar to your relationship with this guy?	[Interview 3, line 61]
How did you go about ending that friendship in that sense?	[Interview 3, line 246]

Figure 5.2   Examples of descriptive questions (from the data set).

Extract 5.5: How description questions can elicit meaning (Int. 5; lines 317–329)

Leading up to this extract, Deborah had been talking about her friends' frustration with her because she never seemed able to go out with them once she had her baby, and how they were 'never gonna ring again'. Instead of asking Deborah, 'what did that feel like?' the interviewer probes for more description about how the 'not ringing' was played out; in her response, we see more of the meaning of friendship to Deborah.

Interviewer: And, and, and how did that feel at the time when your friends, I mean did your friends actually actively say to you 'we're not ringing, we're not ringing you if you're not gunna come out', or did it just more happen ...?

Extract 5.5: continued

Deborah: Yeah, I think once they did [Int: yeah], and I was like cos it
           was, that's what I said 'you only ever ring me when you want
           me to come out with you', it was a bit like that, cos they were
           that kind of people [Int: yeah] you know going out all the time
           and I was before I had my little boy, but things change and
           [Int: yeah] you know I had a boyfriend then as well and you
           know I had my own home and a family kind of thing and it was
           like 'I can't just go out at the drop of a hat' and 'I'm running
           a home here' kind of thing [Int: yeah, yeah], you know what
           I mean erm, but I think now they sort of understand that as
           they've sort of got up to that now, and [Int: yeah] I think I was
           gutted at the time though, I did feel like I lost my friends [Int:
           yeah] because

The next most frequently asked questions in interviews often relate to
the interviewees' felt experience (most appropriate when an Interpretative
Phenomenological Analysis or Grounded Theory analysis is anticipated). Such
questions are useful when the interviewee has given a description of something,
but has said little about what this was like. Extract 5.6 illustrates how careful questioning about emotions can stimulate interviewees' further reporting.

**Extract 5.6: Questions eliciting felt experience
           (Int. 4; lines 207–228)**

Just prior to this extract, Trevor had talked about a friend who had begun
taking drugs and who had pulled out last minute from being a best man
at their friend's wedding. From the first descriptive section (lines 194–199)
it is hard to get a sense of what this was like for Trevor, so the interviewer
proceeds with further questions around this, and Trevor responds with more
emotional detail.

Interviewer: Yeah, and how did that make you feel, knowing that you
              couldn't, couldn't be best man?
Trevor: Er you feel crap and that cos especially when you know
              you're close friends with two people and you start to feel in
              the middle cos you know like you've got two best friends and
              it's like 'hang on' you know, what do you do?

> Interviewer: So, and then, so erm what, what, what do you feel that changed then after that incident, well not being able to be best man, what, how do you feel that, that changed your friendship?
>
> Trevor: Er I don't, er I don't know I mean, just er, you know er it was horrible, you just er, it just kept getting worse and worse and more selfish and selfish, saying nasty things about my friend's wife behind her back and like, and that, and then you know … it was like you're getting more and more let down, just like you know there's no point, you know cos you know when it starts affecting you personally and how you feel you know cos people do change over time [Int: yeah], you know events and life effects people so you know it's understandable but you get to a certain point where you have to think 'hang on this is just not working'.

Regardless of the type of questions you use, it is crucial (certainly as a novice interviewee anyway) that your questions are open-ended and non-leading. Open-ended questions give the interviewee the option of responding in complex ways, and typically means avoiding questions to which the interviewee can only answer yes/no; any response to these will have been heavily shaped by the response options given and actually tell you very little about experience anyway. So, for example, instead of asking 'is it important to you to have friends?' you might ask, 'tell me something about the aspects of friendships that matter to you?'; or instead of 'do you regret moving here?' you could ask 'how do you feel about your decision to move?'. Similarly, questions should be non-leading, which means that they should not imply that one way of responding is preferable to another. However, avoiding closed and/or leading questions is often hard, even for experienced interviewers, as illustrated in Extract 5.7.

Extract 5.7:   The pitfalls of leading questions (Int. 0; lines 90–93 Int. 1; lines 99–103)

Here the interviewer, mid-flow in conversation, asks what seems like an interesting question. The problem with it is that it leaves the interviewee with little option but to agree – it would be hard for him to say that he thought the friendship (with his best friend) would end anytime soon.

> Interviewer: Ok, cool. Erm the, the first friend you were talking about, do you, do you reckon that's a friend for life, I mean …?
>
> Alexander: Yeah he's gunna be my best man at my wedding if I ever have one so, definitely, [Int: yeah], definitely, best, er best mate for life.

(Continued)

Extract 5.7: continued

However, in Louise's interview, the interviewer asks a more open version of the same question, which generates a more differentiated answer.

Interviewer: Yeah ok. How long do you think you'll erm, you'll know these friends for do you think?

Louise: Hopefully like after university and stuff, there's a few that I think we'll try and stay in touch with but you won't for obvious reasons, but there's a few er I reckon will stay

Interviewer: And what are the obvious reasons?

Louise: Like they live too far away and don't you know, I don't know, like one, some of them a ....

5.9 Activity Suggestion

Select a transcript from the corpus and:

(i) scan for longer sections of narrative and identify what seemed to help interviewees give more detailed responses;

(ii) check the use of prompts and identify which ones seemed to help the participants, and which were too leading.

So, descriptive, feeling or meaning-making questions can generate useful data in interviews. Note, though, that the qualitative research interview does not typically focus on *why* people do things or feel things (Kvale & Brinkman, 2009); such lines of questioning tend to feel confrontational to the interviewee as they imply that there are rational and logical explanations for everything we do, which is not always the case. For example, if in an interview you said that you had felt moved to tears upon hearing a particular story, and the interviewer asked you why, you might feel they were implying you should not have felt the way you did, or that it was illogical to feel so. However, if you were asked to *describe* more about the episode of feeling emotional, you may be more willing to share your perception and experiencing of that event.

However, even the best thought-out questions cannot guarantee that the interviewee will give you a lengthy response. To aid both interviewee and interviewer further, you can prepare some back-ups in the form of *prompts* and *probes*. Prompts are sub-questions to help interviewees should they find it hard to answer your initial question (e.g., a prompt to 'What does friendship mean to you?' might be 'What kinds of things are important to you?'). Probes are a type of searching sub-question, and are useful if you want to explore interviewee responses further. Be careful, though, that you do not become too leading in your use of these. Extract 5.8 illustrates the use of these in the friendship interviews.

Extract 5.8:   Probes

Interviewer: So the people that you do lose contact with, what, what's, what are the sort of things that end up meaning that you lose contact with them? [Alexander, Line 234]

Interview: Yeah, so to you that's an important sign of, of friendships that ability to feel comfortable?

Shazia: Yeah, definitely, yeah.

Interviewer: Yeah in that silence. And em that, that ability do you feel, when, when do you feel that happens in a friendship? Do you feel there's a certain point that that happens or [Shazia, lines 100–103]

Other useful examples:
Could you give me an example of that?
Could you say more about that?
Are there other times when you felt similar/different to that?

Even bearing all these things in mind, it is still often incredibly difficult, even for very experienced researchers, to generate a good interview schedule and it may take quite a few drafts before you have a set of questions with which you are happy. These pointers and the examples in Chapter 7 for the data set will help:

1. Write down what you want to know, without giving too much thought to how it sounds.
2. Think about what ordering of questions will make most sense to the interviewee (but be prepared to move from this ordering during the interview depending on what the interviewee brings up).
3. Work on re-phrasing/re-wording questions to improve their clarity and focus, and to make them answerable, respectful and non-leading. For example, you might start with 'What was it like to be rejected by that University?' and reshape it into 'Can you tell me about the day you received the letter from that University?'.
4. Ask yourself whether you could actually answer those questions, and if your responses would help you understand your research question.
5. Try to do a pilot (test) interview to see if the questions are answerable and if they do generate data relevant to the research question.
6. Try to learn by heart the key questions you would like to ask, so that you don't have to keep checking your paperwork during the interview, which is highly distracting to both you and the interviewee.

Conducting the interview

There is an extensive literature on how interviews should be conducted, and a multitude of aspects which should be considered. Here, we focus on the crucial aspects of good interviewing.

Your safety and that of your participant are of paramount importance (see Chapter 6 on Ethics for more discussion on this). Also, ensure that you have a recording device that works, has sufficient battery or charge, and test it out in the environment in which you will be interviewing to ensure it can pick up voices. It is both an ethical and professional issue that you do this to ensure that no-one's time has been wasted and that you demonstrate respect for the interviewee's disclosure to you.

When you first meet your interviewee, be relaxed and friendly; it may take them a few minutes to get the measure of you but they will appreciate your efforts to put them at their ease (indeed, much of the friendship interviews have a minute or two of general chit-chat at the start, often with quite a bit of laughter). When you are ready, remind the interviewee of ethical issues (e.g., why the interview is being recorded and what you will do with the recording; see Chapter 6 for more on this). Once you have checked that the interviewee is happy to continue, you can start; your opening can follow on from the natural conversation you were having with the interviewee or you can have a more distinct start (e.g., see Figure 5.3).

Many new to interviewing feel that the recorder renders them more self-conscious. However, you soon come to ignore the recorder and interviewees

---

This interview is all about people's friendships, and what they think of as a good friend, so the questions all deal in some way with the general topic of friendship. Are you happy to talk about this?

And just to remind you again that you can stop the interview at any point without having to explain why, and you can withdraw your data from the study after the interview if you feel that you'd like to, and again without having to explain why. Are you happy with all this?

Here's the consent form, which I'll ask you to fill in and sign at the end of the interview. It contains details of how the data will be used and who will be able to read it. Have a look through the form and make sure that you're happy with what's on there.

If there's anything you don't understand then please ask me. When you're happy you can pass me the form back and I'll give you it again at the end of the interview for you to fill in and sign.

Thanks. Well, I wonder if a good place to start would be for you to think of a particular friend you have, and to tell me a bit about how you met?

Figure 5.3: Example opening for an interview.

are often far less worried about it than you. One or two aspects of interviewing sometimes unsettle the new interviewer. For example, what should you do if the interviewee asks you a question, or if they go silent on you? Table 5.1 highlights some things that you should be prepared for, along with some pointers on how to handle them.

A good ending to an interview is important for lots of reasons, not least ethical ones. Given that the interviewee has personally disclosed aspects of their life to you, you need to ensure that they do not leave the interview still feeling psychologically exposed. Thus, your final few questions should be relatively light and unsearching. Also, ask the interviewee if there is anything not yet discussed that they feel is important to talk about; then ask them how they found the interview and check that they are happy for their data to still be included in your study.

Table 5.1 Things that may throw you

Possible challenge	Possible response
Interviewee asks you a question (e.g., what does friendship mean to you?)	Interviewers typically do not disclose. Should an interviewee ask for you opinion, or your view, you could say that you would need to think about it, or say it's an interesting question. If pushed, say that you would rather keep the interview time for listening to what is important to them
Interviewee begins talking about topics or issues that are not relevant to your research question	Bring them back to it by asking how them to draw out the relevance, or by simply saying that you're going to return now to a question more directly related to your focus. Don't worry too much though – most talk tells you something interesting
Interviewee keeps insisting they cannot remember events/thoughts you are asking them to recall	Re-frame question or move on
Interviewee asks for your advice, or your approval	Do not give it. Tell the interviewee you understand how important it is to feel things are OK, or to get someone's opinion, but that you are really not in a position to offer that
Interviewee is silent after a particular question	Try not to jump in to fill it. Silence does not necessarily mean that the interviewee cannot, or does not want to, answer; it may mean they are gathering their thoughts or trying to remember. Allow a comfortable lapse before asking whether the question made sense to the interviewee, or if they would like to move to another question
Interviewee gets upset	Interviews, however benign, can provoke emotional memories, so have tissues with you. Give the interviewee time. Tell them you see that they are upset and that they can take as long as they need to. Don't rush to end the interview as it may signal to them that you are uncomfortable. When they are ready, ask them if they feel happy to continue. You could ask if they want to say a little about how they feel now

Thank them for their time, and for their willingness to talk, and you could then perhaps move on to what the rest of the day holds for them etc.

Summary points

1. Interviewing is a key data collection method in qualitative research, and with appropriate compatibility to methods of analysis, sensitivity to context and awareness of co-construction, it can generate useful data to answer a multitude of research questions.

Table 5.2   The Do's and Don'ts of interview questions

Do	Don't
Consider whether interviews are the best method of data collection given your research question	Don't assume an interview is the best way for you to collect data
Think carefully about the wording of questions	Don't be convinced you will be able to think on the spot in the interview
Ask sensible, answerable questions (e.g., tell me about the day you heard you'd been accepted to University)	Don't ask questions full of psychological jargon (e.g., tell me about your self-concept)
Start with easy-to-answer questions, and progress to more searching questions later	Don't start with tricky or crucial questions; the interviewee needs time to orient themselves to the topic and the interview
Ask open, unbiased and non-leading questions that give interviewees opportunity to respond as they wish (e.g., what do you feel is important to understand about the effects of bullying?)	Don't ask yes/no questions, or lead your participant to say what you want them to (e.g., Do you think bullying is bad?)
Consider how broad a question can be before it becomes unanswerable (e.g., tell me about the things that are important to you in being a sister' rather than 'tell me about your experience of being a sister')	Don't leave your interviewee to figure out what you want them to talk about; give them sufficient clarity
Try to get the interviewee to talk freely, with as little intervention from you as possible	Don't keep interrupting the interviewee; it shows that you are more interested in what *you* want to say than you are in what *they* are saying
Have some prompts prepared to help the interviewee, if necessary, or to delve further into their responses	Don't move directly from one question to the next without being sure the interviewee has said all they want to in response to that question
Be ready for silence	Don't jump in to fill every second of silence
Know your questions well, so that you can listen more attentively in the interview	Don't keep checking your papers to see what question is coming next; it is distracting and unprofessional
Think about how you will end the interview	Don't end abruptly; the interview may feel unsettled by this

2. Good interviewing necessitates planning on many levels, from whom to interview, where and when, to what to ask and how to end.
3. Although anyone can ask questions, becoming a good interviewer takes practice; for the novice researcher though, Table 5.2 provides a summary of key tips for interviewing.

Want to know more?   5.10 +

You could start with some of the following:

Denzin, N. K. & Lincoln, Y. S (Eds) *Handbook of qualitative research* (pp. 645–672). London: Sage.

Gubrium, J. F and Holstein, J. A. (Eds) (2001) *Handbook of interview research*. London: Sage.

Holstein, J. A & Gubrium, J. (1995) *The active interview*. London: Sage.

6
Research Ethics in Qualitative Research

Nigel King

Introduction

This chapter will introduce you to a very important issue for psychologists: the ethics of the research we carry out. I will start by defining what 'research ethics' means in general and in relation to psychology, and introduce the main principles and procedures that guide researchers. Next, I will consider the particular issues that face qualitative research projects, arguing that whilst they do not differ from other methodologies in their underlying principles, they do in terms of how these are put into practice. I will take you through some of the distinctive ethical challenges facing qualitative psychology, including issues relating to the new and rapidly growing field of online qualitative research.

What do we mean by research ethics?

Our starting point in thinking about ethics in psychological research must be to consider what the term means in general. In its broadest sense, 'ethics' refers to questions of how we conduct ourselves morally. As a topic of systematic enquiry, it has its origins in classical Greek philosophy, where great philosophers such as Socrates and Aristotle presented a variety of arguments for what constitutes a 'good life'. In the post-classical Western world, Christianity became the basis for ethical judgements, grounding them in scripture. Philosophical and religious positions have continued to influence ethical reasoning to this day – think, for example, about debates over topics such as abortion, animal rights and privacy. However, from the late nineteenth century onwards, developments in ethics have also been closely associated with the rise of professions such as medicine, the law, teaching, nursing, accountancy and so on. Many of the ethical dilemmas we face in society today are addressed in relation to the ethical codes of conduct of such professions.

For instance, much of the controversy around the topic of assisted suicide is bound up with the ethical requirement for doctors not to harm their patients. Those opposed to any kind of physician-assisted suicide argue that it breaks a fundamental ethical principle of their profession. Those in favour counter with the view that to deny such assistance to a desperately ill person is itself a form of serious harm. This example illustrates a point I will return to later: ethical principles rarely tell us unambiguously what we should do in a given situation. Rather, they encourage us to think through with care the consequences of different choices.

The notion of 'research ethics' grew out of professional ethics, especially in medicine. It is concerned with providing guidance to researchers in particular disciplines as to how they should carry out their work in a morally defensible manner. With particular reference to social research, Edwards & Mauthner (2002) state that: 'Ethics concerns the morality of human conduct. In relation to social research, it refers to the moral deliberation, choice and accountability on the part of researchers throughout the research process'. (p. 16).

A major milestone in the development of research ethics was the Helsinki Declaration on medical research involving human subjects, originally published in 1964 and revised six times since – most recently in 2008 (World Medical Association, 2008). It was instrumental in the development of institutional ethical review committees, initially with specific reference to medical research but rapidly broadening to the natural and social sciences. Alongside this has come the evolution of codes of ethical research practice within individual disciplines including, of course, psychology. There are also codes that relate to specific aspects of research, such as work with animals (British Psychological Society, 2007a) and online research (Ess, 2002).

There is naturally some variation in the issues addressed and procedures advocated by different codes of ethic; we will examine those issues specific to psychology in the next section of this chapter. It remains the case, though, that the principles espoused in the Helsinki Declaration underlie contemporary research ethics as a whole. They are:

- Protection from harm (physical and psychological)
- Respect for individual dignity
- Right to self-determination
- Right to privacy
- Protection of confidentiality

A further general principle is the expectation of honesty and integrity on the part of the researcher.

Research ethics in psychology

In the UK, the ethical principles under which psychological research is carried out are detailed in the British Psychological Society's Code of Ethics and Conduct

(BPS Code) (British Psychological Society, 2006). Other countries where psychology has a significant presence usually have similar codes under the auspices of their national associations. The BPS Code covers both psychological research and professional practice, under four key principles: respect, competence, responsibility and integrity. These encompass the ethical issues that all psychologists involved in research must address: informed consent, confidentiality, right to withdraw, assessing risk of harm, deception, debriefing, limitations to the researcher's role, use of incentives, and honesty and integrity in the research process. I will explain each of these in turn below, and highlight their implications for psychological research in general.

Informed consent

Participants should normally only take part in research where they have made an overt decision to do so, and where that decision is based on adequate information about the project. Such information should make it as clear as possible what is expected of participants, what the purpose of the research is and what will be done with the data emerging from the study. It should be provided in a manner that ensures as far as possible that participants will understand it; so, an information sheet for undergraduate students would be written in a language different from one aimed at 12-year-old children. Information may be given in writing or verbally, or through a combination of the two (which in many studies may be the best option). Written consent is usually expected, though there may be occasions where it is not appropriate, and verbal consent is acceptable (ideally, tape-recorded).

There are three sets of circumstances where the expectation of informed consent may be partially or wholly waived: where research involves the observation of ordinary public behaviour; where participants are not competent to give informed consent; or where deception (or withholding of information) is essential to the design of a study. The last of these will be covered under a separate heading. It is generally considered acceptable in observational research not to ask for consent from individual participants when they are in a public place, in which they would normally expect to be observed. For example, if you were comparing males and females in terms of how they greeted friends in a café, you would probably not need to gain individual consent from each person you observed. The point about expectations is important here, though; an ethics committee would be likely to take a different view if in the same setting you wanted to record private conversations between individuals rather than simply note types of greeting behaviour.

Where participants are not fully competent to give consent for themselves, an authorised representative of the participant may be able to give consent on their behalf. In the case of people with severe mental health problems or cognitive impairments, this might be a health professional; for children it is normally be a parent or guardian. Schools have the legal right to act in the place of parents (*in loco parentis*) but will take decisions on an individual study basis as to whether they wish to obtain parental consent to involve children. In the UK, researchers would normally need a Criminal Records Bureau (CRB) check before they work with children or vulnerable adults. A key principle when carrying out research with such groups is that every effort should be made to explain the project to participants in terms they would understand, and to ensure that they are happy to be part of it – even where formal consent is the responsibility of a parent, guardian or professional. In research with all but the youngest children, you would normally seek consent from both child and parent before you proceed.

Confidentiality

This refers to access to participants' personal information disclosed in the course of a psychological study. The default position is that personally identifying information should be anonymised as early as possible during the research process, it should not be used in ways that might reveal identities and only information relevant to the research question should be collected in the first place. In experimental and survey research, it is normal to replace personal names with a code number from the very start. Where there is a need for the research team to identify data with an individual – for instance, in a longitudinal study where a second questionnaire must be sent and its data matched with the first – a code sheet matching numbers to real names will be kept in a secure location, separate from the anonymised data itself.

Most ethical codes, including those of the BPS, state that in certain rare situations, researchers may have a moral duty to breach participant confidentiality. This comes into play when participants reveal information about themselves that indicates there is a very serious and imminent danger that they will harm themselves or others. For example, in a clinical psychological project an individual may score so high on a measure of suicidal intent that the researcher feels ethically impelled to intervene in some manner. The BPS Code rightly stresses that only in 'exceptional circumstances' (p. 11) can concerns for safety warrant a breach of confidentiality, and it is highly unlikely that you will have to face them in the course of undergraduate research. Should you ever experience such concerns, it is essential that you discuss them with your project supervisor, or another appropriate member of academic staff.

Right to withdraw

Participants must be told they have the right to withdraw from a study at any point, without any requirement to explain their decision and without any subsequent consequences for them. They should normally also have the right to ask for their data to be withdrawn from the study after they have provided it. This may be achieved (as noted above) by keeping a secure code sheet matching participant names to code numbers in the data set. Inevitably, such a strategy involves some loss of anonymity, as the researcher could at least identify data with individuals providing it. An alternative strategy is to give participants a code number at the time of the data collection and ask them to quote it if they should later decide to withdraw their data. This provides greater anonymity, though it does rely on participants keeping a record of their code number somewhere they can find it later.

Assessing risk of harm

Before beginning any study, researchers have the responsibility to assess the risk of harm coming to participants through their involvement. For psychological research, the risk of physical harm is usually not an issue, though it occasionally can be the case that procedures potentially create dangers for certain people. In such circumstances, exclusion criteria might be needed to ensure as far as possible that those at risk do not take part in the research. An example would be a study which involved exposing participants to flashing lights; the researchers would need to ensure that anyone with epilepsy was excluded. Much more frequently, we need to take into account possible psychological harm. This could be in the form of significant and lasting distress, embarrassment, reputational damage and so on. Most ethical review committees, including those overseeing undergraduate work, will expect some kind of risk assessment to form part of the application process. Although not always addressed in ethical codes, risks to researcher safety must also be considered.

Researcher safety

The potential for researchers to come to harm is not always addressed directly in codes of ethics, but it is something that individual researchers and their organisations must take seriously. Universities will usually require some kind of assessment of risks to researchers as part of, or in tandem with, the focus on risks to participants as part of the ethical review process. As with participants, the risks may be in terms of physical safety or of psychological harm (or both). For undergraduate level research, universities will have strict procedures to minimise such risks.

Deception

Deception and the deliberate withholding of information are sometimes used in experimental research in particular, when the researcher thinks that to tell participants exactly what the experiment is about would completely undermine what it seeks to achieve. To use a famous example from social psychology, the Asch experiments examining conformity in groups would have been impossible if the real participants had been told that their fellow 'subjects' were in fact confederates of the experimenter, told to give a response that might be in contradiction to the evidence of their senses (Asch, 1956). Deceptions such as this are only considered ethically permissible nowadays where (a) they are clearly necessary to test the hypothesis under investigation, (b) they involve relatively trivial matters that are unlikely to cause participant distress, and (c) participants are informed about the deception as soon as possible after the experiment. The same applies to studies where important information about the aims and/or design of a study is withheld at the start, even if no overt deception is used.

Debriefing

After taking part in research, participants should be given a full account of the purpose of the project and the way in which the data will be used. This is especially important in experimental projects where some degree of deception or withholding of information has been used as. In such studies, researchers may sometimes need to wait until all data are collected before debriefing individuals, to avoid the danger of experimental manipulations being revealed to later participants by earlier ones. This necessitates careful and secure storage of participant contact details in order to ensure they can all be contacted for debriefing.

In some types of research, there is no need for deception or withholding of information, and potential participants are given comprehensive details about studies at the point they are recruited. This applies to most qualitative and survey-based research. Here, debriefing of the kind used in experiments does not really apply; instead, information provided at the end of the study will tend to focus on how and where findings will be disseminated.

Limitations to the researcher's role

When a researcher presents herself as a psychologist, it is possible some participants may feel she is able and willing to offer them assistance or advice on their own mental health problems (or those of family or friends). However, any attempt to do so raises the danger of there being confusion over the professional role she is in, which could place both the researcher and the participant in a difficult situation. It is therefore important that psychologists undertaking research restrict their involvement with participants to that role, even if they are qualified to offer professional help. Especially where the topic of the research is related to areas of professional psychological practice, it is a good idea to have available contact details for suitable agencies and services that can be provided to participants if required.

Use of incentives

Researchers sometimes offer payment to encourage people to participate in their studies. The main ethical issue here is that the scale of the payment should not be such that it might induce participants to expose themselves to psychological and/ or physical risks that they would otherwise be likely to refuse. The BPS Code declares that researchers should:

> Refrain from using financial compensation or other inducements for research participants to risk harm beyond that which they face in their normal lifestyles. (British Psychological Society, 2006, p. 18)

Making judgements about when and at what level it is appropriate to offer inducements is quite a complex matter: how do we know what amount of money would over-ride an individual's normal caution? How can we be sure that the risks in a psychological study are equivalent to those in a person's 'normal lifestyle'? Decisions about use of inducements should therefore always be made with careful consideration of the context of a particular study.

Honesty and integrity in the research process

Ethical responsibilities for researchers do not only relate to direct interaction with participants. They also include the requirement to act honestly and with integrity throughout the research process. Specifically, researchers must:

- declare potential conflicts of interest at the point where ethical approval is sought, and detail how these are to be avoided;
- avoid any fabrication or dishonest manipulation of data or presentation of findings;
- acknowledge fully and fairly the contribution of all those involved in the research project.

Research governance and ethical review processes

The term *research governance* refers to systems and procedures set up to manage and monitor research activity. This includes not only oversight of ethics committees and similar bodies, but also encompasses things such as insurance cover, intellectual property rights, dealing with complaints and monitoring research outcomes and their dissemination. Examples of research governance systems include the Research Governance Framework which covers research in the British National Health Service (NHS) and in local authority social services (2005), and the Economic and Social Research Council's (2008) *Research Ethics Framework*. Within universities, governance of undergraduate research will normally be overseen by course committees, or similar bodies, often in liaison with a departmental or faculty ethical review board. Day-to-day responsibility for monitoring undergraduate projects will usually rest with the member of academic staff supervising the work.

All research carried out by psychologists will these days require ethical review at some level, be it externally (e.g., in the NHS), or via an internal committee (and sometimes both). Exact procedures differ between committees, but in all cases researchers will be expected to complete documentation detailing how the ethical issues described above are to be addressed in the proposed project. Figure 6.1 provides an example of a completed ethics review application form from my own institution, the University of Huddersfield. It is from a current project led by Dr Viv Burr and myself, examining how material from reality TV shows may be used to teach psychology students about research ethics.

It is likely you will be asked to complete a similar form for your own undergraduate dissertation project, although of course the precise design of form will

THE UNIVERSITY OF HUDDERSFIELD
School of Human and Health Sciences – School Research Ethics Panel

OUTLINE OF PROPOSAL

Name of applicant(s): Viv Burr and Nigel King

Title of study: TEACHING ETHICS THROUGH REALITY TV

Department: Behavioural and Social Sciences   Date sent: 2.3.09

	Please provide sufficient detail for SREP to assess strategies used to address ethical issues in the research proposal
Researcher(s) details	Dr Viv Burr, Reader in Psychology Professor Nigel King, Professor in Applied Psychology
Supervisor details	n/a
Aim / objectives	To evaluate the use of reality TV material to facilitate student learning in relation to research ethics in psychology The project is funded by the HEA Psychology Network
Brief overview of research methodology	The project will involve two sessions with participants. Session 1: Reality TV intervention Students will be given a study sheet to read consisting of a number of orienting questions and they will then watch a recording of a reality television programme such as Big Brother. They will then be asked to discuss the recording in groups of 4 or 5, commenting upon the ethical issues that it has raised for them. They will be encouraged to discuss the ethical defensibility of the practices involved, to consider the complexity of the ethical issues, and to reflect upon areas where there may have been differences of opinion in their group. Finally, they will be asked to discuss how the issues they have discussed might apply in a research context. The discussion will be recorded. At the end of the session, students will be asked to provide brief written summaries of the group discussion in relation to: • The ethical issues that were of concern to them with regard to the individuals taking part in the programme. • The ethical issues that were of concern to them with regard to their own participation as viewers. • The application of the above to psychological research projects. Session 2: Design of ethical proposal This will take place one week after session 1, as this would be the likely arrangement if this approach is adopted in teaching in the future. Students will be given a research brief based on one of the key psychological issues from the reality TV material viewed previously, for example attraction, self-presentation or inter-group conflict. They will be asked to discuss how they would design a psychological research study to investigate this issue and to produce a written outline proposal addressing the ethical concerns. As before, the discussion will be recorded, and the anonymised proposals will be reviewed by psychology colleagues not connected with the project. Detailed feedback on their proposals will be provided to students.

Figure 6.1   Example of an ethical review application.

	<u>Analysis of discussion recordings</u> The discussions will be transcribed and analysed using Template Analysis (King, 2004), looking at: • The process of ethical reasoning within the group. • Key learning moments in the discussion • Specific examples of occasions where their ethical reasoning draws on their experience of the reality TV material. King, N. (2004) Using templates in the thematic analysis of texts. In C. Cassell and G. Symon (eds) *Essential GuidetoQualitative Methods in Organizational Research*. London: Sage
Permissions for study	Head of Department – already obtained when bid was submitted.
Access to participants	An initial e-mail has been sent to all second year students in the Division of Psychology and Counselling providing some brief details about the proposed study and asking for expressions of interest. It has been made clear that all details of the study are subject to SREP approval. Once approved, students will be sent a copy of the information sheet and arrangements made to run the two sessions. We are seeking a total of 20 participants. It will of necessity be a convenience sample. We need to run these sessions during this teaching year, and we recognise that for students to devote two or three hours to the project is a considerable investment of time for them. We therefore propose to offer a £40 payment (in the form of a gift voucher) to participants.
Confidentiality	Only the research team will keep a record of which students took part in the project. The research proposals produced by students as part of the project will be anonymised for all uses in the preparation and dissemination of materials based on the project.
Anonymity	Participants will be anonymised in all transcripts as well as in the proposal mentioned above. Only the research team will have a record of participants' real names, for the purposes of providing feedback which is an essential part of the project. A codebook matching real names and pseudonyms will be kept in a secure file, in line with Data Protection requirements.
Psychological support for participants	Given that the materials to be used will be from a broadcast TV programme, and that the intervention will take the form of a group-based teaching session, we do not envisage any need to make special provision for psychological support of participants. In the unlikely event of significant distress occurring for any participant, we will direct them to the normal sources of student support within the University, which in most cases would their personal tutor or the Counselling service.
Researcher safety / support (attach complete University Risk Analysis and Management form)	The project does not raise any researcher safety issues above and beyond those of ordinary teaching activities.
Identify any potential conflicts of interest	None
Please supply copies of all relevant supporting documentation electronically. If this is not available electronically, please provide explanation and supply hard copy	
Information sheet	Attached
Consent form	Attached
Letters	Initial e-mail attached
Questionnaire	n/a
Interview schedule	n/a
Dissemination of results	As a condition of the funding, we will present a paper based on this work at the 2010 Psychology Learning and Teaching conference. We will also develop a pack for psychology lecturers which will be accessible via the HEA Psychology Network website. We will also look for opportunities to disseminate within Huddersfield, such as the 2010 Teaching and Learning Festival. We will submit at least two papers for publication; one to a specialist journal in HE research and one to a more general psychology journal.

All documentation must be submitted to the SREP administrator. All proposals will be reviewed by two members of SREP. If it is considered necessary to discuss the proposal with the full SREP, the applicant (and their supervisor if the applicant is a student) will be invited to attend the next SREP meeting.

Figure 6.1   continued.

TEACHING ETHICS THROUGH REALITY TV

Dr Viv Burr and Prof Nigel King

PARTICIPANT INFORMATION SHEET

We are carrying out a study to examine whether material from reality TV shows can be a useful medium to help students learn about research ethics in psychology. The research will involve about 20 second year students and they will be asked to attend two lecture-type sessions one week apart and then write a brief research proposal. If you agree to join the project, it is important that you complete all parts of the research.

In the first session, we will show students a clip from a reality TV show, such as Big Brother, and then get students into small groups to discuss the ethical issues that they feel are raised by what they have watched- these discussions will be recorded. They will be given some study sheets to help them focus their discussion, and asked to take some notes on what they have discussed.

In the second session, students will be asked to discuss how they would design a psychological research study to investigate a given issue- as before, the discussion will be recorded. Students will then be asked to produce a written outline research proposal addressing the ethical issues. The proposals will be marked and students will get feedback on them.

We will be writing papers for academic journals and giving conference presentations based on this research. We will also be developing teaching materials from it, to share with lecturers at other universities. Participants' identities will be strictly anonymised in all such materials.

If you have any questions you would like to ask us before taking part in this research please contact Viv or Nigel by e-mail (v.burr@hud.ac.uk,n.king@hud.ac.uk).

Thank you for your interest in our project.

Figure 6.2   Example of a participant information sheet.

vary from institution to institution. Besides completing a review form, applicants must also provide copies of materials to be used with participants, such as participant information sheets, consent forms, questionnaires or interview schedules/ guides and so on. As I stated earlier, it is crucial that information sheets (and any other materials for participants) are written in a style and at a language level that participants can readily understand – without talking down to them. Psychological (or other) jargon should be avoided as much as possible. Figure 6.2 shows the participant information sheet used in the study described in Figure 6.1.

Consent forms are commonly designed as a series of statements with a tick-box to indicate the participant has read and agreed to each, followed by a space for both participant and researcher to sign and date. These statements will cover things such as: acknowledgement by the participant that she has read the information sheet and had the chance to ask questions; that she recognises her right to withdraw from the study at any time; that she agrees to the dissemination of findings that include her data. If participants are to be audio- or video-recorded, they need to give explicit consent to this, and to the use of their anonymised quotes in material arising from the study. Figure 6.3 shows a consent form from the project on using reality TV to teach ethics.

CONSENT FORM

Title of Project: TEACHING ETHICS THROUGH REALITY TV

Name of Researchers: Dr Viv Burr and Prof Nigel King

Please tick box

1. I confirm that I have read and understand the information sheet,for the above study. I have had the opportunity to consider the information, ask questions and have had these answered satisfactorily. ☐

2. I understand that my participation is voluntary and that I am free to withdraw at any time, without giving any reason, and without any consequences for me. ☐

3. I understand that all information I provide will be treated as confidential, and will be anonymised. ☐

4. I agree to the audio-recording of discussion groups I take part in during the course of this study. ☐

5. I agree to the use of anonymised direct quotes from the study in publications and presentations arising from it. ☐

6. I agree to take part in the above study. ☐

_____   _____   _____
Name of Participant   Signature   Date

_____   _____   _____
Researcher   Signature   Date

Figure 6.3   Example of a consent form.

Ethics in qualitative research

Although there are philosophical debates within qualitative research about the appropriate basis for ethical judgements (Doucet & Mauthner, 2002; Christians, 2003), qualitative psychologists in practice must address the same principles as those invoked in quantitative research. However, the nature of qualitative research means that some issues must be dealt with in more depth than in quantitative studies; equally, other issues may be less prominent for qualitative than quantitative researchers. I will return to each of the issues discussed above, and explore their implications for ethical research practice in qualitative psychology. When you have read through this section, you might want to try to apply what you have learned to the ethical review exercise shown in the Activity Suggestion box.

Activity suggestion: Ethical review of a qualitative research proposal 6.1

Below is a research proposal for a qualitative psychological project. Bearing in mind the ethical principles and issues discussed in this chapter, read through the proposal and consider its strengths and weaknesses. If you like, you can then use the review form in Figure 6.4 to summarise your views and come to a decision, as if you were a member of an ethical review committee. At the end of the chapter I have highlighted some points that you should have borne in mind in your review. *Do not peek until you have completed your review!*

Research proposal: Working in the fast food industry

Aims

To explore the experiences of young people working in major fast food chain outlets.

Participants

Twenty people aged between 16 and 25 years will be recruited from a cross-section of fast food restaurants in the Huddersfield area. The sample will include 10 males and 10 females, and will seek to include at least five participants from non-white ethnic groups.

Design

Semi-structured interviews will be carried out at the participants' work-places. Interviews will all be taped and transcribed in full. Interviews will cover the following areas:

- Why they chose to work at this restaurant
- Previous experience of working in the fast food industry
- Feelings about colleagues, managers and customers
- What they see as the good and bad points of their work
- Issues of health and safety at work

Arrangements for addressing ethical issues

Potential participants will be given an information leaflet before they agree to take part, and will be asked to sign a consent sheet. They will be told of

(Continued)

6.1 continued

their right to withdraw from the research at any point. Participants' names will be anonymised in all material arising from the project. Information will be available, should participants request it, on health and safety regulations and other employee rights issues.

(Based on material from module 'Introduction to Qualitative Research Methods', Department of Behavioural and Social Sciences, University of Huddersfield, developed by Dr Victoria Lavis and Prof. Nigel King.)

Title of Project	Working in the fast food industry
Ethical issues arising *List all the ethical issues you see as arising from this proposal. (Continue on a separate sheet if necessary).*	
Assessment of ethical provisions *For each of the issues you have listed, note how well (if at all) you feel it has been addressed. (Continue on a separate sheet if necessary).*	
Recommendation **Tick one box**	Accept the proposal as it stands ☐ Accept, subject to minor modifications ☐ Request major modifications and resubmission ☐ Reject outright as intrinsically unethical ☐
Reasons for recommendation *Note your main reasons for coming to the recommendation above.*	
Suggested modifications *If you have made a recommendation other than outright acceptance or rejection, suggest what modifications you would like the researcher to make, in order to make it possible to approve the project.*	

Figure 6.4 Record of the decision of the Research Ethics Committee. (Based on material from module 'Introduction to Qualitative Research Methods', Department of Behavioural and Social Sciences, University of Huddersfield, developed by Dr Victoria Lavis and Prof. Nigel King.)

Informed consent

There are two features of qualitative research that are especially pertinent to the issue of informed consent. First, qualitative researchers tend to have more personal contact with their participants over a longer period of time than do quantitative researchers. Second, qualitative methods are open and flexible, and often evolve over the course of a project; one cannot, for instance, specify exactly which questions will be asked in which order in a qualitative interview study. These features mean that in qualitative research, consent-giving should be seen not as a single action but as an ongoing process of negotiation (Ramos, 1989). This might begin with initial informal discussions with a potential participant, before the signing of a consent form at the start of an interview. However, during the interview itself, there may be a need for further discussion about consent (Rosenblatt, 2000); perhaps because the interaction has moved into areas not anticipated by the researcher. After the interview, negotiation about how data are to be used may also be necessary.

Confidentiality

Confidentiality is often the most difficult ethical issue for qualitative research. Whilst for most surveys and experiments it is unproblematic to keep participants' personal information confidential, in qualitative research such information is often what we are interested in! We use interviews, diary methods, focus groups and so on, precisely because we want to understand the phenomenon we are focusing on in the wider context of participants' lives. As a qualitative researcher you can, then, never promise 'complete' confidentiality to participants, rather you should make it clear what you will be doing with their data and how their identities will be protected from the point where they are first recruited to a study. In most studies, anonymisation is key to achieving this, but how it is to be carried out is often far from straightforward. Simply giving every participant a pseudonym may not be enough, because other details about their views and experiences may potentially reveal their identities. For instance, if you interviewed the headteacher of a school, even if you used pseudonyms for her and her school, anyone who knew that the school was involved in the research would know with absolute certainty to whom you were referring.

Similarly, King & Horrocks (2010) give the hypothetical example of a focus group held with young mothers. If there was only one mother there who had three children, reference to this fact would reveal her identity to other participants reading a report on the findings – and perhaps to people outside the group. The researcher could just not mention the fact that she has three children, but this could be crucial to her experience and thus remove much of value from the study. There can be no universal rule as to how to deal with such dilemmas, but it is always best to anticipate them as far as possible, so that you can negotiate with participants about how to handle the situation. In the young mothers' example, you could agree to agree to consult with individual participants about the use of quotes or paraphrasing that might touch on sensitive issues. It is also important to note that in focus groups, participants must be asked at the start to keep each other's contributions confidential.

A further issue that relates to confidentiality is how to deal with 'off the record' comments. These can be divided into two types: first, comments made at the end of an interview, after recording equipment has been switched off; second, comments made during the interview which the participant asks to be treated as 'off the record' or words to that effect. Taking these in turn, it is quite common for participants to talk further about the research topic after the interview has concluded. This may be because something has occurred to them that they had previously not thought of, or because they feel free to reveal something outside of the formal interview. If you find yourself in this position, you should ask the participants whether they would be happy for you to keep a record of what they have just said, or whether they meant it to be kept entirely confidential. In the former case, you may feel it is appropriate to ask them to repeat the comment on tape; if you are uncomfortable with this, you can at least keep a written note of what was said. If the participant is clear that the comment is not to be included in your data, then you must keep strictly to this undertaking – and the same is true for requests to exclude particular comments made during the interview. If the comment is especially valuable, you might try very cautiously to negotiate a form of it that he/she would be happy for you to use. Sometimes by removing specific details from the point made, and/or by promising a higher degree of anonymisation than normal, participants will feel able to agree some degree of use of the remarks in question. Remember, though, that you must not put undue pressure on them to change their mind and must not question their choice, once they have reflected further on it and come to a decision.

Right to withdraw

Qualitative research does not raise any major issues, regarding the participant's right to withdraw, that differ from those of quantitative research. Participants must be made fully aware of this right from the start of data collection, including their right to withdraw data after it has been collected. In all types of research, there is usually a practical limit to the time period in which data can retrospectively be withdrawn, as to do so will not be in the researcher's hands once it is published or otherwise in the public domain. It is a good idea to give participants some idea as to the extent of the period during which data withdrawal will be possible.

One point to be aware of is that you should never decide for a participant that he/she should withdraw from your study. This can arise with inexperienced researchers, when they are faced with a participant becoming distressed during data collection (such as in an interview). Distress does not necessarily equate to 'harm', and removing control from a participant by insisting they conclude the interview may itself have a negative impact on them. I discuss the topic of dealing with participant distress further in the next section.

Assessing risk of harm

As with all research, in a qualitative project you need to think through carefully the possible sources of harm to participants before you start, and address those that are significant enough to be of concern. In qualitative research, the limitations to confidentiality I noted previously make reputational harm and embarrassment a greater issue than in most quantitative research. The more personal, in-depth nature of data collection also makes it more likely that the conversation will move into areas that the participant finds distressing – though at least in face-to-face qualitative research, this distress is visible, enabling the researcher to respond to it. People may well get distressed filling in questionnaires sometimes, but those running the project would have no way of knowing this. I emphasised in relation to the right to withdraw that you should not assume that distress inevitably equals harm. If participants have given proper informed consent to take part (as of course they absolutely should have done!), they may have done so with foreknowledge that the topic is one that could be emotional for them. Far from being inevitably harmful, the chance to talk to an interested outside party (i.e., the researcher) may be helpful – indeed, that might be one reason why they agreed to participate in the first place. You should still always take participant-distress seriously, but the best response is to give them a moment to compose themselves and then offer them choices as to what to do next. You might say something like: 'I can see you find this upsetting. Would you like to take a break now, or move on to a different topic? We can always come back to this point later if you feel like it. If you want to stop the interview altogether that's fine too.' My experience is that people very rarely choose to terminate the interview entirely because of emotional upset – most often they choose to have a short break and then carry on.

Researcher safety

Since qualitative research often involves extended personal contact with participants, researcher safety must be taken seriously. I would normally be very reluctant to allow an undergraduate student to go to a participant's own home to carry out an interview, unless they were already personally acquainted. Where possible, I would recommend that you use university facilities as a venue for interviews that do not involve friends or family. If your project involves members of an organisation outside the university, a private room in their own premises might be appropriate, but you should never be alone in a building with someone you do not know. (Even for experienced researchers, caution should be exercised in meeting strangers in private for interviews. It is good practice to make sure that a colleague or supervisor is made aware of where and when interviews are to take place, and a fully charged mobile phone should be carried at all times during field work). If your research involves contacting participants by e-mail, it is preferable to use a university student account (or similar) rather than a personal account.

Deception

In qualitative research, deception should not be an issue, as there is no method-ological necessity to mislead participants about the purpose and nature of a study. Indeed, given the emphasis on building trust in much of the literature on collecting qualitative data (McKie, 2002; Warren, 2002), attempts to deceive would be seen as both methodologically risky and morally unacceptable. What *can* be an issue is the amount of information to give participants at the start of a study. There is some-times a tension between giving as full an account as possible of what your research seeks to do and why, and providing participant information in a form that will be meaningful and comprehensible to them. For instance, part of your reason for designing a study in a particular way may relate to theoretical debates within psy-chology that are unlikely to mean much to most participants. Also, you may not want to flag up in advance all the specific topics you might want to probe on, for fear of leading the participant. Judgements about how much information partici-pants need in advance will always have to be made in the context of particular study. One rule of thumb to bear in mind, though, is that you should never with-hold information purely on the basis that you are worried that disclosing it may put people off participating. You must also always answer questions about the study as fully and honestly as possible.

Debriefing

Following on from the previous discussion, there is usually no need for extensive debriefing in a qualitative study, given that you have been open about the aims and purpose of the research from the start. Generally it *is* appropriate at the end of data collection to remind the participant how their data are to be used, ensure they have your contact details should they later have any queries or concerns, and let them know how they can access reports emerging from the study.

Limitations to the researcher's role

The danger of role confusion is often greater in qualitative studies than quantita-tive, because of the closer personal contact that tends to be involved in the former. I made the point earlier that psychological researchers need to clearly indicate the boundaries of their role, and this is especially important here. For qualitative researchers, this commonly means more than just making your role clear at the point participants are recruited. You also need to be careful during data collection not to allow the interaction to take you in a direction where it is hard for you to avoid requests for psychological advice. Having information on sources of help and advice relevant to your study topic can be very useful in dealing with such situ-ations should they occur.

Honesty and integrity in the research process

The expectations regarding conflicts of interest, honest handling of data and acknowledgement of contributions to research, are no different in qualitative than in quantitative psychological research. The more open and multifaceted nature of qualitative findings can on occasion create dilemmas in relation to how data are used. This can happen when funders, host organisations or even co-researchers exert pressure on the researcher to delete certain quotes or revise the way certain themes are discussed. Because qualitative research emphasises that there is never one complete and correct interpretation of a set of data, such changes may not seem like an attempt to undermine honesty to those requesting them. And sometimes there are good ethical grounds for responding positively to such requests, where the upset likely to be caused by using a particular quote (for example) could be avoided by removing or replacing it, without substantially changing the message of the findings. In undergraduate research, you are not likely to face serious dilemmas of this kind, although this can arise in final-year projects conducted with the co-operation of external organisations. My advice would be, wherever possible to discuss in advance the grounds on which you would be willing to alter a report in response to the concerns of those with a stake in the research. This, at least, gives you a basis for negotiating any particular requests at the end of the project.

Use of incentives

There are no distinctive issues for qualitative researchers regarding the use of incentives; the general points I made above apply equally to any qualitative psychological study.

Online qualitative research

The rapid growth of the Internet as a medium for communication between people has led to the development of online research methods in psychology and other disciplines (Joinson et al., 2007). Alongside online surveys and experiments, qualitative techniques have emerged and there is every likelihood they will become more widespread in future (see also Chapter 4). The most common online qualitative methods are e-mail and Instant Messaging (IM) interviews. These differ mainly in that e-mail interactions are non-synchronous – that is, they do not happen in real time – whilst IM is synchronous (in real time). Responses in e-mail interviews tend to be more considered and thought-through than in IM, whilst the latter are more spontaneous; which method is more appropriate will depend on the needs of a specific study.

The use of the Internet for research brings a new dimension to ethical consid-erations, and has led to the publication of dedicated guidelines from professional organisations including the BPS (2007b) and the Association of Internet Researchers (Ess, 2002). I do not have space here to examine all the issues relating to the ethics of online research in detail, but will highlight four areas where particular care is needed. For fuller accounts, see Ess (2007) and King & Horrocks (2010).

Establishing participant identity

One of the most obvious differences between online and face-to-face interviews is that you are not physically present with the participant when you are interacting by e-mail or IM. Frequently, the fact that you can conduct research with partici-pants who are geographically very distant from you is one of the main reasons for choosing an online approach in the first place. One of the difficulties this creates is that it is much harder to be sure your participants are who they say they are than in most other methods. This may be ethically problematic if you wish to exclude certain people from the research – for example, children under 16 years of age. You can never completely rule out the danger of impersonation in online research, but there are strategies you can follow to make it less likely. First, where possible, obtain internet-contact details through a source you can trust. Second, consider asking participants to return a consent form via a medium other than the Internet – such as by post or fax. Third, consider using webcams in at least part of the research; this technology is now much more readily available and can be used in combina-tion with software such as Skype to carry out synchronous interviews. The lengths to which you should go to reassure yourself of your participants' identities should be judged relative to the risks associated with misidentification. Where the risks are high, and you cannot operate an extremely robust identification procedure, you might need to rethink your choice of method. Where risks are low, you may be happy using fairly simple procedures.

Effects of visual anonymity

Research suggests that the visual anonymity provided by internet-based interaction (excepting here the use of webcams) has an impact on the way people behave online (Joinson, 2005). This includes a tendency for people to be more open about personal matters than they might have been face-to-face. Voida et al. (2004) refer to a case in a study using IM where one participant commented on the fact that she had been so immersed in the online conversation that it came as a 'shock' at the end to be reminded that she was providing data for a research project whose findings would be made public. This demonstrates the need to be very clear with partici-pants about what they are consenting to in terms of the way data are to be used.

Maintaining confidentiality

Ironically, whilst people may feel more anonymous online than in other interactions, in fact the nature of the Internet poses serious threats to anonymity and confidentiality. All online interactions are potentially accessible to internet service providers (ISPs) who can be required by law enforcement agencies to turn records over to them in certain circumstances. Furthermore, if you are using a university e-mail account for your research, the institution's systems administrators could access e-mail exchanges with participants. It is unlikely that you will be involved in online research as an undergraduate student where the ethical sensitivities make these significant issues for your participants. A greater concern is that e-mails can very easily be shared accidently (James & Busher, 2007) – all it takes is one mistaken mouse-click! You need to take great care in storing e-mail or other internet-based correspondence securely on your computer.

Managing online relationships

In some online methods, most notably e-mail interviews, exchanges commonly continue over extended periods of time – for weeks, or even months. Because of this, and also because of the tendency towards self-disclosure noted above, participants may come to feel a degree of personal closeness to the researcher that would not transpire in a one-off face-to-face interview. The potential to build strong rapport is in many respects a valuable feature of the method, but it does increase the risk of the relationship straying towards one which is inappropriately personal. Bringing the research relationship to a close can be particularly difficult; it is a good idea to set a time limit for the project from the start so that the participant can be reminded when it is near to the end, and a closing message does not seem to come out of the blue. For an interesting and detailed account of the process of managing relationships in online interviews, see Kivits (2005).

Conclusion: Going beyond the 'tick-box' mentality

It may seem from the discussion above that guidance on best ethical practice in qualitative research is often difficult to achieve and occasionally ambiguous. Take a topic like confidentiality: for an experimental study, your textbook might lay out a set of procedures to follow, to ensure identities are concealed and personal information protected. In contrast, my advice for qualitative studies talks about negotiation, acknowledging the limits to confidentiality and keeping in mind the context of an individual project. I would, however, argue that not only is this less clear-cut approach inevitable, given the nature of qualitative research, it is also very valuable for promoting a proper consideration of ethics in psychology as a whole.

The rise of institutional ethics review boards, whilst stemming from the laudable goal of ensuring the protection of research participants from mistreatment, has sometimes led to highly bureaucratic processes – most notably in the health field (Sibbald, 2008; Stewart et al., 2008). This in turn can lead to a 'tick-box mentality' in which researchers are more concerned to negotiate the review process than to reflect carefully on the ethics of what they are doing. In qualitative psychology, we always need to think about ethical matters with an eye on the contextual detail of a specific study, which often means wrestling with ambiguities and balancing demands of different ethical principles. This can sometimes be difficult, but in the end such painstaking moral reasoning, rather than the tick-box mentality, is precisely what research ethics should be about.

6.2 Notes for the ethical review exercise (Activity Suggestion box, p. 109)

- The proposal only mentions anonymising individuals. You might think it necessary to anonymise the restaurant chains as well, and the town in which they are located.
- The proposal suggests that interviews will take place in the restaurants where participants work. It might be difficult in these locations to find quiet and private places in which to hold interviews. Also, the identities of those taking part are likely to be revealed to colleagues and managers if they are interviewed in the restaurant. You might find this unacceptable given that the research might elicit some negative views on colleagues, managers, customers and/or organisations.
- The researcher has not clearly indicated that participants will have a chance to ask questions after receiving the information sheet.
- The researcher has undertaken to have information on employees' legal rights available, in case of queries by participants. However, you might feel that the researcher should be prepared to direct participants to a wider range of advisory material – for example, in relation to stress management, and health services targeted at young people.

Part 3
Qualitative Analysis: Practical Examples

7

Introducing the Data Set

Stephen Gibson

Introduction

This chapter introduces the data set on which Chapters 8 to 11 are based (see Box 7.1 for details of how to access the data set). Following a brief outline of the background to the collection of the semi-structured interview data which constitutes the data set, the rest of the chapter focuses on the design of the interviews themselves, and covers issues such as sampling, the interview schedule, ethics and transcription. Although not intended as a straightforward methods section, readers of this chapter will nevertheless find information one typically expects to find in such sections of a psychology laboratory report or journal article. The difference here is that through a series of Critical Issues boxes, you will be encouraged to think critically about the data, and to reflect on how alternative strategies for data collection might have yielded quite different data (see also Chapter 4).

It is important to emphasise at the outset that whilst we believe the interviews to be of a very high standard, they are not offered as a model of perfection. Indeed, the idea that perfect or flawless data could ever be collected is one that should be treated with extreme caution. Related to this is the notion that different types of analytic methodologies would typically favour different strategies for the generation of data. It is never a 'one-size-fits all' procedure. So, it will come as no surprise that in seeking to collect data suitable for analysis by the four different approaches covered in Chapters 8 to 11, it was unavoidable that some approaches were occasionally given priority during the process of producing the set of interviews and accompanying transcriptions. The places where this was the case will become apparent as you work through this and the subsequent chapters.

7.1 How to access the resources of the data set

The resources can be found at: http://www.psychology.heacademy.ac.uk/
Webdocs_not_nof/tqrmul/dataset/, where you will find the following items
for each of the five interviews:
(i) Digital video files, split into segments of approximately 15 minutes each
(ii) Digital audio files, split into the same segments as the video files
(iii) 'Playscript' transcript
(iv) Jeffersonian transcript

Background

The idea behind the data set was, quite simply, to collect data that could be analysed from a variety of analytic standpoints in order to provide a useful resource for teaching and learning. This stemmed from the observation that whilst many texts provide guidance on how to conduct qualitative research, there are few that explore the way in which different analytic perspectives might be brought to bear on the same data set '(see Lyons & Coyle, 2007, for an exception)'. Where authors have sought to engage in such an endeavour (e.g., Wilkinson, 2000; Van den Berg, Wetherell & Houtkoop-Steenstra, 2003;), the work has tended to be written up for the benefit of other researchers, rather than specifically with a view to introducing students new to the field to the varieties of qualitative analysis. It was for this reason that we decided to provide a set of resources for pedagogical purposes. Initially, we considered using existing data sets – all of the contributors to this book are qualitative researchers engaged in their own research and all have ready access to such data. However, it quickly became apparent that in order to allow for the collection of data that would be suitable for analysis using the various analytic approaches we had in mind, we would need to collect a data set specifically for the purpose of developing this resource. Our decision to select the range of analytic approaches described in this book was based on a survey we conducted to find out the commonly used approaches in UK-based Departments of Psychology (Forrester & Koutsopoulou, 2008). The collection of a new data set also had the singular advantage of allowing us to consider exactly what it was we felt was needed for the teaching and learning of qualitative methods. In this respect, the decision to use video recordings meant that we could enable students, as far as possible, to see for themselves what the process of data collection actually looks like.

Participants

The five interviewees (three females and two males) were all undergraduate students at Liverpool John Moores University. With only five participants, it is clearly impossible to seek to provide a representative sample (and indeed issues such as 'representativeness' and 'generalisability' are understood somewhat differently in qualitative research; see Madill, Jordan & Shirley, 2000). However, recruitment aimed to maximise sample variability along a number of demographic features such as gender, age, ethnicity and employment history. Participants received course credit and a £20 book voucher for their participation.

Interview design

The interviews were designed to get people talking about their experiences of friendship. There was no specific research question as such (something which is not uncommon in qualitative research), as anything more specific might have risked the interviews being framed in such a way as to produce data more suitable for analysis with some approaches than others. Despite this, of course, a series of decisions had to be made concerning how to conduct the interviews, which inevitably led to the prioritisation of some approaches. In particular, we were mindful that Discourse Analysis (DA) and Conversation Analysis (CA) can, in principle, be used to analyse any recorded talk, whereas Grounded Theory (GT), and especially Interpretative Phenomenological Analysis (IPA), typically require interviews to be conducted in certain ways. As a result, we decided that in order to produce data that would be analysable from each of these four perspectives, we would aim to conduct the interviews in a broadly narrative style, with a focus on getting participants to tell the interviewer about their friendships. This would then allow for subsequent questioning to focus on issues concerning experiences of friendship, and the meaning of friendship – both of which are central features of the style of interviewing typically favoured in IPA (see e.g., Smith & Osborn, 2008), and also suitable for GT.

In contrast, DA and CA are much more cautious about notions such as experience, and instead focus on what Edwards (2006, p. 41) has termed the 'rich surface of language and social interaction'. Where interviews have been used in DA, they have tended to follow Potter & Wetherell's (1987, p. 164) suggestion that interviews can be 'much more interventionist and confrontative' encounters than is the case in other approaches. Whilst Potter and Wetherell stress that such interviews shouldn't typically be explicitly adversarial in nature, even a gently confrontational style of questioning might produce data less well suited for IPA. Having said this, of course, it is difficult, if not impossible, to defend a hard-and-fast distinction between 'narrative' and 'interventionist' interviewing, and you will almost certainly be able to spot places in the interviews where the interviewer seems to be adopting a more interventionist approach, or in which the interviewee seems to react as if such an approach is being adopted.

In contrast, CA typically eschews interviews altogether, and instead works with 'naturalistic' or 'naturally-occurring' data (see Chapter 4). Having said that, there is a growing CA literature exploring interaction in interviews (Roulston, 2006) and other data-gathering practices (e.g., Drew, Raymond & Weinberg, 2006). The novelty of CA's approach to such matters is that rather than treating interviews as a method of getting at some other topic (e.g., friendship), they are instead treated as a topic in their own right, with analyses revolving around the question of 'how do interviews get done'? In this respect, interviews are viewed as one form of institutional talk (see e.g., Heritage, 2005) and can be contrasted with 'everyday talk' or 'ordinary conversation'. It was by recording ordinary, everyday conversations and studying them in fine detail that CA highlighted many basic conversational structures that make up the core findings of the approach.

With these provisos in mind, the interview schedule was designed to be relatively open-ended (see Box 7.2 and Chapter 5 to see the forms of questions used in the interviews). The preamble was written in such a way as to provide the interviewer with a guide to the issues that they might raise with participants before

---

7.2 The interview guide

The interviews are intended to encourage participants to discuss and reflect upon the experience and meaning of friendship. The questions here are a guide only – they do not have to be asked in the order or form presented here.

Preamble (which assumes that they've already been made aware that the video of the interview will be made available online) to include something along the lines of:

'We're interested in people's friendships, and what they think of as making someone a good friend, so the questions all deal in some way with the general topic of friendship. Are you happy to talk about this? Now, as you can probably see, we're using video cameras to record this interview – are you happy with this? And just to remind you again that you can stop the interview at any point without having to explain why, and you can withdraw your data from the study after the interview if you feel that you'd like to. Are you happy with all this? Here's the consent form, which I'll ask you to fill in and sign at the end of the interview. It also contains details of how we plan to make the interview available both in transcript form and by posting the digital video files on the Internet so that anyone will be able to access them. Have a look through the form and make sure that you're happy with what's on there. If there's anything you don't understand then please ask me. When you're happy you can pass me the form back and I'll give you it again at the end of the interview for you to fill in and sign.'

7.2 continued

Initial rapport-building chat might cover issues such as what the participant is studying at university, what year they're in, etc.
Suggested starting question:

> **'As you know, this project is about friendship. Can you tell me about your own friends and what they mean to you?'**

Possible follow-up questions:

> 'What does it mean to be friends with someone?'
> 'Can you tell me about something from your own experience, which demonstrates what it means to be friends?'

Probe for examples of good friendship, being let down by a friend, letting a friend down, making it up to a friend, losing a friend, making a new friend, etc.

Probe for examples of acquaintanceship vs. friendship; friendship vs. good friendship; best friend?

> 'Tell me how you met your friends'.

beginning the interview. Ultimately, the actual questions took up only a few lines, and were intended to be as open as possible. The interview schedule was therefore a very loosely structured type of 'semi-structured' interview, without being completely unstructured (see Chapter 5).

The interviews took place in a small room in the Psychology Department at Liverpool John Moores University, and lasted between 46 and 63 minutes (mean = 54 minutes). Two interviews were conducted by Alasdair Gordon Finlayson, a tutor in the Psychology Department at Liverpool John Moores University, and three were conducted by Tanya Corker, a research assistant (Table 7.1).

Table 7.1 Interview details

Interviewee pseudonym	Interviewer	Interview length (min)
Shazia	Tanya	63
Alexander	Alasdair	50
Louise	Alasdair	46
Trevor	Tanya	57
Deborah	Tanya	54

7.3 Critical issue: Why interviews?

As Willig (2008) points out, the most common way in which qualitative researchers in psychology collect data is the semi-structured interview. Our decision to use semi-structured interviews reflected our recognition that this method of data collection is one with which undergraduate students on qualitative methods courses are likely to have some familiarity. However, simply because something is done frequently, it doesn't necessarily mean that one should continue to go on repeating it out of habit. There are many well-founded critiques of interview methods – some specific to particular ways of doing interviews, and others to the whole endeavour of sitting down with someone and asking for their 'views' on some issue or other.

Recently, Potter & Hepburn (2005) have questioned the way in which a great deal of qualitative research in psychology makes use of interviews in an unthinking way, ignoring the dynamics of the interview interaction and treating interview talk as a more-or-less unproblematic route to accessing such mental entities as 'thoughts' 'feelings' or 'beliefs'.

What other methods of data generation might have been used?
Would they all have been amenable to analysis using IPA, DA, CA and GT?

Ethics

As with any study, it was important that appropriate ethical standards be followed regardless of the fact that the interviews were being conducted for the purposes of providing a learning and teaching resource, rather than for a full-fledged research project (see Chapter 6). However, because it was our intention from the outset to make videos and transcripts of the interviews available on the Internet, we were presented with an ethical dilemma not typically faced by researchers. Clearly, the participants' confidentiality and anonymity could not be maintained. They would be identifiable to anyone who knew them by virtue of the video recordings, and their words would be available for all to read, hear and download. The British Psychological Society (n.d.) advises that '[i]n the event that confidentiality and/ or anonymity cannot be guaranteed, the participant must be warned of this in advance of agreeing to participate'. We therefore put in place a procedure for gaining informed consent from the participants, and gained institutional approval for the project from ethics committees at York St John University (where the project was co-ordinated by Stephen Gibson) and Liverpool John Moores University (where the interviews were organised by Alasdair Gordon-Finlayson).

The project was advertised via the Psychology Department at Liverpool John Moores University, and students who responded indicating a willingness to take part were provided with an information sheet outlining relevant details of the project, and with a time for their interview (see Figure 7.1). The reason for doing this was to provide participants with an opportunity to consider their participation over the course of a few days, to ensure that they were sure they were happy to take part.

Information sheet for participants

Project title: Development of a web-based resource to aid the teaching of qualitative research methods at undergraduate level.

Thank you for your interest in taking part in the project, which is funded by the Higher Education Academy Psychology Network, and involves members of staff at several UK universities. The project aims to develop a set of materials to aid the teaching of qualitative research methods on undergraduate psychology courses. It involves a one-on-one research interview on the topic of 'friendship', which will last approximately 30-60 minutes. The interview will be recorded using video equipment and fully transcribed.

The video and transcript of the interview will then be considered for inclusion in the final set of project materials which will be made available on the internet via the project webpages. This is so that the materials can be accessed by lecturers and students undertaking qualitative methods courses in psychology. Any decision about whether or not to include your interview in the final project materials will be based purely on methodological and technical grounds, and will in no way reflect a judgement about you as an individual, or about what you say in the interview.

The materials are designed to provide a resource for learning and teaching which should be in use for some years to come, and as such we hope that by participating in the project you will see yourself as contributing to the teaching of psychology at undergraduate level. **However, it is important that you are aware that, as these will be available on the internet, anyone will be able to access these materials.** Although we will make efforts to remove personally identifying information such as names of other people mentioned in the interview, you will still be identifiable in the video recordings. If you are not happy to give your consent to this, then please feel free to withdraw from the project. Please also note that the topic of the interview, friendship, may be an emotive one, and if you feel that you may experience distress talking about this then please consider whether you really want to participate. You also have the right to withdraw your contribution from the study at any time after the interview until the materials are made available online. You will be able to see the video materials and transcript in full prior to them being made available online so that you can choose to edit your interview, or withdraw it from the study entirely, if you wish.

The details of when and where your interview will take place are as follows:

Date: Time:

Place:

If you need to cancel or re-arrange, please contact Tanya Corker at <EMAIL ADDRESS>. In the meantime, if you have any further questions about the project, please contact Alasdair Gordon-Finlayson (a.r.gordon-finlayson@ljmu.ac.uk) or Stephen Gibson (s.gibson@yorksj.ac.uk).

Figure 7.1   The participant information sheet.

RESEARCH CONSENT FORM

Development of a web-based resource to aid the teaching of qualitative research methods at undergraduate level.

Name of research interviewer: ....

If you wish to get in contact with the research team at any point, please email Alasdair Gordon-Finlayson (a.r.gordon-finlayson@ljmu.ac.uk) at the School of Psychology at Liverpool John Moores University, or Stephen Gibson (s.gibson@yorksj.ac.uk) at the Faculty of Health & Life Sciences, York St John University.

This project aims to develop a set of materials to aid the teaching of qualitative research methods on undergraduate psychology courses. It involves a one-on-one research interview on the topic of 'friendship', which will last approximately 30–60 minutes. The interview will be recorded using video equipment and fully transcribed. **The video and transcript of the interview will then be considered for inclusion in the final set of project materials which will be made available on the Internet via the project webpages.** This is so that the materials can be accessed by lecturers and students undertaking qualitative methods courses in psychology. The materials are therefore designed to provide a resource for learning and teaching which should be in use for some years to come, and as such we hope that by participating in the project you will see yourself as contributing to the teaching of psychology at undergraduate level. **However, it is important that you are aware that, as these will be available on the Internet, anyone will be able to access these materials.** Although we will make efforts to remove personally identifying information such as names, you will still be identifiable in the video recordings. If you are not happy to give your consent to this, then please withdraw from the project. You also have the right to withdraw your contribution from the study at any time after the interview until the materials are made available online. You will be able to see the video materials and transcript in full prior to them being made available online so that you can choose to edit your interview, or withdraw it from the study entirely, if you wish.

The following statements are to enable you to indicate your consent if you wish to participate in the project. Please read and complete this form carefully. If you are willing to participate, circle the appropriate responses and sign and date the declaration at the end. If you do not understand anything and would like more information, please ask.

Figure 7.2   The consent form (first part).

Following the interviews, participants were asked to complete a consent form (see Figures 7.2 and 7.3). This was shown to participants before the interview began, so that they were aware what they would be asked to sign after the interview. The form was then completed at the end of the interview.

The interviews were transcribed (see section on 'Transcription' below for details), and the participants were then given the opportunity to review, edit and, if they wished, withdraw their contribution prior to it being made available online. None of the participants themselves indicated that they wished anything to be removed from their interview, although it was subsequently decided to remove part of Louise's interview as it referred to some delicate personal circumstances

I have had the research satisfactorily explained to me in verbal and written form by the researcher.

YES / NO

I understand that the research will involve a video-recorded one-on-one interview on the topic of 'friendship' lasting 30–60 minutes.

YES / NO

I agree to digital videos and transcripts of the interview being made available via the project webpages.

YES / NO

I understand that, as a result of the materials being made available on the Internet, my anonymity and confidentiality cannot be maintained.

YES / NO

I understand that I may withdraw from the interview at any time without having to give an explanation.

YES / NO

I understand that I may withdraw my contribution from the study at any point after the interview has finished and before the materials are made available online.

YES / NO

I understand that I will be given the opportunity to view the materials before they are made available online in order that I can choose to edit or withdraw my contribution if I so wish.

YES / NO

I agree to extracts from the transcripts being used in academic publications, such as books and journal articles.

YES / NO

I agree to the materials being used as the basis for presentations at academic conferences.

YES / NO

I freely give my consent to participate in this project and have been given a copy of this form for my own information.

Signature: ....

Print name: ....

Date: ....

Please provide an email address at which we can contact you when we have the materials ready for you to review: ....

Figure 7.3   The consent form (second part).

of one her friends. The point at which this section has been removed is indicated clearly on the transcripts and recordings.

It was pointed out to participants on the participant information sheet and the consent form that they would only be able to withdraw their data before the materials were made available online. The reason for putting this limit on the timeframe in which they could withdraw their data was that once materials were on the Internet, and people had started to download and use them, they were in the public domain and we therefore would be effectively unable to recall them.

Although we were unable to maintain the anonymity of participants, we nevertheless sought to take some measures to limit straightforward identification. Clearly, the participants would be identifiable to anyone who knew them, but in order to obscure personal details about the participants, we took a number of steps. First, the participants were referred to by pseudonyms, as is common in qualitative research. Second, where the participants referred to the names of other people, or to local areas or halls of residence during their interviews, these were edited out of the interviews. You will notice that on the video and audio files there are occasionally times when the sound recording goes quiet for while. This is because the participant mentioned some such piece of information, and in the transcript this is indicated by either a transcriber's comment in double brackets, or (in the case of names) the use of a pseudonym.

It might be pointed out that we could have taken further steps to protect anonymity, such as pixelating the participants' faces on the video recordings. However, the ability to use the materials as a teaching and learning resource would have been seriously hampered by the obscuring of features such as facial expression and direction of gaze. The point of providing video-recordings is to preserve this information, as far as possible, in order to allow for an appreciation of its importance in how we make sense of the interview data. To remove it would therefore negate the point of video-recording the interviews in the first place. Of course, this shouldn't be taken to imply that all possible ethical questions are somehow resolved – or that you should necessarily agree with the various choices that we made – rather, we hope that the procedures adopted and materials used will help inform debate regarding the ethics of making data available via the Internet (see Critical Issue box below).

7.4 Critical issue: Making data available on the Internet

The practice of making data available on the Internet is becoming increasingly common in some approaches to qualitative research in psychology and related disciplines. For example, many conversation analysts and

7.4   continued

discursive psychologists advocate sharing one's data online in order to facilitate reader engagement with analyses, and to allow readers to more easily develop alternative interpretations of the data. There are many excellent examples of this practice:

> Emanuel A. Schegloff's website: http://www.sscnet.ucla.edu/soc/faculty/schegloff/sound-clips.html
> Mike Forrester's data at the ethno/CA website: http://www2.fmg.uva.nl/emca/Forrester.htm
> Loughborough's Discourse and Rhetoric Group (DARG): http://www.lboro.ac.uk/departments/ss/centres/darg/audio_video_materials.htm

What do you think? Do the advantages of making data available via the Internet outweigh the potential ethical problems?

Transcription

As with interviewing style, transcription is another area where different practices are typically favoured by the different approaches covered in Chapters 8 to 11. Whereas IPA, GT and some variants of DA tend to use more-or-less standard orthographic transcription (which renders the interaction in a form resembling a 'playscript'), some other versions of DA, and most notably CA, typically feature the use of much more fine-grained transcripts which make use of a set of transcription conventions developed by Gail Jefferson (see Table 7.2 for the Jeffersonian conventions used in the present transcripts, and see Jefferson, 2004, for an extensive inventory). Box 7.5 presents an example of the same section of one of the transcripts in both Jeffersonian and 'playscript' transcription conventions.

Table 7.2   Jeffersonian transcription conventions

Transcription element	Meaning	Transcription element	Meaning
↑ or ↓	Marked rise (or fall) in intonation	:::	Sounds that are stretched or drawn out (number of :: indicates the length of stretching)
Underlining	Used for emphasis (parts of the utterance that are stressed)	[ ]	Overlaps, cases of simultaneous speech or interruptions.

(Continued)

Table 7.2:   continued

Transcription element	Meaning	Transcription element	Meaning
UPPER-CASE LETTERS	Indicate increased volume (note this can be combined with underlining)	° word °	Shown when a passage of talk is noticeably quieter than the surrounding talk
.hhh	A row of h's with a dot in front of it indicates an inbreath. Without the dot an outbreath	=	When there is nearly no gap at all between one utterance and another
(comment)	Analyst's comment about something going on in the talk	(.)	Small pauses
> word <	Noticeably faster speech.	<word>	Noticeable slower speech
⸮	Rising intonation at the end of an utterance	(1.4)	Silences (time in seconds)
(h)	Outbreath/laughter in word(s) when speaking		

Source: From Forrester (2002, p. 11); based on Psathas (1995).

7.5 Comparing Jeffersonian and 'playscript' transcripts

The following extract is from Louise's interview, and lasts for a total of 19 seconds:

Playscript
57 INT: When you are with each other, what, I mean what do you get up to? What do you do?
58 LOU: Like in the day or … just generally?
59 INT: Well generally, in the day, in the evening, whatever, both, all three.
60 LOU: Oh generally, just the typical watch telly together and then drink together before we go out and then go out, like do each other's fake tan and stuff [laughs], so …

Jeffersonian
230 INT: =.hhh when you are with each other what
231   (0.2)
232 INT: I mean w what d'you get up to what d'you do?
233   (0.5)
234 LOU: like in the day or::
235   (0.5)
236 INT: we[ll]

continued **7.5**

237	LOU:	[js] generally
238		(.)
239	INT:	generally [in the day] in the evening or whatever (.) both
240	LOU:	[>well we generally<]
241		(0.2)
242	INT:	all thre[e]
243	LOU:	[x] typical watch telly together an erm
244		(1.1)
245	LOU:	drink together before we go out °n then go out°
246		(0.7)
247	LOU:	°like°
248		(0.4)
249	LOU:	do each other's fake tan n stu HA ha ha ha .hhh so ha ha .hhh

Activity suggestion: Transcribing everyday talk **7.6**

Have a go at producing a transcript of a section of one of the interviews, and compare it to those provided on the website.
   How does it compare?
   Did you hear anything differently?

Critical issue: Transcription as theory **7.7**

As Elinor Ochs (1979) has pointed out, transcription is theory. This means that we shouldn't treat a transcript as a straightforward route to the 'reality' of any given interaction, but rather as the outcome of a series of theoretical decisions and assumptions about how to represent talk as text. It might, for example, be tempting to treat a Jeffersonian transcript as somehow better, or more complete, than a 'playscript' transcript. However, this idea should be treated with extreme caution – certainly, a Jeffersonian transcript is more appropriate if you are looking at the data with a view to assessing the operation of features such as pauses, overlap and intonation – but such a prioritisation of paralinguistic features in a transcript may detract from a focus on the content of what was said. Moreover, as becomes apparent when you have a go at Jeffersonian transcription yourself, it can sometimes be difficult to 'hear' all the interactional features that might be relevant.

When you consider some of the issues highlighted in the Critical Issue box above, you will understand why many conversation analysts emphasise the importance of making one's recordings available to readers of a research report – other researchers can consider the recordings themselves and may be able to offer alternative 'hearings' of the data that shed new light on the analysis. This is likely to become a more common practice; however, even here we should be cautious of treating the audio or video recording itself as the ultimate arbiter of reality (Ashmore, MacMillan & Brown, 2004). Due to the nature of the research process itself, only certain things get recorded, and what one records will always frame one's analysis to a greater or lesser extent.

Summary points

This chapter has introduced some relevant features of the data set which underpins the next four chapters, as well as points the way to a critical engagement with the decisions underlying its development. We have:

1. considered what might be involved in thinking through some of the ethical issues in carrying out a study;
2. looked carefully at the kinds of material you would want to produce so as to make sure participants understand what a study is about;
3. provided some outline to the kind of interview guide one would produce when carrying out an interview based study;
4. drawn attention to issues relevant to considering the use of recorded material as a data resource for researchers; and
5. highlighted the significance of different transcription formats used in the qualitative methods used in this book.

Now that you're familiar with the basics of the data set, you're ready to turn to Chapters 8 to 11 to see how different analytic approaches might be applied to the data.

8

QM1: Discourse Analysis

Sally Wiggins and Sarah Riley

Introduction

For discourse analysts, words do more than reflect facts about the world. Instead, talk, or any other text that we may use to communicate, is understood as accomplishing some kind of social act. Thus, when Shazia (interview 1 in the data set) states that she'd rather have 'a few people that mean a lot to me than hundreds of people that I know so little about', discourse analysts do not see this statement as a reflection of Shazia's beliefs about her friendships, but as an active construction of a particular version of reality that has consequences for Shazia's interactions with others and her understanding and experiences of herself. Put simply, for discourse analysts, words *do* something in interaction and we are therefore interested in analysing what that something might be.

There are different versions of Discourse Analysis (DA), none of which has a step-by-step procedure. This makes DA a flexible method that can address a range of research questions, but this plurality can be daunting for a novice researcher. Students may also be put off DA because it has a particular theoretical standpoint about knowledge that may seem different or alien from what they've previous learnt in psychology. We have therefore used this chapter to introduce some of the key points that underlie the theory of knowledge that discourse analysts share. We follow this introduction by describing some of the processes involved in analysing data from two versions of DA, which are commonly referred to as Discursive Psychology (DP) and Foucauldian Discourse Analysis (FDA).[1] First, though, we

---

1 We use the term Foucauldian Discourse Analysis (FDA) because that is the most common term for this kind of work in psychology (see e.g., Willig, 2001, 2008). FDA is inspired by the work of French philosopher Michel Foucault as well as other post-structuralist philosophers.

give you a taste of what discourse analysts do, by looking at Extract 8.1 from interview 1 of the data set:

> ### Extract 8.1:   Data set sample extract (Int. 1; lines 454–462)
>
> (This same extract is considered early on in this and the next three analysis chapters.)
>
> Shazia: I'd rather have some, a few people that mean a lot to me than hundreds of people that I know so little about, that doesn't, it's, it's not, you can't even call it a friendship it's just an acquaintance [Int: yeah], but I don't, I'm not really bothered about people that I'm just acquainted with and like just fellow students and stuff like that, I kind of push those kind of, cause I don't like people knowing exactly what I'm feeling and thinking all of the time, so I think if I've got these few people around me that are close to me I can confide with them and that's it, I don't have to, yeah I don't like other people knowing too much about me [Int: OK, OK], I don't know if it's because I don't really like them or because I keep them away for a reason, but yeah, so only a few people close to me.

You will see from Table 8.1 that discourse analysts are interested in the detail about what is said, including which words are used and how are these put together in conversation. Discourse analysts are interested in the consequences of using these accounts and not others and so are also interested in which words are absent. The kinds of questions asked in DP work at times overlap, therefore, with those of FDA, since both are interested in understanding the ways in which accounts are constructed (put together, built up) rather than being concerned about any putative underlying cognitive states (cf. Interpretative Phenomenological Analysis [IPA], Chapter 10). What distinguishes the two versions is often the focus on the detail of discourse, with DP focusing as much on *how* things are said as *what* is said.

Also note that for DP, a more detailed transcript is normally used to highlight such features, so with Extract 8.1 we may have to stop short of addressing all the DP questions posed above. We can, however, start to pick out the words used to describe people, places or events: 'acquaintance' (line 3), 'fellow students' (line 5), 'few people' (lines 8 and 12) and also 'I'd rather have' (line 1) and 'I don't like' (line 6). So already we can start to see Shazia managing her identity: that is, building up an account of what she is 'like' and how that affects her friendships with others.

We can say little about how the two speakers respond to each other in this short extract, as we have not shown the interviewer's question prior to line 1, and there are only minimal responses from the interviewer herself (lines 4 and 16).

Table 8.1   Questions discourse analysts tend to ask of a piece of text from either a Discursive Psychology (DP) or Foucauldian Discourse Analysis (FDA) perspective

From a DP perspective	From a FDA perspective
Which words are being used to describe people, places or events? What other features of the talk are present, such as pauses, intonational features and repetitions?	What 'world', or version of reality, is being constructed in this account?
How does each speaker respond to each other's talk?	How do people understand themselves in this world and, from these understandings, what can they do and say?
What do the speakers do so that their account sounds factual? How do they negotiate that they or others may have an interest in presenting a particular version? How is accountability managed and how do people draw on psychological concepts, such as identities or mental states?	What is the social and historical context that allows this world to make sense?

What this tells us about the context of this talk is that it is a very particular kind of interaction – different, say, from two students chatting to each other, as one person appears to have a much more 'passive' role in the interaction.

From an FDA perspective, we might explore the way that Shazia appears to be constructing two different types of friendship groups, distinguished in terms of size, meaningfulness, privacy, intimacy and exposure. Shazia presents herself as someone who has a few meaningful friendships, which allow her intimacy without having to sacrifice her privacy, as she would do with a large group of friends. Shazia constructs this account by using contrasting terms such as 'a few people that mean a lot to me' with 'hundreds of people' who are not like friends, but acquaintances. She then makes a link between the type of friendship group she has and her need for privacy 'cause I don't like people knowing exactly what I'm feeling and thinking all of the time' (lines 6–7).

In asking ourselves why Shazia feels the need to justify having a small group of friends, we could surmise that this account makes sense within the context that as a student Shazia is aware of other people who have large groups of friends. In this context, Shazia may be vulnerable to being labelled unpopular, unsocial or otherwise socially problematic. Her account thus functions to ward off such labels by constructing her small friendship group as a positive choice. To social-historically contextualise this account, we might also note that a central aspect of the modern self is being able to compartmentalise public and private aspects of the self (Burkitt, 1991); Shazia's stress on the importance of protecting the private nature of herself makes sense within this discourse.

8.1 Definitions

Discourse refers to any form of talk or text, and in some forms of Discourse Analysis (DA), to any form of meaningful interaction between people, such as bodily movements or visual signs. One of the skills in learning how to 'do' DA – as with other methodologies – is in learning the language of the approach. This is particularly important for DA, an approach that primarily rests on the assumption that language is an active, not a passive, process.

So, the first lesson to learn is this: the term 'discourse' is preferred over alternatives such as 'language' or 'communication', and is more commonly used in the literature. This is because 'discourse' refers to both talk and text, and it captures the social and constructive element of interaction. That is, 'language' may implicate a linguistic emphasis, with a focus on grammar, punctuation or other technical aspects of the language system. 'Communication', on the other hand, is a word that buys into the notion of language as simply a medium; a way for my thoughts to be transferred into your head. 'Discourse', by contrast, highlights the way in which language is used in interaction (e.g., chatting with friends, e-mailing or talking in a tutorial) and privileges the talk rather than the people using it.

Background

The main aim of DA is to understand how talk and text construct particular versions of reality; in this sense, it is broadly *social constructionist.* Social constructionism refers to a theoretical position that questions taken-for-granted knowledge about the world and understands knowledge as produced in social processes. This means that we are interested in what discourse is *doing* in different settings and with the consequences of talking (or writing, or interacting) in a particular way.

8.2 Critical issue: Social constructionism

Knowledge, it is argued, is *constructed* (i.e., built up, brought into being) through our social practices, rather than already in existence, ready to be discovered. Thus, what we consider to be 'facts' about the world are instead considered to be culturally shared agreements about reality at a particular time and place. For example, we generally consider emotions to be internal states, yet in Shakespeare's time, emotions were considered public displays and so the concept of repressed anger would not have made sense to people then.

The main assumptions of DA can be summarised as follows: Social life is primarily made up of talk and text; that talk *does* things; and that there are multiple realities. Let us unpack these a little further. When we say that *social life is made up of talk and text*, we mean that discourse is fundamental to the way we live our lives; everything we do relies to some extent on discourse. Even when we are alone, or not talking, the actions we perform are understood through prior knowledge or interactions that have been produced through talk. For example, at a child's birth the announcement of 'it's a girl'! or 'it's a boy'! brings with it a whole set of understandings about that child, which may affect what the baby is called, the way people interact with the baby, how they interpret the baby's behaviour – even the colour they use to paint the baby's bedroom! It is because of the significance of talk and text to social life that we focus upon it. To understand psychology and social life, we must therefore understand the discursive processes that take place in different social settings.

Our second assumption is that *talk does things*. When we think of talk, usually we think of it as neutral, in that it reflects our external world and helps us share our internally created thoughts and ideas with others (sometimes referred to as the 'conduit metaphor' of talk). However, for discourse analysts, language does not neutrally describe our world, it actively constructs it in interaction; and the words we use to construct our thoughts and ideas are embedded in social values. In Extract 8.1, for example, Shazia is understood as managing her identity in particular ways.

Discourse is thus active in producing our understanding of our world. In starting to think about the two forms of DA that we focus on in this chapter, DP is particularly interested in the immediate interpersonal work that talk does, and with how psychological notions (e.g., mind, identities, emotions) are produced and managed in interaction. For example, rather than trying to understand the emotions that a person feels (as IPA might do), DP would focus on how emotional expressions (such as 'hopping mad' or 'blind with love') can characterise emotions in particular ways; as brief lapses in one's behaviour, for example, rather than personality traits (see Edwards, 1999).

For FDA, talk is understood as bringing into being the nature of what we are talking about, talk constructs the objects/subjects that we 'know', giving us a place from which to understand ourselves and our world. For example, describing someone as 'heterosexual' draws on an understanding that sexuality is something people are (heterosexual) rather than something that they do (e.g., men who have sex with women). FDA, then, is interested in identifying the social understandings that our talk draws upon. These social understandings become part of our 'common sense' and often take the form of relatively coherent ways of talking about objects and events in the world, what Edley (2001, p. 198) calls the 'building blocks of conversations'. Foucauldian discourse analysts are interested in exploring the possible ways of being that are opened up or shut down when we use these building blocks.

We can see these differences in our brief consideration of Shazia's account above. The DP analysis looked at how Shazia's identity was constructed and how this was built up using familiar terms (e.g., *I'm not really bothered about*) that tap into lay understandings of psychology and personality. In contrast, the FDA analysis was more interested in the construction of two types of friendship groups – 'large but meaningless' or 'small and intimate' – and how this construction allowed Shazia to argue that her small friendship group was a matter of positive choice.

The third assumption of DA is of *multiple realities*: there are multiple ways, rather than one true way, to understanding something. The metaphor of a map is useful here: a piece of land may be represented by a geologist's map in terms of the types of rock it is made of, or by an ordinance survey map that will give you information about roads, contours, buildings and trees. The maps are both 'true' representations of reality. So discourse analysts argue that in explaining our social world, we can draw on many different versions to make sense of it. For example, by focusing on different aspects of a really good night out, you might tell a very different, but equally 'true', story to your friends than you would to your parents. It is the fact that we can construct different versions that makes language so interesting for discourse analysts – we ask 'why this version and not another', and this leads to a further question: 'what is the consequence of using this version and not another'?.

8.3 Want to know more?

For a clear and thorough discussion of social constructionism, see Vivien Burr's (2003) *Social constructionism* (2nd Edn). London: Routledge.

For more detail on Discursive Psychology, see:
Hepburn, A. & Wiggins S. (2007) *Discursive research in practice: New approaches to psychology and everyday interaction*. Cambridge: Cambridge University Press.
There is also a classic text by Edwards & Potter (1992) *Discursive psychology*. London: Sage.

For more detail on FDA, see:
Willig, C. (2001) Introducing qualitative research in psychology: Adventures in theory and method. Buckingham: Open University Press; or
Willig, C. (2008) Discourse analysis. In Smith, J. *Qualitative psychology*. London: Sage.
A classic text is Parker (1992) *Discourse dynamics*. London: Routledge, which is available at www.discourseunit.com

For an example of Foucauldian Discourse Analysis with a geneological analysis see:
Arribas-Ayllon, M. & Walkerdine, V. (2008) Foucauldian discourse analysis. In: Willig, C. & Stainton-Rogers, W. (Eds) *The Sage handbook of qualitative research in psychology*. London: Sage.

Steps in the research process

You should now have a sense of why language is important to discourse analysts and the kinds of questions they ask. If you want to use DA in your own work the next steps would be, as with all research, to choose your topic, decide on a research question, design your study and carry out the data collection in order to build a corpus of appropriate data to analyse and write up. In DA the data needs to be audio- and/or video-recorded and then transcribed for coding and analysis. In the sub-sections below, we work through these stages using the data set materials to illustrate.

Devising a research question

In *discursive psychology* research, the sorts of research questions that are commonly used are those that reflect a concern with the ways in which people manage psychological matters in everyday life, such as identities, accountabilities and mental states. For example, 'how do sex offenders account for their criminal activities?', 'how do participants in weight management ('dieting') programmes attend to the issue of blame'? If we were focusing on the data set provided, the sorts of research questions DP might ask are:

- How do the participants construct their identities when discussing friendship, and how do these identities change at different points in the interview?
- How is responsibility for making or breaking friendships managed?
- How are mental states or personality traits (such as 'outgoing' or 'clever') invoked to manage one's account of friendship problems?

By now you will be getting the sense that 'how' questions are quite popular in this type of analysis! Certainly, DP researchers are interested in the processes involved in social interaction, and thus 'how' questions work well, though they are not the only way in which you might phrase a research question within this framework. Note that these types of questions avoid any 'why?' type phrases; this is because DA is not concerned with causality, but with the implications of talk for our understanding of everyday life.

In *Foucauldian discourse analysis*, we might ask research questions that aim to explore the understandings we use to explain our world; the rights and expectations these understandings convey on a person; and the social and historical context that allow these understandings to make sense to the speaker. Research questions in FDA often focus on how discourses construct 'subject positions' and how these (re)produce power relations. 'Subject positions' is a term used to describe relatively coherent ways of understanding an aspect of the self. These are associated with particular rights and responsibilities in terms of what we can do and say. For example, being a 'student' allows someone access to the library but not behind the librarian's desk.

8.4 Critical issue: Language use and power relations

Discourse analysts often bracket off parts of words, as in the term '(re)pro-duce'. We do this because it helps us flag up the multiple meanings and power relations in the terms we use. By saying '(re)produce' we are empha-sising the idea that language constructs (or produces) a particular reality, but it does so by drawing on concepts that are already available to us in our socio-historic cultural context – as such it 'reproduces' culturally domi-nant ideas.

In terms of our friendship data set, a FDA might ask:

- How is friendship talked about?
- What are the subject positions available in contemporary friendship discourse?
- What are the social and historical contexts that allow this talk on friendship to make sense?

Note that your research question will probably develop during your study. You may start off with a general question such as 'how is friendship talked about', but as you start to analyse your data you may notice a re-occurring theme that seems to articulate something important. You would then focus on this in more detail, devel-oping a more specific research question, such as 'how is meaningfulness bestowed on friendships'? In this sense, DA might be said to be *data-driven*.

Designing your study and collecting data

DP tends to favour 'naturally occurring data' (for further discussion see Chapters 4 and 11). For FDA, nearly anything is text and can therefore be analysed. This is because writing, images, actions and everyday objects are part of symbolic systems that can be read for the meanings they employ including, for example, the instruc-tions from a single tube of toothpaste (Parker, 1994). To design your study use your research question to structure your ideas about what methods you will use to col-lect your data. For example, if you are interested in the management of food and identity you might ask families to record their mealtimes. See Chapter 4, part 2 Gibson & Riley and Chapter 5 for ideas to generate qualitative data appropriate for DA. You will need to collect enough data to do an interesting analysis but not so much that you become swamped. This is a judgement call that you can make with your supervisor and by reading other studies similar to your own.

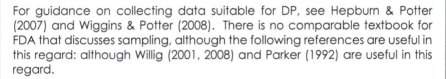

Want to know more?   8.5

For guidance on collecting data suitable for DP, see Hepburn & Potter (2007) and Wiggins & Potter (2008). There is no comparable textbook for FDA that discusses sampling, although the following references are useful in this regard: although Willig (2001, 2008) and Parker (1992) are useful in this regard.

Transcription

Once you have your data in either audio or video format, the next step is to transcribe it – that is, to type or write up the sound file into a Word document which will then be read and analysed alongside listening to and/or viewing the audio/video files. We will not go into much detail here, other than to note the different transcription styles of DP and FDA as these have implications for analysis.

For *discursive psychology* research, which overlaps at times with conversation analytic work (see Chapter 11), the level of transcription required is more detailed than that for FDA, and the system devised by Gail Jefferson is most commonly used (see Chapter 7). At first glance, such transcripts can appear strange or difficult to read, though they are essential for this type of analysis. They enable researchers to examine where overlaps in speech occur, how something has been said, and so on.

Foucauldian discourse analysis often uses a simplified and less detailed transcription notation, for example, short pauses may not be timed. The level of detail you need will be a pragmatic decision based on providing enough information to give a sense of how the person spoke and to be able to address your research question.

Coding

The next step is to start coding the data; deciding which areas to focus on, and how to begin analysis. To keep your focus, you should always be guided by your research question. For all DA, coding is an iterative process, interpreting and re-coding the data; similarly you may cycle between the stages of coding and analysing data. It is therefore important to give yourself plenty of time for these stages, as this is where your ideas may develop significantly.

For *discursive psychology*, coding involves sifting through the data, collecting instances of a particular phenomenon, such as when participants refer to ending a friendship. Often you will need to code the data once, then start analysing, then go back to re-code or search for further extracts – so don't expect to do it once and be finished with it. For example, you might start off with instances of participants' accounts of ending friendships (e.g., 'we don't really talk any more'), then later decide to focus on a broader focus of changing friendships (e.g., 'we spend more time in a bigger group of friends now').

When you are coding, try to be as inclusive as possible to avoid missing any potentially important extracts. Cut and paste these extracts into a new Word file ready for analysis. Always include a few lines before and a few lines after a section of extract to provide a little more context to work with.

8.6 Activity suggestion

Look at interview 3 (Jeffersonian-style transcript) of the data set materials, and up to line 351 code for instances where the interviewee (Louise) invokes mental states, psychological terms or personality characteristics. Make a list of the lines where you have coded and a brief description of what Louise is saying there. Compare your codes with ours below.

Did you make similar or different coding decisions? Why do you think that might be?

The extracts we picked out were:

Lines 119–139: talk about a girl who 'didn't like the people she was originally living with' and how her group had already made a 'bond'
Lines 152–163: being 'close' and smoking forming a 'bond'
Lines 205–229: 'feels like I've known her for years', 'know when we need our own space'
Lines 282–310: 'not my type of thing', 'she's not a very sociable person', other four were 'quite close'
Lines 336–351: 'all close together', 'little posse'.

There is no one right way to code for *Foucauldian discourse analysis*. However, if you're starting out with FDA it can be useful to have some steps to follow as you build up your confidence and develop your own style and practice. In this spirit we offer the following stages as introductory guidelines.

1. *Noting general impressions, subjects and objects.* Create large margins either side of the transcript, in which you can write notes. On the left-hand side write down key words that seem to summarise chunks of your data (a 'chunk' can be sentence, paragraph or argument), from these notes you will start to get ideas for the key themes of your participants' talk. On the right-hand side write down a summary of what the person is saying – this helps to sensitise yourself to the style and content of your participant's talk and to help you think of the arguments, objects and subjects that are being used to construct particular realities.

2. *Identifying key themes and marking them on the transcripts.* As you work through stage 1 you will start to notice that you are writing down similar terms; see if you

can find an overarching term for them and use this term as a theme. Aim to find several themes that can either summarise much of your data or that allow you to focus on patterns of talk that are relevant to your research question. You may need to repeat stages 1 and 2 several times before you have themes that can do this. The aim of cycling through stages 1 and 2 is to develop your thinking from descriptive to more conceptual themes which seem to incorporate a lot of your data.

When you're happy you've done this theme identification you can move onto stages 3 and 4. Keep in mind both your research question(s) as well as what the participant is saying, so that your coding is data-driven. This allows you to explore issues that you may not have thought of before, but which are relevant for your participants and hence for your study. Being sensitive to your data in this way is essential for doing original and interesting research and is especially important if you have a very broad research question which you aim to make more specific during the research process. Note that the same extract can be coded in more than one way. Whilst there is no 'good' number to have, a rule of thumb for an undergraduate project might be to aim for two to five themes.

3. *Collecting instances to produce a series of extracts.* Go through your data, marking any section in which one of your themes is discussed. Be as inclusive as possible, including oblique as well as overt references. You can do this by writing next to the section, highlighting it or using the notation facilities in software such as NVIVO (see Gibbs, 2002) .

4. *Identifying discourses: Sorting the extracts for different ways of talking about the theme.* Cut and paste all the extracts that relate to a theme into a Word document, noting where in the data the extract comes from. One method is then to physically cut this document so that you have slips of paper, each with an extract on. Then sort the slips of paper into piles that seem to represent a discourse, that is, share a particular way of talking about the theme. Repeat this process several times until you have found a way to conceptually categorise the different ways that the theme is talked about. Don't be disheartened by the cyclical nature of this process, each time you do it you are developing your thinking about your data.[2]

Activity suggestion 8.7

Returning to interview 3 (this time the simpler playscript transcription version), read through the transcript applying stages 1 to 4 as outlined above. If you're struggling to 'break into' the data, consider the activities that Louise describes with her friends. For example, we noticed the way that Louise

---

(Continued)

---

2 You can do a similar procedure on NVivo, however, there something about the physical and repetitive nature of sorting that can help you make imaginative associations.

8.7 continued

talked about spending time with people, such as going out or watching films (e.g., lines 73, 202, 305, 469). In the right-hand margin we had written 'going out' and 'watching films' to summarise this talk and in the left-hand margin had written words, such as 'time' or 'effort', which seem to conceptualise this talk. Cycling through stages 1 and 2 we thought that Louise talked about 'time' and 'effort' in ways that seemed to orient around distinctions between different kinds of friendships. We then went back to the transcript, marking any talk that seemed to distinguish different kinds of friendships. Collecting these extracts together (stage 3) and sorting them (stage 4) allowed us to describe the different social worlds that appeared to be constructed in Louise's talk. For example, Louise appeared to distinguish between long-term meaningful friendships and a kind of 'everyday' friendships with people she enjoyed spending time with but wouldn't necessarily make much effort to stay in touch with. Look carefully at these examples and the process we went through and you'll see what we mean.

Analysis and interpretation of the data

Discursive psychology: At the end of your DP coding you would have created a Word document of coded instances, which, in the example we used, were of when Louise had evoked mental states, psychological terms or personality characteristics When starting to analyse your corpus of coded data the first thing to do is to read through this data (having already read through the entire data set a few times), making notes about what strikes you, stands out or appears odd. You will need to do this a few times, re-reading the data and listening to and/or watching the data as you do so. For example, you might note that participants often use the phrases 'I don't know' or 'you know' when talking to the interviewer. Alternatively, the way in which participants answer questions might seem to be odd in some respect. For example, in interview 5 (Deborah), on being asked what they do together as friends, the participant may seem dismissive of their activities as 'silly' or 'juvenile'.

The following extract is taken from lines 293–308 in the Jeffersonian transcript of interview 3 (Louise), which we can use to start analysing the data by picking out features that are relevant for DP.

For many students starting out in DP, it can often help to be guided by a list of 'devices' that can be searched for in the data (see box below). It is important to remember, however, that doing DP is not just about 'device spotting' (see Antaki et al., 2003), though this might help you to get started.

Extract 8.2:   Notions of being sociable (Int. 3; lines 293–308).

1	Louise:	there's one girl who
2		(0.9)
3	Louise:	isn't she doesn't come out with us cos she's not a very: sociable
4		person she's the type who'd rather stay in and watch films
5		(0.5)
6	Louise:	so we do watch films with her occasionally but=
7	Alasdair:	=°m[:°]
8	Louise:	[she] goes home quite a lot you see
9		(0.5)
10	Louise:	so we don't really see that much of her and she
11		goes out with other friends from other ha:lls so
12		(0.4)
13	Louise:	but the other four of us ↓we are
14		(1.2)
15	Louise:	quite [close]
16	Alasdair:	[but th]is

Critical issue: Discursive 'devices'   **8.8**

Here is a non-exhaustive list of the kinds of features that discursive psychologists might look for in discourse. These features are often form part of how speakers negotiate fact, interest and accountability. Note that these can overlap with conversation analytic concerns (see Chapter 11).

* Emotion categories – such as 'I was so upset'. The focus is often on how these are used to contrast with cognitive categories, for example, 'I was too upset to think straight', and can be used as a resource for holding others accountable.
* Extreme case formulations – such as 'the worst day of my life'. These are often used to strengthen an account or may be used ironically.
* Script formulations – for example 'we watch films together'. This presents an event as if it were typical or routine, and thus can imply something about the speaker or subjects.
* Pronoun use and 'footing shifts' – that is, when the speaker moves from saying 'I' to 'we' or 'you', for example. This is often used to manage accountability for events.
* Assessments – such as 'she was lovely' or 'I hate her'. These can be used to do subtle work in managing blame or accountability.
* Three part lists – such as 'here, there and everywhere'. These are common in much talk, especially in political speeches. They often add credibility and authenticity to accounts.

In our analysis of Extract 8.2 we thought that it was particularly interesting the way in which responsibility (or accountability) for being friends, or not, with someone was managed in rather subtle ways: we noticed how Louise uses pronouns to mark out this 'one girl' (line 1) as being separate from 'us' and 'we' (lines 3, 6, 10 and 13). Hence, what 'we do' (line 6) is directly contrasted with what 'she' is like (lines 3–4). When it is spoken this way, the other girl becomes the odd one out. Her not going out with Louise's group of friends is blamed on her not being 'a very sociable person' (line 3), rather than anything that the group might have done. In this way, it is not Louise who is being unfriendly or unsociable; rather, the friction is caused by the other girl's *personality* ('she's the type...', lines 3–4). Note how this is worked up in a rather scripted way – 'we do watch films with her' (line 6), 'she goes out with her friends' (lines 10–11) – as if these events were commonplace. This makes it a more believeable story, and more forgiveable too; if this girl was only 'unsociable' on one occasion, then that would not be reason enough to exclude her from the group.

We also noticed an apparent ambiguity. Look at lines 3–4, then at lines 10–11. It doesn't sound like this girl is 'not very sociable', if they don't see much of her and she goes out with other friends. Such variability in talk is expected within discursive research. Rather than trying to find out what Louise 'really' thinks of this girl (which would be the focus of an IPA, see Chapter 10), we can look to see what this variability is doing in the talk itself. The claim of her not being sociable is used to account for why she doesn't go out with Louise and the other people (hence, they cannot be blamed for her not joining in). Then, when Louise tells of how they try to engage with her – by watching films together – this is hampered because the girl is often out or with other people. Hence the contradictory account of this girl serves the purpose of rationalising and justifying Louise's attempts to be her friend.

8.9 Activity suggestion

Choose a section of an interview from the data set at random. Note down anything that interests you about the way the talk is structured. Think about what is 'going on' in the talk, it may help to ask yourself the following questions:

> *What sort of 'business' is the speaker involved in (e.g., blaming, justifying, describing)?*
>
> *What would happen to the talk if I exchange words (e.g., replacing the word 'girl' with 'young woman'?)*
>
> *What discursive devices can I identify and what kind of 'work' might they be doing?*
>
> *What is being constructed in this piece of text and how is this achieved?*

Foucauldian discourse analysis: Having followed stages 1 to 4 of the coding stages outlined above you would now have coded your data in terms of the different ways that a topic has been talked about, thus identifying the discourses that make up the meaning-making around your research topic. Now you need to focus on how these discourses are constructed and the consequences of using these discourses.

To consider how each discourse is constructed, look at each pile of extracts you produced in stage 4 of coding and consider how the arguments used sound plausible. Although you can look at the kinds of discursive devices that DP analysts are interested in, FDA tends to focus on construction in terms of the broader sense-making that's occuring in the text. This means considering both the 'building blocks of common sense' which we talked about at the beginning of this chapter. For example, we could argue that Shazia (Extract 8.1) draws on a common sense understanding that in good friendships confidences are shared safely and that privacy is an important value.

To analyse the function of the discourses you've identifed, ask yourself 'what possible ways of being are opened up or shut down by this talk?' This question focuses your analysis on the consequences of using these constructions, including implications for subjectivity. For example, the talk in Shazia's extract constructed her small friendship group as a positive choice, warding off any label of her as failing socially.[3] Exploring the implications for subjectivity and locating these understandings within their social and historical context allows FDA to analyse power relations. Another way to do this is to think about the role of institutions in supporting or benefiting from these discourses. In Louise's example (Extract 8.2), we can think of the various ways the university is structured – halls of residence and mass education teaching styles – that encourages large group identities.

Activity suggestion **8.10**

Again, take a section of an interview from the data set and read it with the following questions in mind:
> *What reality is being constructed here?*
> *What common sense understandings are drawn upon to make this talk sound plausible?*
> *What is the implication for the speakers and those spoken about in terms of what they can say, think or do?*
> *What are the wider discourses that allow it to make sense?*

---

3 In DA there are broadly two forms of consequences in talk: those that function at the interactional level, the focus of DP; and those that focus on subjectivity and power relations, which is the focus of FDA. Some discourse analysts argue that it is valuable to do 'mixed level' research which draws on both DP and FDA. For example, see Wetherell & Edley (1999) and Riley (2002).

Writing up the analysis

The analysis and writing up stages are interlinked and should be allocated signifi-cant time as many discourse analysts find that they develop their analysis as they write up their study. A similiar structure in writing up is used across different forms of DA and, as with other qualitative methodologies (see Chapter 12), this section of your report is more likely to be titled, 'Analysis' or 'Findings' rather than 'Results'. This section will usually provide an outline of the key findings, such as the different discourses identified, before going on to describe the findings in more detail. The analysis may contextualise the findings by making links to the literature review or the research questions. When writing up DA you may not note down everything that you picked out in your initial analysis: it is more important to identify one or a few important patterns in the talk that is relevant to your research question and be clear and focused when making an analytical point. Putting line numbers on extracts and then referring to these is helpful, and it may also be necessary to refer to the intonational features of the talk, particularly for DP analysis (although this has not been done in the example below).

Example of Discursive Psychology writing up: Managing accountability for friendships

Throughout the data, participants deal with the complexities of managing friend-ships, their formation, progression and decline. Part of this complexity is the implication of responsibility or accountability for making or breaking friendships. If one is always 'losing' friends, then that might say something about the individual and their ability to form relationships with others. On the other hand, it is difficult to place the blame entirely on others as this might appear self-centred or false. We can see an instance of how participants might deal with such complexity in Extract 8.3. At this point in the interview, Alasdair (the interviewer) has just asked Louise (interviewee) if she is close to other people in her flat.

The first thing to note about Extract 8.3 is the use of pronouns to categorise individuals as part of, or separate from, groups of friends. Thus, in line 3, the girl (who at this point isn't given a name), is referred to as 'she' in contrast to 'us' (lines 3 and 13) and 'we' (lines 6, 10 and 13). This is built upon through reference to the girl's reported behaviour or characteristics: she's not very sociable, she watches films, she goes out with other friends. Note also how Louise provides some evi-dence of trying to engage with the girl – making an attempt to be friends – with the comment 'we do watch films with her occasionally' (line 6). This is worked up in a rather scripted way, and repeated in the reporting of the girl's apparent absence in the flat (line 10). As with claims about the girl's personality ('she's not very socia-ble', 'she's the type'), this presents the issue as an ongoing problem, rather than a one-off event. If someone is a particular 'type' of person, it is harder then to make

> ### Extract 8.3: Making 'doing sociable' accountable (Int. 3; lines 293–305)
>
> | 1 | Louise: | there's one girl who |
> |---|---------|----------------------|
> | 2 | | (0.9) |
> | 3 | Louise: | isn't she doesn't come out with us cos she's not a very: sociable |
> | 4 | | person she's the type who'd rather stay in and watch films |
> | 5 | | (0.5) |
> | 6 | Louise: | so we do watch films with her occasionally but= |
> | 7 | Alasdair: | =°m[:°] |
> | 8 | Louise: | [she] goes home quite a lot you see |
> | 9 | | (0.5) |
> | 10 | Louise: | so we don't really see that much of her and she goes out with |
> | 11 | | other friends from other ha:lls so |
> | 12 | | (0.4) |
> | 13 | Louise: | but the other four of us ↓we are |

them behave differently. This works to place the emphasis on the girl as being the root of the problem; it is not what Louise and the others do that is to blame.

Example of Foucauldian Discourse Analysis writing up: Constructing friendships at university

From a social constructionist perspective, identity is not something a person has, but something that is produced in relationships with others through our talk and interactions. When students arrive at university they enter an environment where previous relationships (e.g., with parents and school friends) are often absent and where they are surrounded by large groups of peers (in halls of residence, lectures, etc.) from where new relationships may be formed. In this context these new friendships become important indicators of identity. Indeed, in our study the importance of friendships was taken for granted, and people without friendship groups were understood as needing support to develop them. However, not all friendships were considered equal and three different discourses of friendships were identified: 'meaningful', 'everyday' and 'meaningless'.

Meaningful friendships involve time and effort. They are characterised as a special relationship between people who resonate with each other in some way. These relationships tend to be experienced at the individual and private level, rather than in a group context. As such, people have only a small number of these. For example, Louise describes a specific person in her social group (Extract 8.5).

Extract 8.5

Yeah, yeah, she's like if I had, if there was something wrong with me or something then she's the one I'd go to out of the whole of the flat, so yeah she's a particular one.

Similarly, Deb distinguishes a special person out of a large social group, whom she now sees in and out of university and with whom she plans to travel abroad (Extract 8.6).

Extract 8.6

Deb: I know loads of people, but I don't know what it was, just, we just clicked.

Alternatively, 'everyday friendships' are based on proxemics (such as living near each other in halls), involve relatively little effort, are good while they last (in the sense that they are enjoyable and not fake), are functional (its important to have them), and tend to be experienced when in a group. Louise gives such an example (Extract 8.7).

Extract 8.7

Louise: Yeah, yeah, there's erm, we've formed like a group of about fif-teen of us, we're all quite close group cause we all live on the first floor you see, of where we stay, so there's a couple who are from other halls, so it's really good, quite a sociable group and everyone, there's people who are closer than others, but then we're all close together, so it's cool, I like it.

The third type of relationships, 'meaningless relationships', are a downgraded version of everyday friendships, made up of people who do not share a closeness. For example, see Shazia's (see extract one) talk of 'acquaintances'.

Constructing different types of friendships creates a variety of subject positions based on the dichotomies of popular/unpopular, social/unsocial, intimate/acquaintance, and discerning/indiscriminant. These dichotomies are used to position the speaker on the positive side of these binaries (popular, social, intimate, discerning), closing down the possibility that the person is somehow failing in their relationships, a concern made particularly salient by the university context where friendships provide important sites for identity.

Activity suggestion **8.11**

Can you identify three similiarities and three differences between the DP and FDA writing up examples? These may be about the content, style or focus. For example, could you tell which type of DA was being used by the titles alone? Is there a difference in the use of extracts or on the level of focus on specific talk?

The examples above are much shorter than they would be in a 'real' report – can you think of ways the analyses might have been developed?

Summary points

1. For discourse analysts, talk actively creates and structures our social world, it is therefore worth studying in its own right (and not as a vehicle to inner beliefs or motivations).
2. Discourse Analysis (DA) examines the detail of talk and interaction to explore the consequences of constructing reality in particular ways.
3. DA allows us to question 'natural' or common sense understandings about the world and to explore how these are deployed in interaction to construct particular versions of the world that have consequence for what people can think, say or do.
4. There are different versions of DA, which, whilst sharing a social constructionist epistemology, have a different approach to the analysis of talk or texts.
5. Discursive Psychology tends to focus on the micro-management of fact, interest and accountability, and the ways in which people invoke psychological terms such as mental states, identities or personality characteristics.
6. Foucauldian Discourse Analysis tends to focus on the wider discourses that allow talk or text to be made intelligible; the implications for subjectivity in these accounts; and the role of institutions in supporting these discourses.

9

QM2: Grounded Theory

Alasdair Gordon-Finlayson

Introduction

Grounded theory methodology is a powerful qualitative approach that strives to arrive at a *theoretical* understanding of psycho-social phenomena that is *grounded* in the data collected from the lives and contexts of the participants. There is a strong coding procedure at the heart of grounded theory, but it is more than just a simple technique for coding qualitative data: it is an approach to research that provides an extensive analytical framework focused on the production of theory.

Grounded theory was initially developed by two American sociologists, Barney Glaser and Anselm Strauss. They came from different theoretical backgrounds: Glaser's interests were in standard hypothetico-deductive research whilst Strauss was more interested in the perspective of the *symbolic interactionists* like Herbert Blumer and G. H. Mead. Glaser & Strauss (1965) collaborated on a study looking at the process of dying in hospital and two years later published the seminal *Discovery of Grounded Theory* in which they formalised the research methodology they had devised (Glaser & Strauss 1967).

! | 9.1 Definitions

Symbolic Interactionism is a perspective conceived by George Herbert Mead (1863–1931), a social psychologist. Symbolic Interactionism has influenced modern thinking about the role of the interpretation and meaning in the social world. Herbert Blumer, who formalised Symbolic Interactionism in the mid-twentieth century, summarised the basic tenets as:

1. Human beings act towards things on the basis of the meanings they ascribe to those things.
2. The meaning of such things is derived from, or arises out of, the social interaction that one has with others and the society.
3. These meanings are handled in, and modified through, an interpretive process used by the person in dealing with the things he/she encounters. (Blumer 1969, p. 2)

Grounded theory entails an *inductive*, rather than a deductive, approach to doing research. A hypothetico-deductive model of research design involves beginning with a theory, and then developing hypotheses to test whether that theory holds true. In contrast, grounded theory starts with the detail of individual cases and uses the logic of induction to move from there to developing a theory that holds true for those cases.

Background

Defining grounded theory

We can distinguish some fairly clear characteristics that define whether a study is grounded theory – or not. We can identify three major traits that influence the logic, the procedures and the product of a grounded theory study, and illustrate these with examples from the common data set produced this book. Once we've looked at what grounded theory actually is, I will summarise the procedures and show in the next section how I applied this to the transcripts from the data set.

Critical issue: Disputes in grounded theory 9.2

The development of grounded theory has been marked by a split between Glaser and Strauss on methodological and epistemological grounds (for more on the story, see Morse et al., 2009). Glaser maintains that Strauss and others, especially Juliet Corbin, had adapted the methodology too much to still be claiming to be doing grounded theory, whilst others remain uncomfortable with the both the positivism of Glaser's position as well as the pragmatism of the Straussian version of grounded theory (see Clarke, 2005; Charmaz, 2006).

The disputes in grounded theory often serve to highlight some of the most telling problems in qualitative research. Where does interpretation end and analysis begin? How do we approach the problems of language and representation? To what extent can we follow a set of instructions, and where does our creativity and individuality enter into the research process? How does qualitative research function logically?

The interested researcher will find much to explore in these areas – the challenge is sometimes not to allow oneself to be paralysed by the 'meta-questions', to remember to get stuck into your own data, to continue to *do* grounded theory, not just *talk* it.

Grounded theory is ... theoretical

The goal of grounded theory is the generation of theory. If the product of a study is not theoretical, that study really can't be called grounded theory. We are usually aiming for a *substantive* theory, rather than *grand theory*; that is, the theory we arrive at will make sense in terms of its own context rather than positing universal laws that govern all of human behaviour. In our example, our grounded theory should be able to make sense of how friendships are formed and maintained as people enter university, or even just one particular university if there are specific local issues that come up. However, we're not trying to explain how all kinds of human relationships form.

It is not only the goal of this approach that is theoretical; researchers themselves need to develop what is referred to as *theoretical sensitivity*. This refers to a set of characteristics and skills in researchers, many of which only come with experience, which come into play as they produce codes and categories. Theoretical sensitivity at this stage enables the generation of theory, enabling them to become 'more in-tune to the meanings embedded in the data' (Corbin & Strauss 2008, p. 231). Charmaz, who advises use to code for *actions* rather than *themes* in our search for theory, says:

> Theorizing means stopping, pondering and rethinking anew... To gain theoretical sensitivity, we look at studied life from multiple vantage points, make comparisons, follow leads and build on ideas... When you theorize, you reach down to fundamentals, up to abstractions, and probe into experience. (Charmaz, 2006, p. 136)

This sensitivity to theory also drives the way that the data are collected, in a sampling process called *theoretical sampling*. This is a gradual sampling strategy (see Definitions box below) used in grounded theory, in which participants are selected to further explore ideas that the researcher is developing from data already collected. It might be that a participant is sought who can clarify a certain question, or that participants are chosen to ensure that all the possibilities of a given theoretical construct are present.

!

9.3 Definitions

Sampling in qualitative research. In contrast to quantitative, nomothetic research, sampling in qualitative research is often *purposeful* rather than representative. As we are not attempting to statistically generalise certain characteristics of our sample to the population, we can choose participants based more on their *individual characteristics* and what we hope they can bring to our project – what we can learn from them. This selection can either be *a priori* (choosing participants at the start of the project) or *gradual* (choosing participants individually whilst continuing with the analysis), and there are different strategies for each. Many Grounded Theory projects start with an *a priori* sample and then use a gradual strategy to select further participants once the analysis of the initial data has got underway.

For instance, when reading through Deborah's interview (interview 5, lines 375–392) I noticed reference to some of her old friends being uneasy with her new role as a student – they had previously known her only as a single mum living in a deprived area of Liverpool. This led me to think about how friendships are affected by radical changes in how we identify ourselves – how did Deborah's friends really feel about this move, did it threaten them in any way, did they feel that they needed to pull back a bit from her? To answer these questions, perhaps I need to find some participants who, rather than being university students themselves (even though this is who we are looking at in the project as a whole), have had friends go off to university leaving them behind. Also, is there something specific about university here? Perhaps I could speak to one or two people with friends who have joined the armed services, or been posted overseas by an employer. This would help me investigate a tentative theoretical construct I'd called 'changes of universe – influence on current friends'.

The process of theoretical sampling continues right up to the end of the project. The point comes when you've gathered enough data to fully develop all of your conceptual categories and are satisfied with the grounded theory you've developed. This is known as *theoretical saturation,* where no matter what new data you collect, no new detail or properties are added to your conceptual categories.

The idea of the entire research process as focused on theory is fundamental to the process of doing grounded theory. The logic of the coding process (described in detail below) is to move from (i) concepts that are generated directly from (i.e., *grounded in*) the data, towards (ii) related collections of these concepts, or conceptual categories, that are more general and more explanatory (therefore functioning as theoretical), and finally to (iii) the statement of the grounded theory itself. This *inductive* move from the particular to the general is not unique to grounded theory, but grounded theory relies on it utterly.

Grounded theory is ... analytical

The idea of grounded theory is to become analytical in your approach to the data and the developing theory. Grounded theory is produced by reflecting on qualitative data; it is an *analysis* informed by the researcher's theoretical sensitivity. This enables the inductive move from the detail of your participants' lives to a theory that explains the underlying processes and dynamics in more general terms.

In grounded theory, analysis and reflection take place in *memos*, which are written throughout the life of the project. A memo is your written reflections of your analysis, and there a few examples of memos later in this chapter. Memos can serve many functions, including reflecting on definitions and properties of emerging concepts, comparing cases to each other, advancing tentative ideas about developing theories, and so on. They can also include diagrams which might represent, for example, the relationship between concepts that you are trying to refine.

The most visible analytic technique is the coding process by which the data are broken down into their conceptual components (*open coding*) and these concepts arranged into categories (*axial coding*), and it is the identification of the relationship between these categories (*selective* or *theoretical coding*) that produces the grounded theory that is the culmination of the research process. Later on in this chapter we will look at memos and coding in more detail, as they are really the 'nuts and bolts' of the grounded theory process.

The analytical nature of grounded theory is also evident in the strategies that various authors have advanced for developing one's thinking about the research project. Corbin and Strauss have a list of 13 *analytic tools* (2008, p. 69), some of which have been commonly adopted by other grounded theorists (including the asking of questions, constant comparison and negative case analysis), whilst others have not proved as popular (e.g., the 'flip-flop technique' or 'waving the red flag'). Their approach provides a fairly easy-to-understand set of tools that you can consider as you progress through your project.

Constant comparison is *the* central analytic technique, adopted by all grounded theorists. At all stages of the project, the researcher is continually comparing *concept to concept*, to determine where they might fit in the greater scheme of things. This comparison reveals possible relationships between concepts, which will lead to the structure of the conceptual categories.

In order to flesh out these ideas, the researcher compares *incident to incident* or *case to case*, investigating how the details of these concepts differ in individual instances. This ensures the richness and variety within higher-order conceptual categories, which might otherwise be lost in a drive towards over-simplification in order to generate theory. The risk of this over-simplification is that whilst you might end up with a fine-sounding theory, you could also easily lose the ability of your theory to provide an explanatory framework for individual cases. This *fit* is a hallmark of good grounded theory that must never be sacrificed in the name of an alluringly simple theory. For instance, when reading Deborah's transcript I started to develop an early notion that 'new friendships' with other university students and 'maintained friendships' with old school friends tended not to mix at all. However, when I compared this with the case of Louise (interview 3) I had to reconsider this, as Louise talks of having had school friends stay with her at university and mix socially with her friends from halls. The tentative idea of exclusivity had to be abandoned, but this led to the developing of a more sophisticated model of how friendships function.

Another analytic tool that is used by all grounded theorists is *asking questions*. You should constantly examine your own analysis as you proceed, generating questions that you need answered. Sometimes the answer can come from further analysis, at other times they might be self-evident. However, on other occasions you will find that you do not have the data to answer a given question, and need to go out again and conduct more interviews or observations in order to gather the data necessary to address the question. In starting to look at the interviews in our data set, I wanted to examine how friendships are formed and maintained by university students. Early on it struck me that the participants seemed to lack a clear definition of what friendship was. As I continued to immerse myself in the data, I kept the question of 'How does this person define friendship'? in my head. It engendered a certain sensitivity to the issue that later with the identification of a 'lay taxonomy' of friendship oriented to by these participants. The Procedure Highlight box gives an example of a memo that asks this sort of question.

Procedure highlight: Questioning memo   **9.4**

Theory memo – 3 December: A 'lay taxonomy' of friendship?

What we have here is a way of seeing where friends rank against other friendships in terms of closeness (but what of lifelong friends you hardly ever see?).

The first question is about the nature of the taxonomy: is it clear groups, or is it more a spectrum? Maybe I'll try diagramming someone's friends to investigate this. What is the structure of this taxonomy? My first effort was a sort of Venn diagram – does that hold? Or is it more something like a central point ('me') and people clustered around 'me' with various radii of closeness? Worth diagramming that too, perhaps.

I suspect that this taxonomy then determines how friends are treated – how much effort is expended on maintaining the friendship, etc. The next question is: what mobility exists in this taxonomy, and how and why do friends move from one category/level/status to the next?

Grounded Theory is ... cyclical

Grounded theory involves cycling backwards and forwards during the research process in several ways. Firstly, the logic of the theory-generating process, driven by memo-writing and structured by coding procedures, involves moving between the data and analysis, continually reflecting on the links between what we see and what we understand theoretically. These iterations lead to our theory becoming more mature, more conceptual and more 'high-order'.

This logic of theory generation also holds for the iterations of analysis and data collection that make up the process of theoretical sampling. As we reflect on developing theory, we make decisions on who to speak to next – we gather additional data and build this into our analysis, then look again for more data, and so on.

Additionally, we also cycle between the developing theory and the literature. In grounded theory much has been made of the *delayed literature review*. Essentially, the grounded theorist doesn't undertake an exhaustive literature review before commencing with data collection or analysis, as this would prime them with theoretical ideas. In turn, this would make it harder for them to develop a novel theoretical framework from the data collected during the project.

However, it is impossible to go into the research process totally naïve to the subject area – indeed, you may well be researching an area in which you are already considered something of a specialist. A middle ground is sought, where we first reflect on our own understanding of the field, whatever that might be. From such an understanding we might formulate a set of *sensitising concepts* that will, perhaps, help define where we start looking, and how we develop important elements like our interview guides. By going to the effort of identifying these pre-existing ideas, we allow ourselves to be sensitive to the possibility that emerging concepts might be influenced by them, giving us the opportunity to reflect more carefully and ensure that concepts can be developed independently of these preconceptions. As we start to reflect on the conceptual categories that are being developed through the analytical process, we *then* turn to the literature to see what others have already said on the topics.

?

9.5 Where are we now?

Grounded Theory is theoretical, analytical and cyclical. Key concepts that have been introduced so far include:

- Theoretical sampling
- Constant comparison
- Coding
- Theoretical sensitivity
- Memo-writing
- Theoretical saturation

As we go through the rest of this chapter we'll deal with these in more detail and consider some concrete examples of them in the analysis of real data.

Grounded theory is not ...

Not all people who claim to be doing grounded theory are doing grounded theory – either because they're not fully informed about what defines grounded theory, or perhaps because they think that calling their research 'Grounded Theory' lends it a respectability and trustworthiness which may not be entirely deserved.

One journal editor (Suddaby, 2006) was moved to put together a list of some common misconceptions. Grounded theory is not:

- ... an excuse to ignore the literature – the literature review is delayed, perhaps, but it is still conducted.
- ... presentation of raw data – grounded theory involves analysis and abstraction, moving away from raw data to the level of theory.

- … theory testing, content analysis, or word counts (though it can involve these things).
- … simply routine application of formulaic technique to data – the procedures exist to enable the analysis, but they are not the analysis itself.
- … perfect, and researchers need to balance pragmatism with any perceived 'tenets' of the methodology.
- … easy – though it might appear to be quite simple.
- … an excuse for the absence of a methodology – when writing about grounded theory we need to be explicit about how we have adhered to the logic of the inductive and analytical process.

Activity suggestion **9.6**

As the point of this workbook and associated data set is to provide material that students can work with on their own, I am not going to present a completed grounded theory study in this chapter. That job I leave to you! To continue with the Grounded Theory process started for this chapter, you might:

(a) carry on with the coding and memo-writing process and develop a richer explanatory framework for the topic in question;
(b) pick up on tentative ideas from the memos and use *theoretical sampling* to collect more data to develop your own ideas and build on the concepts I've started to develop;
(c) continue the process until you feel that you've reached or are close to *theoretical saturation*.

The theoretical ideas that I put forward later are only an example of what a theory produced by an undergraduate might sound like, and definitely need to be further refined through the grounded theory process. What I have done is provide enough detail for you to get an understanding of grounded theory, to start your own work and complete the process that I've described here.

Sample analysis extract

Let's have a look at the excerpt from the Shazia interview that is discussed in other chapters to see how we'd approach this when doing grounded theory.

The first step in the analysis is open coding (see later sections for more detail on these steps). The first section highlighted above has been coded as 'quality not quantity in friends' – the process of open coding involves labelling the text in order to identify concepts underpinning the data. The open coding continues for the rest of the transcript, and as the coding progresses, the researcher starts to write memos about developing ideas that she might have about friendship.

> ## Extract 9.1:   Data set sample extract (Int. 1; lines 454–462)
>
> Shazia: Yeah I'd rather have some, a few people that mean a lot to me than hundreds of people that I know so little about, that doesn't, its, its not, you can't even call it a friendship it's just like an acquaintance [Int: yeah], but I don't, I'm not really bothered about people that I'm just acquainted with and like just fellow students and stuff like that, I kind of push those kind of, cause I don't like people knowing exactly what I'm feeling and thinking all of the time, so I think if I've got these few people around me that are close to me I can confide with them and that's it, I don't have to, yeah I don't like other people knowing too much about me [Int: OK, OK], I don't know if it's because I don't really like them or because I keep them away for a reason, but yeah, so only a few people close to me.
>
> Quality not quantity in friends
>
> How much you know about people
>
> Acquaintance vs. friend
>
> Not bothered with acquaintances
>
> Don't want people to know my thoughts
>
> A few close confidants
>
> Keeping people away

9.7   Procedure highlight: Memo on closeness

Open code memo – 14 November: 'A few close confidants'

Shazia talks about 'close' friends, which would also seem to imply 'distant' friends (she says 'acquaintances') – this resonates with when she talks about actively keeping some people 'away' from her. This idea of 'closeness' vs. 'distance' doesn't seem unusual at all, it's a fairly common metaphor, so interesting to keep an eye on where this goes.

As other open codes are developed, the researcher might notice a set of codes constellating around the idea of how people define friendships. These codes don't only come from Shazia's interview, but from other people, too. Upon examination, this cluster can be seen as a set of coherent concepts that hang together, so they're grouped in an axial code, tentatively entitled 'Definitions of Friendship'.

Procedure highlight: Memos on defining friendship **9.8**

Axial code memo – 25 November: 'defining friendship'

There seem to be different ways of defining who one's friends are, and the quality of each friendship. For Shazia, it's about closeness vs. distance, but Deborah talks about it in terms of 'true' friends [vs. 'untrue' friends?! She doesn't say!]. Alexander at times bases his judgements on friendship quality on the level of trust that's between two people, shown in their interactions by permission to be humorously insulting to each other – but even he talks in the metaphor of distance (see Int. 2; lines 164–170)

The concept of 'closeness vs. distance', or proximity – as I began to think of it – becomes a property of the category 'defining friendship', and I was starting to get an idea of what friendship structures might look like, and diagrammed this out in a memo to see if it made sense (Figure 9.1).

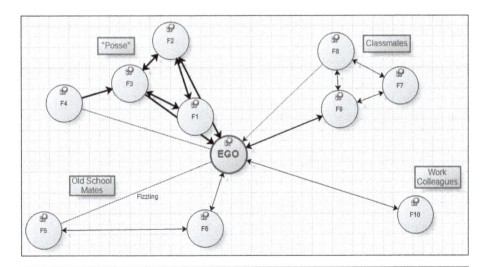

Figure 9.1   Diagram from 'defining friendship' memo.

Essentially, I was just sketching out how people might relate to each other to stimulate my thinking, to generate some theoretical ideas.

Finally, the ideas in this axial code about 'defining friendship' are related to other categories that have been developed in the study. Eventually, a theory is vadvanced that explains how friendship works for our participants in their context of starting out at university and balancing the demands of new friends and a new life with older friends that they might have left behind.

9.9 Activity suggestion: Diagramming

Try mapping out your own friends, either in the way I've done it or however it makes sense to you. As you do this, what do you have to take into account about the nature of your friendships? Try writing a note of about 300 words (a memo) summarising the main issues you encountered whilst mapping your friendships like this. Don't write about the detail of the friendships themselves, try to engage with the *theory* of how friendships form.

Analysis

The analytical process runs throughout the life of a grounded theory project – it starts as soon as you have collected some data, and continues until you have finished your report or paper describing the research.

Memo writing

For many beginning grounded theorists, the core procedure at the heart of grounded theory appears to be coding, and this is sometimes what attracts people to this research approach. The assumption is that coding is easy, that it is a clear, step-by-step proccss easily followed.

These sorts of presumptions, though, are not true. One can see how they might have arisen; for instance, coding is something that one can read a set of instructions about … one such set is below. However, when you start to do grounded theory properly, it becomes obvious that coding is simply a structure on which reflection (via memo-writing) happens.

> *It is memo-writing that is the engine of grounded theory, not coding.*

It is in memos that the interpretative and theory-generating processes *happen* in a grounded theory project. Memo-writing starts at the very beginning of the research process, perhaps in some form of a research journal, where the researchers reflect on how they came up with the specific research problem and what their intuitive understanding of the field is. It continues all the way through the analytic process, and the final product of a grounded theory project, that is, the theory itself, is produced from memos written at a late stage of this process.

Procedure highlight: What can memos do? 9.10

Corbin & Strauss (2008) write that 'memos and diagrams are more than just repositories of thought. They are working and living documents' (pp. 117–118). Memos can appear as journal entries, as formal definitions of ideas we're playing with, as diagrams of processes that we're observing or social contexts we become aware of, and so on. They can be used to define codes that we have come up with, or to flesh out the properties of conceptual categories we're developing. We can use them to ask questions, to make comparisons, to record insights, to jot down suggestions for future theoretical sampling or ideas that we might want to follow up later in the literature.

As you do grounded theory, I cannot urge you strongly enough to keep writing memos, sketching ideas out, recording your sudden inspirations. This is where the work of grounded theory takes place, and it's also where your final theory starts to take shape. In fact, you may find that the process of producing your final report is in part based on re-writing some of your more important memos, rather than simply sitting at your computer and doing everything in one go.

Keep a pen and paper with you at all times so that you can jot down an idea on the bus before you lose it forever. If you're more the technical type, find out if your phone has a voice recording feature and how to work it (and maybe how to transfer those recordings to your computer), or perhaps carry a Dictaphone or digital recorder around with you. A sudden flash of inspiration or insight that isn't recorded straightaway is usually lost forever!

Early in the analysis phase

Memos from the early stages of a grounded theory project (see the next Procedure Highlight box) can be short: they may be simply thoughts jotted down as you read through your transcripts for the first time; or to catch the sense of open codes that you're generating. This is fine: remember that there's no one assessing your memos, so don't hesitate to get the idea down on paper or on the screen so that you can come back to it later.

Memos and diagrams are always 'works in progress', right up until you finish your report. Memos are always tentative and never more so than at this early stage.

9.11 Procedure highlight: Early memo example

Open code memo – 28 November: 'negotiating proximity'

This comes from early in Louise's interview – she says that it's difficult living with others, but that 'we've learnt to live with each other'cause we know when we need our own space and we know when it's time to be like with each other'.

These sorts of negotiations may be of interest … balancing privacy and togetherness, essentially negotiating proximity to one's friends on a day-to-day or hour-to-hour level. More intense obviously in a flat-sharing situation, but does this happen in other contexts too? I mean, sure of course it does, but how might this be different?

Analysis through the project

As the project goes on, we carry on memo-writing. I recommended that you spend some time writing memos, at least every time you sit down and 'do' your project – I also tend to force myself to stop and write a memo every time I decide on an axial code, or get some sort of insight into patterns between axial codes.

As the project matures, your memos might get a bit more formal. Because your ideas are starting to come together, and the concepts and categories are starting to develop into viable theory, it becomes necessary to set them out clearly in black and white. Even though they start to look more formal, though, it's important that they remain quite flexible and that you're able to change your mind in them.

I tend to keep memos as separate documents that I re-visit from time to time, expanding on the ideas in them as my understanding of the ideas develops.

Very early on, I'd decided that one interest of the project was going to have to be how friendships begin and end, and there was plenty of material in the data set about these 'friendship careers'. After doing some coding, I drew this as a diagram (Figure 9.2).

The diagram shows friendship careers as having a beginning, middle and end. We meet people because of happenstance ('circs' in the diagram) or because we're actively looking for new acquaintances ('seeking'). Once we have friends, that relationship is maintained, and sometimes it comes to an end. Nothing really earth-shattering there, you'll agree!

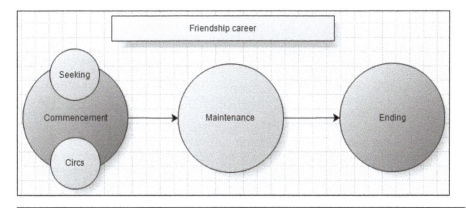

Figure 9.2 'Friendship career' diagram.

After I'd done the diagram, I left it for some time. I came back to it a bit later, having done some more coding from other transcripts.

Procedure highlight: Memo from the middle of the project **9.12**

Category memo – 9 January: 'friendship careers'

So this was an idea from fairly early on, that there's somehow a lifetime for a friendship that involves a structure and a progression. There's a start to a friendship (perhaps most of this is about circumstances, though there's evidence, for example in the transcript of Alexander, of actively seeking out friends).

There's maintenance of the friendship – for instance, Louise talking about her various groups of friends (college vs. university; Int. 3, lines 119–133) and how she has to actively seek out the old friends (the ones that she's not so thrown together with on a day-to-day basis) to keep things going.

I think that here is where the link to defining friendship is made... because some of what a friend 'is' feeds in, I'm guessing, to this job of maintenance. Deborah talking about how she just picks things up with her old school friends, even if she hasn't seen them for a while – it sounds very different from Louise. Is this contrast a property of 'maintaining old friendships'? Was Deborah 'better friends' with her old mates than Louise with hers? I don't really think this is the case. So, what's the difference?

Perhaps they expect friendship to be different things – that what Deborah is happy to call friendship is not what Louise would call friendship, so actually they're getting the same 'amount' of relationship (ack! surely a better way of saying that?!) but interpreting it in different ways.

(Continued)

9.12 continued

My feeling right now is that this 'getting an amount of relationship' is probably a blind alley. I'll keep an eye out for the way that they talk about it, see if it comes up.

Then, of course, there's the ending of relationships. Naturally, this only applies to friendships that have ended, rather than those that are still alive... but where they have ended, there seem to be two sorts of endings: fizzles and bangs. Fizzle is an in-vivo concept from Louise (line 190), relationships sometimes just fizzle out as contact is slowly lost and not refreshed. Eventually you're just not friends any more. More dramatic is when there's some sort of active split from a friend – for Alexander, this is, for example, when there's been a breach of trust ...

(and so on).

The category memo in the Procedure Highlight box above shows that ideas are starting to link up. The idea of a 'friendship career' is already linked to 'defining friendship' here, tying two fairly complex ideas together.

Wrapping things up

Later, 'defining friendship' evolved into the 'taxonomy of friendships' discussed earlier, and the concept of 'friendship maintenance' had developed as an important social action undertaken by everyone (to varying degrees). Elsewhere in the analysis, I'd been looking at the ending of friendships in more detail, and this now tied in with both 'maintenance' and 'taxonomy' in a way that started sounding something like the beginnings of a theory.

9.13 Procedure highlight: Late theory memo

Theory memo – 12 February: '... Let's have a stab at pulling these ideas together'

Our relationships with our friends form a taxonomy of 'types' of friendship ('bezzie mates', 'our posse', 'classmates', etc.). These types vary specifically with regard to (a) personal proximity (e.g., 'close friends') and (b) frequency of contact. Maintenance of these relationships has to take this into account: close friends that are now only seen during university vacations require maintenance in a way different from more distant but day-to-day relationships with people in our research methods workshop.

> Without active maintenance, less frequent types of friendship are likely to atrophy, whilst more frequent friendships that are not actively maintained can lead to inter-personal friction and 'falling out'. However, the higher frequency contact of this type means that it's more likely that one is going to attend to that relationship and not let it go too far.

It can be seen that we are now moving towards a more theoretical stance, and it might not be too far from this sort of memo to finalising our grounded theory.

Coding

Many or even most of the memos that you produce in a grounded theory study will start from the coding process. It should be clear by now that whilst coding is important, it's not the primary job in grounded theory. Unfortunately, many students 'fetish-ise' coding, mistaking it for the main task. This can lead to an underdeveloped theory that is extremely vague and not able to properly explain or account for the lives of the participants.

Coding is nowadays quite often done on a computer (not *by* a computer!), but the alternative is to develop a system of index cards and filing boxes. If you don't have access to qualitative analysis software like NVivo or MaxQDA, this latter is likely how you'll proceed. There's nothing wrong with this; in fact many people prefer not to use a computer for coding, worrying that the demands of the program will end up shaping how the coding will be done.

When developing your own system for recording your coding, make sure that you can always quickly trace between your memos, your coding and the original data. Quote substantially in memos if you need to, remember to note page and line numbers etc., so that you can easily go back and look at the original context of an idea.

Open coding

The first stage of coding, known as *open coding*, begins as soon as there is some data to work with. Open coding essentially means to take a chunk of text from our data and to give it a label (code title). The size of the chunk varies considerably: early on, one might go through a transcript phrase by phrase, or line by line, coming up with a code title for almost everything said. Later, once you have some ideas to work with and have perhaps developed some questions in a few memos, you might happily code a whole paragraph with one title. Open code titles are either '*in vivo*' or 'constructed'. *In vivo* codes use the actual words of the participants as the title, and can be particularly useful if:

- the participants already have a shorthand for talking about concepts (Louise talks of friends that have 'fizzled', a good *in vivo* term that I maintained throughout my analysis); or
- you're perhaps not sure what a given code deals with, and want to give it a tentative title that doesn't leap to conclusions about what a participant means.

Most code titles, though, will be constructed ones, and this naming of concepts is the first step away from the particular towards the theory you'll eventually build. You're not expected to do line-by-line coding on all the data that you collect. This would take far too long, and coding can already be quite a time-consuming task. As your project matures, your coding speeds up, and as you start to develop a set of open codes, you'll notice ideas repeating themselves in the data. *Focused coding* is the process of choosing some of your most useful and relevant open codes and applying them to larger chunks of data, and it is about now that coding starts to speed up a bit. One open code that I 'promoted' to a focused code was 'trivial activities', and in it I collected descriptions of some of the mundane, day-to-day things that friends do together – watching television, chatting between lectures and so on. These later became important when trying to explain exactly how friendships can be maintained – the 'trivial activities' turned out to be important glue between people.

Also, it is about now that your ideas about what's important in the data start to become more abstract, and it's time to move on to the next stage of coding.

9.14 Activity suggestion: Open coding

Take an excerpt from one of the interviews, and start with some 'quick and dirty' open coding. What do you find difficult about this? Compare your codes with a friend – what have you each picked up on, where do you differ from each other?

Which of the open codes you've come up with do you think you might go on to re-use as focused codes as the analysis progresses?

Axial coding

Axial coding is where the ideas you've identified in your focused codes are related to each other as elements of conceptual categories. I like to start this process quite concretely, writing my open codes on cards and taking them one by one and comparing them to each other. If the relationship is clear and close, I put the cards into a single pile, if not then into different piles. As each open code is considered – paying extra attention to the focused codes – the piles of related ideas (i.e., the **categories**) start to grow. Each category itself is then also labelled, either using a new label or re-applying one from one of the codes that form part of it.

One set of open codes I ended up with included the following (the bold codes are focused codes):

- That thing between us
- **Cycles of contact**
- Travelling to maintain group
- **Keeping in touch by phone**
- **Actively sustaining contact**
- Maintaining presence at a distance
- Visiting outside semester

These were all about maintaining friendships with people that participants had left behind when they started university. For some (e.g., Alexander and Shazia) this was a physical distance, where students had moved to Liverpool to study, but for others (Deborah and Trevor) it was more of a social distance, as they still lived in Liverpool and still saw their 'old' friends fairly frequently. I called this category 'Keeping in touch with old mates' initially (later just 'Keeping in touch').

I've mentioned earlier that when we develop an axial code, this is usually a good time to stop and write a memo. This memo has to tentatively define what it is we're dealing with, and to outline the properties of that category. For the 'Keeping in touch' category, the important property was 'presence' (or lack of it). Once this was identified, I found myself more attuned to the idea of presence in friendships and I could actively seek out more instances of this idea in the data to build on this concept in following memos.

In doing axial coding, we are also looking for the relationships between the conceptual categories, especially relationships that might indicate aspects of a developing theory, such as causal connections or indications of basic social processes. I find it useful to develop a 'map' of my conceptual categories once there's enough detail to see how a few of them relate to each other. The spatial arrangement of the categories can sometimes very easily show the nature of the relationship between them.

In Figure 9.3 we can see a part of a conceptual map that I put together about halfway through the project. I've simplified it a bit – the original was quite messy with loads of open codes strewn over the page, but this is the essential structure.

In this case, laying out the conceptual categories confirmed that there was support for the early idea of a 'friendship career' with a beginning, middle and end (as per Figure 9.2). However, I was uneasy about the way that the 'beginning' categories hung together, so I didn't try to force a relationship onto them at this stage, merely grouping them loosely to deal with later. Importantly, the link between 'maintenance' and 'definitions' (later 'taxonomy') is made quite clearly. Once I'd identified this link through this mapping exercise, I set about writing this

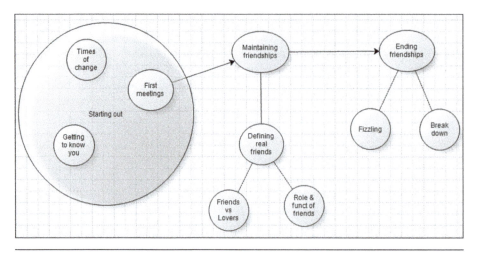

Figure 9.3   Mapping the conceptual categories.

as a memo, part of which is in Procedure Highlight box 'Memo from middle of project' above.

As we continue to write memos, as we build a theory explaining our area of research, and as we continue to look for more data to flesh out our ideas, the axial coding structure firms up. This brings us to the final stage of analysis.

9.15 Activity suggestion: Extending your memos

Memos are living documents that you come back to time and again, honing your ideas as you go. Remember that memo you wrote for the 'Diagramming' activity? Once you've thought about the idea of friendship, read some of the other transcripts, watched the videos or listened to the audio files of the interviews, it's time to revisit. Write an addition to that memo (best to give it a date and perhaps a title) that extends how you think about the ideas you developed there. Try to write something substantial – more than just a couple of hundred words – and as you write, note how the process of writing and reflecting is itself great for generating new ideas and new perspectives. Don't forget to write these down too!

Selective theoretical coding

During the final stage of coding in grounded theory comes selective coding: one chooses a central *core category* from the categories developed thus far, and then organises the other categories around this core category. Corbin and Strauss call this *selective coding*, whilst Glaser calls it *theoretical coding* (though there are other differences, too). Identifying one core category is not necessarily easy, and Corbin and Strauss provide some tips:

1. It must be abstract; that is, all other major categories can be related to it and placed under it.
2. It must appear frequently in the data.
3. It must be logical and consistent with the data. There should be no forcing of the data.
4. It should be sufficiently abstract, so that it can be used to do research in other substantive areas, leading to the development of a more general theory.
5. It should grow in depth and explanatory power as each of the other categories is related to it. (Summarised from Corbin & Strauss, 2008, p. 105).

It would be premature for me to choose a core category for this study, given that I have purposefully not completed a full grounded theory analysis. For the sake of argument, though, and based on the analysis undertaken so far, we could perhaps lean towards 'friendship maintenance' as a core category. It already has quite a central position in the diagrams we've produced, and unites the two directions that the analysis has indicated: the idea of friendship careers and the importance of how we classify our friendships. We could certainly spend a bit of productive time writing a memo or two exploring the possibility of this category as our choice for the core category.

Critical issue: Is software always helpful? 9.16

Different researchers have used different methods (or 'technologies') to help them with their coding. Whilst initially this was always some form of paper-based methodology – index cards, or perhaps literally cutting up photocopies of transcripts and making collections of related texts – more and more researchers are turning to specialised computer packages to help manage their data and represent their coding.

How do you think that using a computer would affect your analysis?

The practical side of things might seem attractive: coding can be faster and it's easy to search through long transcripts for key words or represent codes graphically. But how does this affect the way you *do* coding and diagramming? Does the medium you work with have an affect on your analysis? (And if so, what might the effects of paper-based technologies be?)

Generating theory

Having completed the coding process, all that remains is for us to formulate a final statement of the substantive grounded theory that we have arrived at. This theory must be more than simply a description of what we have found in the data – it must have the power to explain, in socio-psychological terms, the dynamics of the contexts in which our participants carry out their lives. Whilst it must be framed in terms of the specific situation that we have been examining, there should be an orientation towards articulating more extensive principles, that might also point towards more generally applicable hypotheses should we or someone else want to take the work further.

Again, in terms of this worked example we are not really in a position to do this – and further, I would very much like to avoid suggesting a theory based on the common data set, as this might limit the possibilities for theory generation for anyone who wants to attempt this for themselves.

This is not to say that there is only one 'right' theory that can be generated from this data. The interests of individual researchers will move them in different directions as they engage in the analysis. Remember, though, that any theories that are produced from this data set must be able to explain aspects of friendship as lived by Shazia, Deborah, Trevor, Alexander and Louise, so you would expect different researchers grounding their work in the same data not to differ too dramatically.

Writing up the analysis

Grounded theory reports tend to be fairly conventional in their presentation, to the extent even that they usually follow the convention of starting with the literature review, in spite of the fact of the delay to the literature review demanded by the logic of the research process.

As mentioned earlier, it is vital that grounded theorists be clear and transparent about the details of their research process. You may wish readers to give credence to your analysis based on their own trust in the process of grounded theory research; in this case you need to provide enough detail to show them that you have indeed fully implemented the entire approach. Failing to do this may well lead a reader to believe that you may have just lifted the open/axial coding process from the method and applied that to a set of interviews with people selected with little forethought to what the requirements of the project might have been.

The analysis section of your report (see Chapter 12) will always be the most substantial, perhaps accounting for half of the total of the report. There is no single way for the analysis section to be structured, but perhaps the most common way is to discuss the core category in detail and as many of the other categories as necessary to elucidate the grounded theory you are advancing. Do not forget to provide a clear and succinct phrasing of the theory itself! You might often find that the process of producing your results section is mostly that of combining and clarifying some your later memos – the analysis section can seem to write itself!

Remember also that this is *Grounded Theory*, so you must ensure that you illustrate your propositions with examples from the transcripts or field notes that you analysed. Your reader needs to be able to follow at least a couple of the major ideas all the way through, from transcript to theory.

Finally, in the discussion section you need to be able to plainly show how your own Grounded Theory advances our understanding of the area under investigation. You may choose to end with one or more testable hypotheses derived from your data – this is, however, by no means necessary.

Summary points

1. Grounded Theory is an analytic approach to qualitative research that aims at deriving *theory* that is *grounded* in the data of the participants.
2. Grounded Theory involves an *inductive* move from the particular to the general.
3. Some features of Grounded Theory include theoretical sensitivity, theoretical sampling and theoretical saturation.
4. The logic of the Grounded Theory process involves *cycling back and forth* between the data and the analysis until a substantive theory is developed.
5. Grounded Theory proceeds for the most part by the production of reflective documents called *memos*. In these memos, the researcher uses the *constant comparative* method to develop and flesh out the conceptual content of the developing Grounded Theory.
6. Coding in Grounded Theory starts with open (and focused) coding, which leads to the development of a structure of conceptual categories. A core category is selected from these, and a theory is developed that emerges from the relationship between the core category and other major concepts.

Want to know more? **9.17** +

One of the best ways to understand how qualitative writing is done is to read qualitative research reports. For Grounded Theory, a search on any abstracts database for the term 'Grounded Theory' in the title or abstract of a paper will produce lots of results. However, as noted earlier, not all Grounded Theory writing is necessarily good, even in professional journals! Remember to be critical when you read papers claiming to be Grounded Theory. Have they actually done theoretical sampling? Have they been clear about the coding process?

Some example papers using Grounded Theory can be found in:

Cutcliffe, J. R., Stevenson, C., Jackson, S. & Smith, P. (2006) A modified grounded theory study of how psychiatric nurses work with suicidal people. *International Journal of Nursing Studies*, **43**(7), 791–802.

(Continued)

9.17 continued

Rasmussen, B., O'Connell, B., Dunning, P. & Cox, H. (2007) Young women with Type 1 Diabetes' management of turning points and transitions. *Qualitative Health Research*, **17**(3), 300–310.

Schraw, G., Olafson, L. & Wadkins, T. (2007) Doing the things we do: A grounded theory of academic procrastination. *Journal of Educational Psychology*, **99**(1), 12–25.

Weaver, S. E. & Coleman, M. (2005) A mothering but not a mother role: A grounded theory of the nonresidential stepmother role. *Journal of Social and Personal Relationships*, **22**(4), 477–497.

10

QM3: Interpretative Phenomenological Analysis

Rachel Shaw

Introduction

Interpretative Phenomenological Analysis (IPA) is a qualitative method that has particular resonance for psychologists. It is influenced by the theoretical traditions of *phenomenology* and *hermeneutics*. From phenomenology, IPA takes its focus on wanting to understand the meaning of human experience. From hermeneutics, IPA pays particular close attention to the interpretative activity involved in the analytic process when people are doing research with people. A further significant feature of IPA is that it is an *idiographic* (as opposed to a *nomothetic*) method of inquiry. Nomothetic analysis dominates mainstream (quantitative) psychological research and involves population level explanations resulting in probabilistic conclusions for example, there is a 70% chance that person A will respond to situation B in the predicted fashion, C. Idiographic analyses are conducted at the level of the individual case and so are able to make specific claims about the individuals studied.

Definitions 10.1 !

Phenomenology is the 'study of human experience and the way in which things are perceived as they appear to consciousness' (Langdridge, 2007, p. 10).
Key figures: Edmund Husserl, Martin Heidegger, Merleau Ponty
Hermeneutics is a method initially devised to interpret Biblical texts but now a more widely known theory of interpretation.

(Continued)

10.1 continued

Key figures: Friedrich Schleiemacher, Wilhelm Dilthey, Martin Heidegger, Hans-Georg Gadamer.

Idiographic – Relating to study of the individual, who is seen as unique; it often involves subject phenomena. The term is usually found in various qualitative methods within the humanities and social sciences.

Nomothetic – Relating to study of a cohort of individuals, usually at the population level; it aims to derive laws that explain objective phenomena. The term usually applies to quantitative methods in the natural sciences.

10.2 Want to know more?

Langdridge, D. (2007) *Phenomenological psychology: Theory, research and method*. London: Pearson Education.

Van Manen, M. (1990) *Researching lived experience: Human science for an action sensitive pedagogy*. Albany, NY: State University of New York Press.

Palmer, R. E. (1969) *Hermeneutics*. Evanston: Northwestern University Press.

Background

Understanding human experience

The central objective of IPA is to understand what personal and social experiences mean to those people who experience them. Thus, IPA researchers ask their participants to describe to them events or objects they encounter, emotions they feel, relationships they have and so on. The unit of study in IPA research, therefore, is an *experiential account*. IPA is a *critical realist* method, which means that it assumes that reality exists, but that our access to it is never direct (see also Chapter 2). In other words, although we accept that events 'actually exist' in reality, we realise that our only access to those events is through a particular lens, that is, through the particular perspective of the person describing the event at a particular place and time. Hence, in IPA we are not simply seeking to understand people's experiences, we are also seeking to understand people's experiences at a particular point in history, a particular time in their life, in that social, cultural, political and economic context.

IPA research aims to understand what it is like to walk in another's shoes (whilst accepting that this is never truly possible) and to make analytic interpretations about those experiences and about the person as the 'experiencer'. IPA is an empathic method in that it wants to understand experience from another's perspective. It can also be critical by questioning the ways in which participants describe events or relationships to you; it is considered appropriate to go beyond what the participant says to make sense of their account from the position twice removed, that is, as an analyst making interpretations of a participant's own sense making whilst talking ('thinking aloud') in the interview.

Double hermeneutic

Doing an IPA project is a dynamic process. This means that you, as the researcher, are interacting with your participants and with their data. The researcher is therefore active in the analytic process. Furthermore, because we are people studying people, we must attribute the same assumptions to ourselves as we do our participants. As explained earlier, IPA researchers encourage participants to describe and reflect on experiences they encounter. This involves thinking about what experiences mean – that is, interpretation. As the researcher we are also carrying out an interpretative activity in attempting to make sense of what participants tell us. Thus, a dual interpretative process is at work that is known as the *double hermeneutic.*

Definitions **10.3** !

Experiential account. This is an account given by an individual, which focuses on concrete experiences and his/her reflections about those experiences.

   Critical realist. This is a philosophical position, which maintains the presence of an objectively knowable and mind-independent reality, whilst acknowledging the roles of perception and cognition.

   Double hermeneutic. 'The participant is trying to make sense of his/her world and the researcher is trying to make sense of how the participant is trying to make sense of his/her world. This double hermeneutic neatly illustrates the dual role of the researcher. In one sense the researcher is like the participant, drawing on mental faculties they share. At the same time, the researcher is different from the participant, always engaging in second order sense-making of someone else's experience' (Smith & Eatough, 2007, p. 36).

Case study approach

As explained above, IPA is an idiographic method, which means it is focused at the individual level. One of the most common data collection techniques is the *semi-structured individual interview* (see Chapter 5), although participant diaries and written descriptions would also generate appropriate data.

Basing the analysis on individual experiential accounts initially fulfils IPA's commitment to idiography. This focus on the idiographic must then continue throughout the analytic process. In practice, this means that a case study – a research study with one participant ($n = 1$) – is sometimes appropriate for an IPA project (a case study usually involves multiple interviews with one person). It also means that in studies with more than one participant, the analysis proceeds on a case-by-case basis.

In IPA there must be a fully worked-up analysis on case one before moving onto case two. Comparisons between cases are made later on. This procedure differs from methods such as grounded theory and Discourse Analysis which work on the whole corpus – complete data set – from the outset to identify categories or discourses across the sample. This also means that IPA studies usually have small samples, which can be useful if you would find it difficult to recruit large numbers for your project.

! | # 10.4 Definitions

Semi-structured individual interview. A method of data collection involving an interviewer and one interviewee. It is guided by a flexible schedule (or *aide mémoire*) including topics to be covered during the interview, but the wording and order of questions may vary. This method involves actively listening to participants to ensure you get their story and probing for further information when unanticipated topics come up.

This can be compared to the structured interview, which is best described as a verbal questionnaire with fixed ordering of questions and tick-box or short answer responses.

Sample analysis extract

Before moving on to illustrate the processes involved in IPA in detail (below), we can turn to the extract identified in the two previous chapters and consider how an IPA analyst might approach this fragment of the interview– and, of course, this can be directly compared to how other analysis methods presented in this book would begin analysing this same extract.

Extract 10.1: Data set sample extract (Int. 1; lines 454–462)

Shazia: Yeah I'd rather have some, a few people that mean a lot to me than hundreds of people that I know so little about, that doesn't, its, its not, you can't even call it a friendship it's just like an acquaintance [Int: yeah], but I don't, I'm not really bothered about people that I'm just acquainted with and like just fellow students and stuff like that, I kind of push those kind of, cause I don't like people knowing exactly what I'm feeling and thinking all of the time, so I think if I've got these few people around me that are close to me I can confide with them and that's it, I don't have to, yeah I don't like other people knowing too much about me [Int: OK, OK], I don't know if it's because I don't really like them or because I keep them away for a reason, but yeah, so only a few people close to me.

As a method concerned with making sense of people's experiences, an IPA analysis would proceed as follows.

Step 1. It would summarise the experiences that Shazia describes:

(a) Shazia has a preference for a few close friends rather than lots of people she knows little about.
(b) She is not interested in acquaintances but close friends in whom she can confide.
(c) She does not like other people knowing how she feels.

Step 2. It would look at what this means:

(a) Shazia draws on her own concrete experience to make conclusions about what friendship means.
(b) Friendship is important to Shazia and she distinguishes between friends and acquaintances.
(c) Trust is central to friendship; a close friend acts as a confidante.

Step 3. It would look at Shazia's self-reflections to explore what Shazia herself makes of her experience:

(a) Shazia is aware that she does not divulge her inner feelings to acquaintances; Shazia values her privacy.
(b) For Shazia, trust is something which grows out of being close with someone; this is what being a friend means to Shazia.

It is worth noting at this point, and in comparison to forms of discourse and conversation analysis, that the actual transcription of the talk used in IPA, as was noted in Chapter 7, is more in line with a 'playscript', that is, a verbatim transcript of simply what participants said, written down in sequence with only occasional reference to any non-verbal actions or events.

10.4 Activity suggestion

Select a short extract from one of the interviews in the data set and have a go at following the steps 1 to 3 above.

Analysis

This section is not meant to be prescriptive; rather, it aims to provide an account – a running commentary, if you like – of the sorts of activities that are involved in IPA.

Initial thoughts on reflection and quality

Throughout the analysis, it is advisable to keep a *reflective diary* where you can make notes of anything which comes to mind. It is also advisable to keep copies of notes made, key extracts and themes identified at each stage of the analysis. As discussed in Chapter 6, transparency is an important indicator of quality and means of establishing *trustworthiness*. It is useful, therefore, when conducting your analysis to make the process as transparent as possible. This helps you to remember analytic decisions made early on when you are in the later stages of the analysis. It is also particularly useful when writing up, to help make clear to readers the processes you went through to produce your analysis. Keeping records of analytic activity in a reflective diary can help provide an *audit trail* demonstrating how you got from the raw data to the interpretation presented in the results (see Smith, Flowers & Larkin, 2009 for a more detailed discussion of validity issues in IPA research).

10.5 Definitions

Reflective diary. A diary kept by the researcher throughout the whole process of the research: recording the initial idea about what to study; defining the research question; collecting the data; reading through transcripts; conducting the analysis; and structuring the final write-up.

Trustworthiness. 'How do you persuade your audiences, including most importantly yourself, that the findings of your enquiry are worth taking account of? What is it that makes the study believable and trustworthy?' (Robson, 2002; p. 93).

Audit trail. A record of procedures carried out during the analysis. The audit (or paper) trail should fully illustrate what you did in your analysis: what decisions were made, what summaries you wrote, what interpretations you made, aspects of the analysis you questioned, reflections made. In theory, an outsider should be able to look at your audit trail and see exactly how you got from the raw data to the claims made in the analysis which led to the conclusions drawn.

Want to know more? **10.6** +

Guba, E. G. & Lincoln, Y. S. (1985) *Naturalistic inquiry*. Newbury Park, CA: Sage. http://www.amazon.co.uk/Naturalistic-Inquiry-Dr-Yvonna-Lincoln/dp/0803924313/ref=sr_1_2?ie=UTF8&s=books&qid=1260551867&sr=1-2
Robson, C. (2002) Real world research: *A resource for social scientists and practitioner-researchers* (2nd Edn). Oxford: Blackwell.
Yardley, L. (2008) Demonstrating validity in qualitative psychology. In Smith, J. A. (Ed.) *Qualitative research in psychology: A practical research guide* (2nd Edn). London: Sage (pp. 235–251).

Familiarising yourself with the data

The first stage of any qualitative analysis method is to familiarise yourself with the data. Working with transcripts from individual interviews recorded in digital audiovisual format, can mean watching or listening to the interview and reading the transcript. It is a good idea after listening to or watching the interview to go through the whole transcript again for a more detailed read. Whilst you are doing this, you can make notes in your reflective diary of anything in particular which takes your interest or of things which you think might be significant to this person's story. It is also useful to write a summary of the person's account to get an idea of the gist of the content in the interview (see reflective diary extract 1).

Reflective diary extract 1 **10.7** "

Shazia has had one best friend since childhood, Eva.
 Shazia finds it difficult to trust people. She prefers close friendships to lots of friends.
 Shazia likes to feel comfortable in her friendships. She wants her friends to understand her.
 Shazia has moved around schools/universities and has experienced losing friends in the past. Perhaps this makes Shazia a little insecure about her friendships; it also makes her realise what makes a good friend, one she can trust.

Identifying initial themes

Once you are familiar with the data, you need to start reading the transcript again but this time you need to pay much closer attention. You need to break down the transcript into small sections and describe what is being said in each section rather than reading for gist, as in the previous section. You are now faced with two activities that will help identify initial themes: (a) writing *descriptive summaries* of what the participant says – what issues are identified, what events are relayed, what feelings are expressed; and (b) making *initial interpretations* about what these issues, events and feelings might mean, that is, how do they help us understand Shazia's experiences of friends and her sense of what constitutes friendship?

Often it is advised that one should write the descriptive summaries in the left-hand margin of the transcript and that initial interpretations should be written in the right-hand margin. This is a useful way of organising the analysis, but if you find a way that suits you better whilst achieving the same goal, that is fine too. Descriptions of the content in small sections of the transcript are important, so that your analysis stays close to the data and is therefore *data-driven* (as opposed to *theory-driven*). Initial interpretations of small sections of an experiential account are important because they form the first step of interpretative work and are linked directly to the data, again ensuring that any interpretations made further on in the analytic process can be traced back to the raw data. It is advisable to keep a record of these descriptive and interpretative notes, whether in hard copy in the margins of the transcript or elsewhere, to help with your audit trail.

10.8 Definitions

Data-driven research is inductive; that is, interpretations are derived from the analysis of the data rather than existing theory; it usually asks exploratory research questions. Sometimes referred to as a bottom-up approach.
Theory-driven research is deductive; that is, conclusions are based on whether the analysis fits with existing theory; it usually states a hypothesis which is then tested. Sometimes referred to as a top–down approach.

Writing descriptive summaries

At the beginning of the interview, Shazia is asked to talk about one particular friend. The friend she picks is Eva who Shazia has known since the age of six , when Eva moved to the UK from Germany.

Extract 10.2:   Descriptive summary example (Int. 1; lines 21–33)

They have lots of shared experience	Int:	Aw OK. So that's, it's kinda like a mutual learning for both of you as well?
Shazia was slightly older and acted like an advice figure	Shazia:	Yeah, yeah, we've been through like everything together as well, like everything that happened to her for the first time, cause I'm a bit older so I'd like, it's like things with school as well, so I'd do things first and she'd be like 'Well what do I do for this?' and I'd help her and you know, so like that really, yeah.
Initially they shared school related things	Int:	So is that more with em schoolwork or more personal things?
They grew up together and experienced everything for the first time together	Shazia:	Both really, like it'd start with school work because like when you're really young not much happens to you, but you, like first boyfriends and other things like that, and going out clubbing, and doing everything your not meant to [laughs], yeah.
	Int:	[Laughs]. So you were more of, you were more of, it's because you were the older one you sort of, did you, do you feel like you took her under your wing a little bit?
They helped each other out, taking each other under each others' wing	Shazia:	For some things, but a lot of it, she matured faster than me for some things, so then she actually took me under her wing as well so it's, it's a mutual thing I think, yeah.

In Extract 10.1 we see that Shazia talks about her friendship with Eva as shared experience: Shazia and Eva have grown up together, gone through their teenage years together, and shared the experience of their first boyfriends and going out together. At this early stage in the reading of the transcript the descriptive summaries simply sum up the content of what is said. It is important not to get carried away with ideas about what could be implied from what is said – that comes later when writing initial interpretations.

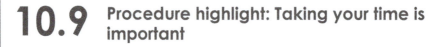

10.9 Procedure highlight: Taking your time is important

Interpretative Phenomenological Analysis is data-driven, so you must ensure that you adequately describe the data in the early stages of the analysis. Learning to write descriptive summaries can be challenging but it is important not to jump ahead into making interpretations too soon. If you find you are coming up with lots of ideas as you write your summaries, you can make a note of them in your reflective diary.

Activity suggestion

Select a transcript from the corpus and as you make your way through this chapter and follow the procedures described using that transcript. By reading and doing at the same time you will be able to act out the processes and so help understanding in a practical way.

We then start to see a slight shift in what Shazia talks about in the interview. Prompted by the interviewer, Shazia describes feeling anxious about growing apart from Eva when she left to go to university. In Extract 10.3 we see that Eva quashed that fear.

Extract 10.3:   Another descriptive summary example (Int 1; lines 143–153)

	Int:	So how, how, how'd you think she felt when you first came to university and you, you talked about your friends you had made?
Shazia worried initially about growing apart from her friend, Eva	Shazia:	She wasn't, to be honest she's not really bothered, like I'm always the one that worries more, like I was like when I told her that I was worried about when like, cause I told her about halfway through my first year, I told her like I
Eva quashed Shazia's concern		was really worried that we were gonna grow apart, and she was like 'This is sad were not gonna grow apart and stuff' [laughs] 'Oh fair enough' [laughs], but no she's fine, it's like she just, as long as I keep her up to date with stories and stuff she don't really, not really bothered [laughs].

	Int:	Yeah. Then how, how does she, has she talked about how she feels since you've gone?
Shazia and Eva feel the same way about each other They haven't changed since Shazia went to university	Shazia:	She doesn't say, nothing's really changed since I've gone and she doesn't feel any different, I don't feel any different.

In writing these descriptive summaries we begin to glimpse what being friends with Eva means to Shazia. For an example of the reflections about what this tells us about Shazia's interpretation of friendship, see reflective diary extract 2.

Reflective diary extract 2   10.10

Shazia has Eva as her closest friend. She was worried about the impact university would have on her friendship with Eva but Eva assured her they would remain close. Since she's been at university, Shazia has started to make new friends. I wonder whether friendships develop differently at different points in a person's life. At university it's almost as if you are thrown into a situation and must do with it what you can. Although Shazia is happy in her friendship with Eva she must now make new friends to deal with this new chapter in her life. I wonder if friendships change over the life course as we mature and do different things in our lives.

Before we move on to making interpretations, though, let's continue working sequentially through the transcript. A little later, Shazia is asked to speak about her friends from university (Extract 10.4).

This extract represents what we might assume is a fairly typical description of what happens when a group of young people are thrown together quite arbitrarily and how friendships develop through living in close proximity. We see that Shazia went out regularly with the people who lived on her floor and these people formed the basis of her early friendships at university. These summaries are the groundwork for later interpretation; breaking down the transcript into chunks facilitates the process of thinking in detail about each aspect of Shazia's account. In Extract 10.4, Shazia was focusing on her new life as a student at university and how she made friends in that context. Later on, the interviewer asked Shazia about her experience of friends at school.

When she was around 11 years of age, Shazia went to a grammar school, which meant leaving behind the friends she had made at primary school with whom she had grown up. The school was an hour's bus ride away, which meant that Shazia met people from outside of her local area for the first time. In Extract 10.5, Shazia describes how difficult it was to leave her old school friends at this particular point in her life.

Extract 10.4: Working through the transcript 1 (Int. 1; lines 166–175)

	Int:	How did you find it when you first came to university in terms of making new friends?
Shazia lived in Halls for her first year while at university	Shazia:	Mm I made quite a, well I made quite a few quite fast cause I lived in ((HALLS OF RESIDENCE NAME)) first year, cause I was at a year in Liverpool last year [Int: OK] and every-one on our floor, we all end up like
She quickly made friends with the girls (and boys) on her floor		for the first two weeks we all went out together to all of the Freshers' things, every, the whole floor, like twelve of us, we just all went out together, so we all became quite close in that week, the first two weeks, and then, and then after that it all started, like all the girls we all stayed close, there was about five of us, and then we all
The girls stayed close friends but they quickly became irritated by the boys		started getting a bit annoyed with the boys cause they were pretty nasty [laughs].
	Int:	They're boys [laughs]
	Shazia:	Yeah em leaving toilet seat up and things which is really annoying [Laughs].

Extract 10.5: Working through the transcript 2 (Int. 1; lines 242–253)

Shazia didn't want to leave her old school friends	Shazia:	I didn't really like it there at first for a couple of months but then I got used to it, but obviously cause like leaving all my old school friends behind cause
Shazia had grown up with her old school friends		I'd been with them since nursery, nurs-ery to middle school so it was really hard leaving those but I think second-ary, oh secondary, I just didn't like the
Shazia didn't enjoy secondary school at all		whole secondary school experience because obviously like confidence levels are really low and growing up and everyone's like maturing at different rates and it's just really crap [laughs], so yeah.

	Int:	It's a hard time to make that transition.
The timing was bad – she was entering puberty and had low confidence making it a difficult time to start making new friends	Shazia:	Yeah.
	Int:	I guess as well isn't it cause …
	Shazia:	Especially at that age as well when everyone starts getting spots and everyone's taller than you [laughs].

These descriptive summaries emphasise the unpleasantness of Shazia's experience of changing schools and being separated from her old school friends. Then something surprising happens. The interviewer asks Shazia how she felt about leaving her old school friends behind and Shazia told her that she was actually ready for a change (Extract 10.6).

Extract 10.6: Working through the transcript 3 (Int. 1; lines 278–288)

	Int:	And then how, how did you feel about the friendships that you were leaving behind, the friendships you had known throughout?
In some ways Shazia was pleased to have a fresh start because she often felt left out of her friendship with her two closest friends from middle school	Shazia:	Em I, I didn't really want to, cause that had em, right there were three of us that were quite close but in a way I didn't, in some aspects I wasn't really bothered cause I was always kind of the third wheel [Int: OK], em those two, the, my other two friends, cause they always like, they were into dancing and they used to go to dance classes and stuff, like they did ballet and tap and all that so they always had that thing in common, they lived right behind each other and stuff
Although they still lived close by, Shazia grew apart from her old school friends and hasn't seen them since		and em, yeah so in some ways I was bothered but then cause I thought well I'm gonna be living, I'll still be living in ((NAME OF TOWN)) I can still see them anytime [Int: yeah], but it didn't really work like that cause you all grow apart anyway and I haven't seen them since I'd have to say.

Here we start to see how Shazia has reflected on this time of her life. It is important to remember that this is a retrospective account, which is especially significant when discussing events from several years ago. The implications of this are that the experiential account we are analysing is not simply a description of what happened at the time but Shazia's evaluation of what happened as well. Given her lived experience since this time in her life, Shazia has put some thought into the meanings of her friendships back then and has come to the conclusion, with hindsight, that leaving those friends behind may have been beneficial. These flickers of reflection in Shazia's account appear to be particularly significant in answering our research question – what does friendship mean? This is an example of something you might make a note of in your reflective diary to be returned to at the later stage of making interpretations and identifying themes.

10.11 Procedure highlight: Using the diary during analysis

Identifying the participant's own reflections is a key part of an Interpretative Phenomenological Analysis. It is important to make a note of the participant's own sense making in your reflective diary so it can be used in the next stage of analysis when you begin to make interpretations. Although we are concerned only with description in the early stage of analysis, as we go through the transcript we become more familiar with the data and with Shazia as a person. These sorts of reflections and initial interpretations recorded in the reflective diary represent the interrelationship between early and later stages of analysis. This is why the diary is central to the process – it helps you stay on track with describing the participant's experience but also records ideas you have about the meaning of her account.

Reflective diary extract 3

The way Shazia talks about this loss of friendship is unusual. She describes feeling upset about leaving her old school friends, whom she has known since nursery, and almost blames her parents for taking those friends away from her. However, she then says that she was glad of the change because those friendships were not as good as they might have been. This is intriguing because it appears to be contradictory. What is making her think that losing those friends was good for her? Does she feel guilty for blaming her parents? Is she directing blame away from her parents by invoking some positive benefit?

Activity suggestion   **10.12**

Take a minute to stop and look at the progress you are making in your own analysis. Reflect on the descriptive summaries you have written. Question them – is there anything you don't understand, does the participant contradict him/herself, are there any issues you want to highlight as potentially significant to understanding this person's experience of friendship?

At the end of the interview, Shazia is asked what friendship means to her.

Extract 10.7:   Towards the end of the transcript (Int. 1; lines 786–794)

	Int:	OK, em so can you sum up then what friendship means to you?
Friendship is comfort, non-judgemental, caring	Shazia:	Right, [laughs] em I think friendship is something that you don't, it's like a situation where you can form like a relationship with someone, and you can just be fairly comfortable and
A friend will always be there for you		know that no one's gonna judge you, no one's gonna pick at everything you, if they do pick they're not gonna like be nasty about it, and they're
Friendship involves trust		always gonna be there, and they do care about you, and someone you
A friend is someone you can enjoy yourself with, someone you have a lot in common with		can trust and stuff, but it's someone that you can have a laugh with and go out with and stuff, and probably that you've got common, a lot in common with as well, I think you need to have a lot in common cause otherwise you're just gonna grow apart then, yeah I think that's it [laughs].

Unsurprisingly, Shazia's definition includes all the components she has discussed previously throughout the interview. As the descriptive summaries in Extract 10.7 illustrate, the aspects of friendship that Shazia highlights are borne out of the stories she has told in the interview: she likes to feel at ease with her friends, to enjoy herself with them and that to do that you need to have things in common. She also emphasises the importance of trust, caring for each other and that friends should be dependable.

Going through the process of writing descriptive summaries provides the essential groundwork on which the remainder of the analysis is based. As we have demonstrated, it is also important to reflect upon and make notes in your reflective diary about aspects of the account that stand out as you go along. This will help inform the next stage of making initial interpretations.

?

10.13 Where are we now?

We have now completed the initial stage of the analysis. We have read through the transcript several times and have become familiar with the data. Having written descriptive summaries (see Extracts 10.2–10.7) of chunks of the transcript and recorded our thoughts and reflections about it in our reflective diary (see reflective diary extracts 2 and 3), we can now move on to making interpretations and identifying themes.

Making initial interpretations

The process of identifying themes can seem unfathomable but hopefully breaking down these two stages of activity – writing descriptive summaries and making initial interpretations – will help demystify the process. As you have seen in the previous section, writing descriptive summaries is a fairly transparent process of summarising what the participant talks about, whilst making notes of reflections and ideas about the data in the reflective diary. In the stage of making initial interpretations, we use those descriptions as the buildings blocks on which to make suggestions about the meanings we can attribute to Shazia's experiential account and come to an understanding of what friendship means to Shazia. In this phase of analysis, it is necessary to start again from the beginning of the transcript: read through the summaries and the sections of the transcript itself and think about what inferences can be drawn from the data to help answer our research question – what is the meaning of friendship.

If we return to Extract 10.2, what we glean from this initial description of Shazia's friendship with Eva is illustrated below.

When making these initial interpretations, it is useful to ask questions of the descriptive summaries – for example, what is significant about spending lots of time together at this critical juncture in Shazia's life? One answer is that sharing novel experiences meant that Shazia and Eva embarked on a joint journey of discovery through their teenage years; they lived these experiences together. Another answer to this question is that sharing significant life events at such a pivotal time – the teenage years – means that Shazia and Eva began their journeys

> > (quotation mark graphic)

Extract 10.8:   An initial interpretation (Int. 1; lines 21–33)

Int:	Aw OK. So that's, it's kinda like a mutual learning for both of you as well?
Shazia:	Yeah, yeah, we've been through like everything together as well, like everything that happened to her for the first time, cause I'm a bit older so I'd like, it's like things with school as well, so I'd do things first and she'd be like 'Well what do I do for this?' and I'd help her and you know, so like that really, yeah.
Int:	So is that more with em schoolwork or more personal things?
Shazia:	Both really, like it'd start with school work because like when you're really young not much happens to you, but you, like first boyfriends and other things like that, and going out clubbing, and doing everything your not meant to [laughs], yeah.
Int:	[Laughs]. So you were more of, you were more of, it's because you were the older one you sort of, did you, do you feel like you took her under your wing a little bit?
Shazia:	For some things, but a lot of it, she matured faster than me for some things, so then she actually took me under her wing as well so it's, it's a mutual thing I think, yeah.

Annotations (right margin):
- Joint journey of discovery
- Developed together as young women – intertwining selves/self-development
- Reciprocity of advice / Mutual relationship

of self-discovery together. In other words, it becomes difficult for Shazia to separate her memory of growing up and her identity-forming from her memory of being friends with Eva.

When conducting an interpretative analysis such as this, it is important to ensure that the claims made can be evidenced in the data; that is, you need to be able to demonstrate how you got from the raw data to the interpretation (Figure 10.1).

10.14 Activity suggestion

Like before, as you read this section, follow the procedures described using your chosen transcript. Students often find the interpretative part of the analysis challenging. Remember that you need to find a balance between being creative and free to make interpretations and ensuring that any interpretations you make can be traced back to the original raw data (i.e., the transcript).

Providing an audit trail is important for you as the analyst to ensure that interpretations made are based in the data. This is because the themes you identify are based on these early descriptions and interpretations. For instance, out of the initial interpretations of Extracts 10.7 and 10.8, we get a sense of the power of Shazia's friendship with Eva. It has penetrated the development of Shazia's sense of self, which has meant that being Eva's best friend is incredibly important to her. Figure 10.1 illustrates one interpretation of this: Shazia and Eva having intertwining selves; that is, their senses of self have developed in parallel because of their close relationship in these formative adult years.

We must remember in an idiographic analysis that any inferences we make are specific to the experiencer, namely, Shazia. We do not know, for example,

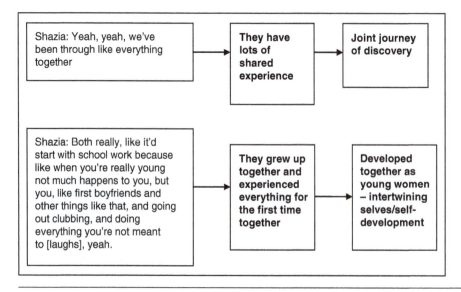

Figure 10.1   Audit trail.

whether Eva feels the same way as Shazia; all we know is what Shazia tells us. This does not weaken our analysis though because one of the key aims of IPA is to understand experience from the experiencer's point of view; we want to know what being friends with Eva means to Shazia. What we glean from Shazia's experiential account helps us to empathise with her and to start to understand life from Shazia's perspective.

Extract 10.9:   Further interpretation (Int. 1; lines 786–794)

Int: OK, em so can you sum up then what friendship means to you?

Shazia: Right, [laughs] em I think friendship is something that you don't, it's like a situation where you can form like a relationship with someone, and you can just be fairly comfortable and know that no one's gonna judge you, no one's gonna pick at everything you, if they do pick they're not gonna like be nasty about it, and they're always gonna be there, and they do care about you, and someone you can trust and stuff, but it's someone that you can have a laugh with and go out with and stuff, and probably that you've got common, a lot in common with as well, I think you need to have a lot in common cause otherwise you're just gonna grow apart then, yeah I think that's it [laughs].

Friendship is non-judgemental (aligned with first portion)

Trustworthiness is central to friendship (aligned with middle portion)

Shared experience and interests is important to maintain a friendship (aligned with final portion)

In Extract 10.9 we see Shazia's notion of friendship condensed into three constructs: friendship as non-judgemental, trust as fundamental to friendship, and friendship as shared experience. Throughout her account, Shazia spoke about concrete experiences in her own life which have led her to these conclusions. Shazia is self-aware and has contemplated how her behaviour has impacted on her development of friendships. Through all of her lived experience, Shazia has come to realise what friendship means to her. From this we begin to see aspects of Shazia's character, her values and beliefs, as she starts her life as an independent young woman.

The initial themes identified through these processes of writing descriptive summaries and making initial interpretations are presented in Figure 10.2.

Shared journey of discovery	Reciprocity
Eva as consistent friend	Trust
Friend as confidante	Empathy
Lost friends/new opportunities	

Figure 10.2   Initial themes in Shazia's experiential account.

The themes in Figure 10.2 were developed through several readings of the transcript (familiarising oneself with the data initially, reading for gist, dividing the transcript into small chunks), writing descriptive summaries, and a detailed interpretative analysis of the transcript and the summaries with reference to the reflective diary. IPA is an active method that requires the analyst to engage with the data in a detailed way in order to do justice to the experiential account provided by the participant.

10.15 Procedure highlight: Interpretation is systematic

Sometimes researchers talk of themes 'emerging' from the data. This is an unfortunate expression, because it implies that themes simply exist in the data to be discovered. IPA is a creative method which requires the analyst to be proactive and engage with the data. Themes are not waiting to emerge but are borne out of close readings, careful consideration and systematic interpretation.

Clustering themes

Now that most of the hard work has been done, the analyst is concerned with making sense of the preliminary interpretations and themes identified. Keeping in mind the extracts from which each theme developed, this phase of analysis involves looking for connections between the initial themes in order to further reduce the data. In effect, a qualitative analysis involves taking large amounts of raw data and then going through various stages of activity in order to reduce them into meaningful chunks. In this method, those stages involve summarising, distilling from those summaries some key meanings, establishing recurrent or salient themes from those initial interpretations, looking for relationships between themes and creating a narrative account of what this experiential account can tell us about the meaning of friendship. See Figure 10.3 for an indication of how themes might be clustered.

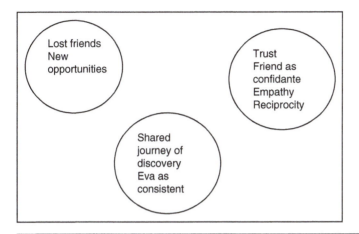

Figure 10.3   Clustering of initial themes.

There may be several ways in which themes could be related; Figure 10.3 demonstrates one way of doing this. At this stage in the analysis it is important to start thinking explicitly about the end result – your findings – the story you want to tell about Shazia's experience of friendship and what friendship means to her. In this case, the decision to cluster themes in this way was borne out of the different aspects in Shazia's account: the development of her relationship with Eva, her previous experience of lost friends which brought new opportunities for personal growth and the constructs she feels are crucial to friendship. Once initial themes are grouped together in this way, the next task is to assign a title for each new (final) theme.

Establishing the final themes

The final superordinate themes are derived from the clusters and represent the central concepts in the analysis of Shazia's experiential account Figure 10.4.

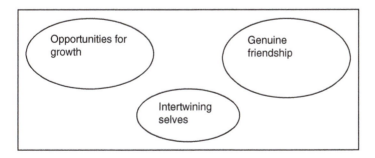

Figure 10.4   Final themes.

It is this set of final themes which will be presented in the results section of a research report. Now that you have established your final themes you need to return to the transcript and identify the extracts which represent each theme. It is sometimes a good idea to create a new Word document for each theme and copy and paste into them each relevant extract representing each theme. This will facilitate with the process of writing up your findings.

10.16 Activity suggestion

Using your selected transcript and analytic work you have done so far:

(i) Write a list of the themes you have identified.
(ii) Cluster the themes by thinking about how they link together or perhaps contradict each other.
(iii) Draw up a set of final themes.

Continuing with other cases

It is perfectly acceptable for IPA studies to be conducted with only one participant ($n = 1$). IPA is an idiographic approach and so works in detail at the individual level, as the previous sections of this chapter have illustrated. Single-case studies in psychology tend to be found only in clinical psychology or developmental psychology (e.g., child language studies), but IPA offers an ideal method for extending this form of design. However, it is possible to have multiple participants in an IPA study too, and it is at this stage, when the analysis of the first case is complete, that you would move on to the second person in your sample. When working on the second case you need to repeat the steps above, ending with an established final list of themes for case two. It is possible that some themes will overlap but they may not; as we know, IPA focuses on idiosyncrasies (things that are unique to individuals) as well as aspects of their accounts which they may share. IPA research is usually carried out with relatively small samples; undergraduate projects often have three to six participants but there is no specific requirement regarding participant numbers.

10.17 Want to know more?

Smith, J. A., Flowers, P. & Larkin, M. (2009) *Interpretative phenomenological analysis: Theory, method and research.* London: Sage.
Smith, J. A. and Eatough, V. (2007) Interpretative phenomenological analysis. In E. Lyons & A. Coyle (Eds) *Analysing qualitative data in psychology.* London: Sage (pp. 35–50).

Writing up the analysis

Writing the results of your analysis involves creating a narrative account of the participant's account and the analyst's interpretations of it. This is often referred to as the final stage of analysis because work is still on-going to produce an account that

---

Genuine friendship

Friendship can mean different things to different people. In this theme we explore Shazia's interpretation of genuine friendship and what her friends mean to her. The friend Shazia talks about at the beginning of the interview is Eva. Shazia has been friends with Eva since early childhood, which means they have grown up together:

> Shazia: Yeah, yeah, we've been through like everything together as well, like everything that happened to her for the first time, cause I'm a bit older so I'd like, it's like things with school as well, so I'd do things first and she'd be like "Well what do I do for this?" and I'd help her and you know, so like that really, yeah.
>
> Int: So is that more with em schoolwork or more personal things?
>
> Shazia: Both really, like it'd start with school work because like when you're really young not much happens to you, but you, like first boyfriends and other things like that, and going out clubbing, and doing everything you're not meant to [laughs], yeah.

In many ways, Shazia and Eva embarked on a joint journey of discovery. They did school work together, had boyfriends together, started going out as teenagers together and misbehaved together. Having someone close to share these novel experiences was important to Shazia and the strength of her friendship with Eva becomes particularly clear when she describes her feelings about going to university and the possibility of losing her friend:

> Int: So how, how how'd you think she felt when you first came to university and you, you talked about your friends you had made?
>
> Shazia: She wasn't, to be honest she's not really bothered, like I'm always the one that worries more, like I was like when I told her that I was worried about when like, cause I told her about halfway through my first year, I told her like I was really worried that we were gonna grow apart, and she was like "This is sad we're not gonna grow apart and stuff" [laughs] "Oh fair enough" [laughs], but no she's fine, it's like she just, as long as I keep her up to date with stories and stuff she don't really, not really bothered [laughs]

In this extract Shazia tell us of her concern during her first year away at university which demonstrates how much she thought about Eva while they were apart. There is a hint of insecurity in Shazia's worry that she may lose her friend or that the nature of their friendship would change. Shazia's trust in Eva is demonstrated by the way her fears are quashed by Eva's no-nonsense response. As we see in other areas of her account, for Shazia, trust is a defining feature of friendship. She also values dependability. In the extract above, Shazia is reassured by Eva's consistent and dependable friendship through which a sense of mutual trust has grown.

Figure 10.5   Short example of a written-up interpretative phenomenological analysis.

is persuasive, defensible and which adequately represents the participant's story. It must also convey the interplay between what the participant said, her own reflections on her experiences and the analyst's interpretative activity. These features make an IPA feel dynamic and creative. They are also what make it compelling and enlightening. In your write-up you need to present each theme in turn, briefly define the theme and then proceed to demonstrate the significance of the theme for understanding the meaning of friendship. This is achieved by providing data extracts and interpretative commentary about those extracts. The short extract in Figure 10.5 illustrates what a written-up IPA might look like.

Summary points

You have come a long way and learned a great deal about what is involved in using Interpretative Phenomenological Analysis (IPA) as a qualitative method. It is good to note:

1. IPA is an idiographic form of inquiry that is directly influenced by the philosophical schools of phenomenology and hermeneutics.
2. As an idiographic approach, IPA focuses on the individual level of a person's experience and involves what is known as a 'double hermeneutic' – the analyst is seeking to make sense of how the participant (e.g., person interviewed) makes sense of their experiences.
3. In IPA there is a close interdependence between keeping a reflective diary, processes of description and interpretation, and the production of an audit trail as the background to establishing transparent trustworthiness in analysis.
4. IPA is data-driven and thus procedures for adequately describing data in the early stages of analysis are important.
5. Making initial interpretations in IPA can involve asking questions of the descriptive summaries made during the initial stages of analysis.
6. The final stages of analysis involve considered strategies of clustering themes and producing a super-ordinate set of themes in order to develop a coherent understanding of the topic under examination.

10.18 Want to know more?

Some very good examples of published IPA papers include:

Dickson, A., Knussen, C. & Flowers, P. (2007) Stigma and the delegitimation experience: An interpretative analysis of people living with chronic fatigue syndrome. *Psychology and Health*, **22**(7), 851–867.
Eatough, V. & Smith, J. A. (2006) 'I feel like a scrambled egg in my head': An idiographic case study of meaning making and anger using interpretative phenomenological analysis. *Psychology and Psychotherapy*, **79**, 115–135.

Flowers, P., Smith, J. A., Sheeran, P. & Beail, N. (1997) Health and romance: Understanding unprotected sex in relationships between gay men. *British Journal of Health Psychology*, **2**, 73–86.

Smith, J. A., Brewer, H., Eatough, V., Stanley, C., Glendinning, N. & Quarrell, O. (2006) The personal experience of Juvenile Huntington's Disease: An interpretative phenomenological analysis of parents' accounts of the primary features of a rare genetic condition. *Clinical Genetics*, **69**, 486–496.

Smith, J. A. & Osborn, M. (2007) Pain as an assault on the self: An interpretative phenomenological analysis of the psychological impact of chronic benign low back pain. *Psychology and Health*, 22(5), 517–534.

11

QM4: Conversation Analysis

Michael Forrester

Introduction

Within psychology there is a concern with studying naturalistic everyday interactions between people. One activity stands out as something we do without thinking about it much – talking to other people or *conversing*. In recent years an approach to the study of conversation has emerged in the sub-discipline known as *Conversation Analysis* (CA). This chapter will provide a brief introduction to some of the central principles of CA and show how these might be applied when looking at the conversations that make up the 'friendship' interviews.

CA as a qualitative methodology began life in sociology and was associated with researchers who used the term *ethnomethodology*. One of the sociologists involved with this approach, Harold Garfinkel (1967), commented that ethnomethodologists study how people spontaneously produce ways or 'methods' of behaving. These sequences of activities that people produce might appear fairly random, and at times uncoordinated, but in fact are very orderly. When we go about the world 'making sense of it', our sense-making practices are methodical in ordinary conventional ways. Ordinary people's own methods are produced so that everybody around them can see how ordinary and normal they are. And if necessary, they are things that we can describe and explain. We are all familiar with the type of situation where a young child trying to get the attention of a parent might be told, 'can't you see I'm talking on the telephone?' (a description of what is going on and simultaneously an explanation of why the child will have to wait). The study of everything that makes up social life, the myriad social procedures, conventions, activities and practices is called 'ethnomethodology'.

> **Definitions** **11.1** !
>
> **Ethnomethodology** is the study of the methods people use to produce and interpret social interaction. Ethnomethodology focuses on providing a rational analysis of the structures, procedures and strategies that people themselves use when they are making sense out of their own everyday world and their interactions within it.

Now, given that taking part in conversation is a very common everyday activity, a close relationship grew up between ethnomethodologists and researchers in sociology who had started using portable equipment to record conversations (Sacks, Schegloff & Jefferson, 1974; Sacks, 1992). At last, there was a way to examine what people say, and *how* they speak when they talk. This group of conversation analysts began to identify many different kinds of structures within conversation. From the beginning it was apparent that there were many regular patterns in these conversations – identifiable when detailed transcriptions were made of them. The approach the conversation analysts adopted when examining such data was ethnomethodological –a focus on how people themselves produce and recognise their own 'sense-making' practices as they are going along. Conversation analysis took to heart the ethnomethodological focus on what people actually say and do. Before getting into considering the background to CA, let's consider first a sample transcript and notice some of the similarities to and differences from the other methods described in the data of Chapters 8 to 10.

Sample analysis extract

> **Extract 11.1:   Data set sample extract (Int. 1; lines 454–462)** ""
>
> 1   SHAZ: yea I'd rather have
> 2   (0.4)
> 3   SHAZ: some
> 4   (0.4)
> 5   SHAZ: a few people that mean a lot to me
> 6   (0.7)
> 7   SHAZ: than::
> 8   (0.8)
> 9   SHAZ: hundreds of people that
> 10   (0.7)

(Continued)

Extract 11.1:   continued

```
11   SHAZ:  I know
12          (0.2)
13   SHAZ:  >so little about<
14          (0.5)
15   INT:   mhh[mm]
16   SHAZ:      [that]
17          (0.4)
18   SHAZ:  doesn't
19          (0.3)
20   SHAZ:  it's (.) it's not you can't even call it a friendship its just like an
21          acquaintance
22          (0.4)
23   INT:   yea
24          (0.4)
25   SHAZ:  but
26          (0.3)
27   SHAZ:  ↑I don't (.) I'm not really bothered about
28          (0.9)
29   SHAZ:  people that I'm just acquainted with and like
30          (0.6)
31   SHAZ:  just fellow students and stuff xxx
32          (0.6)
33   SHAZ:  I kind of
34          (0.6)
35   SHAZ:  push those k- ↑cause I don't
36          (0.4)
37   SHAZ:  ↑like
38          (0.6)
39   SHAZ:  people (.) knowing exactly what I'm
40          (0.2)
41   SHAZ:  feeling and thinking all the time
42          (0.8)
43   INT:   mm[mmm]
44   SHAZ:  [so I think] if I've got these few people around me (.) that
45          are close to me I can confide with them
46          (0.5)
47   SHAZ:      [and that's it] I don't have to (.) yea
48   INT:   [mmhhmm]
49          (0.6)
50   SHAZ:  >↑I don't like< other people knowing:: too much about me
51          (0.3)
52   INT:   okay
53          (0.5)
54   INT:   oka[y::]
```

```
55   SHAZ:      [so I don't] know if it's because
56              (0.5)
57   SHAZ:   I don't really like them or (.) because I keep them away for a
58              reason but
59              (1.2)
60   SHAZ:   yea so having a few people close to me
61              (0.6)
```

The layout of this short section from a conversation analytic is quite striking in that you will immediately notice a host of curious symbols and typography (described in Chapter 7; see also examples in Chapter 8). These serve to represent elements of the talk-in-interaction and draw our attention to the fact that CA is very focused on the structure of talk, the sequence of the interaction and the numerous things that people do when having an everyday conversation. Notice:

1. The transcript is designed to focus on 'talk-as-interaction', the who, how and what we do as we are conversing.
2. *How* a person says something is potentially significant and can indicate something of what they are doing.
3. The transcript is organised so that we can analyse the various structures that people use, such as turn-taking, and identifying when trouble in the talk might occur.
4. The *way* a person says something (e.g., the >words< arrows in line 13 indicate that Shazia said something at that point that was noticeably faster than the utterances around it) can form part of the analytic rationale that the CA researcher employs.
5. All utterances can be analysed with a focus on the sequence of the interaction. In a sense, CA often asks, 'why that (utterance) now'?
6. By analysing the fine-detail of the structures of the conversation we can understand how, and what, the people themselves in the interaction understand and orient to, in the ongoing talk-in-interaction.

Procedure highlight: Steps in the analysis **11.2**

Step 1: Record conversations either in audio or video-recorded form
Step 2: Transcribe the conversations in full using an orthography to describe all relevant actions (see the orthography in Chapter 7)
Step 3: Identify elements and structures in the conversation
Step 4: Highlight **participant-oriented** evidence for the methods that people use for doing 'talk-in-interaction'

The first part of this chapter will provide a background to the analysis by concentrating on three elements of CA: turn-taking, the sequential nature of conversations and the structural nature of interaction. Let's discuss each of these in turn.

Background

Taking turns in conversation: How people use a 'locally managed system'

Basing their analysis on many recorded and transcribed conversations Harvey Sacks and his colleagues developed a model of conversational turn-taking which described its 'locally managed' nature. The model explains what people themselves do when conducting a conversation together, that is, sorting out who has the current turn at talk, who might have the next turn and so on. The whole thing is conducted 'locally' on a 'turn-by-turn' basis in the immediate setting of the interaction. This model is called the *local management system* (LMS) of conversation. It is a system because it is highly organised and orderly, it is local because it always takes place in the immediate local context, and it is 'managed' because it is the people talking who are managing it as they proceed.

11.3 Procedure highlight: Local management system (LMS)

The LMS is based on two components, and a set of rules which operate on these components:

    A: a turn-constructional element

This can be any kind of an utterance, or even a gesture or sound (such as 'ehm'). Known as a *turn-constructional unit* (or TCU), this can be any length at all.

    B: a turn-allocation element expressed

Allocation of turns works in two ways:

 (i) somebody choosing or selecting the next person to talk, or
(ii) the next person selecting themselves.

This place in the conversation where turn-allocation can occur is known as a *transition-relevant place* (or TRP). Often this is a short pause and it is very common for speaker change to take place at TRPs.

Consider how you ask somebody a question. Towards the end of the question, the pitch and emphasis of your voice will typically change (even before you actually get to the end). This indicates to the person you're talking to that you are just about to give up your turn at talk and hand it over. If you are the person being spoken to, you know precisely when to enter the conversation and select yourself as the next speaker. Sacks et al. (1974), in identifying the turn-taking constructional and allocation units (TCUs and TRPs), identified a set of rules at work here. Once you've read these they will seem rather obvious, but it is very likely that you've not really been aware of the fact that conversations work in this way.

Critical issue: Turn-taking rules **10.4**

Consider the comments beside these turn-taking rules – does all this happen when you talk?

RULE 1: This rule applies to the first transition-relevant place of any turn.

(a) If the current speaker selects the next speaker during the current turn, then the current speaker must stop speaking and the next speaker must speak next. And he/she must speak next at the first transition-relevant place after this 'next speaker' selection.

Imagine how weird it would be if, the minute you ask somebody a question and they are about to answer, you start talking!

(b) If the speaker does not select a next speaker during a current turn, then anybody else present (other parties) can self-select and the first person to do this will gain 'speaker rights' at the next turn.

It is quite a skill to learn to recognise just the right moment to come into a conversation without appearing rude, don't you think?

(c) If the current speaker has not selected the next speaker and nobody else self-selects, then the speaker can continue (although this is not a requirement). In doing so, he/she gains a right to have a further turn-constructional unit (TCU).

Don't we all know a 'Mr Boring' who seems to just manage to keep self-selecting, even though we're not sure how he does it?

RULE 2: When rule 1(c) has been applied by the current speaker, then, at the next transition-relevant place, rules 1(a) to 1(c) apply again, and keep re-applying until speaker change is accomplished.

The whole system is 'recursive' going around and around as the talk proceeds. Does this mean we sometimes feel 'stuck' in a conversation?

This system and all the elements in it amount to an array of procedures, strategies and social convention designed and used by ordinary participants (what ethnomethodology calls *members methods*) going about the 'doing' of everyday conversation. And importantly, these practices and the structures which make them up are produced so as to address at least one inherent problem of interaction: the taking of turns. When you stop to think about it, turn-taking in conversation could be very messy and disorganised with everybody not really knowing what's meant to be happening next, and indeed children take some time before they learn conversational skills (Wootton, 1997). The *LMS* ensures that things proceed smoothly, most of the time, and indeed many features of conversation result from its existence. Here are a few (see Sacks et al., 1974 for a complete list):

1. Speaker changes occur with relative ease.
2. Most of the time only one speaker has a turn at talk.
3. Transitions (from one turn to the next) are exceptionally sophisticated and very often occur with no gaps or overlaps.
4. The length of any person's turn is not normally fixed in advance, and neither is the order of turns.
5. The distribution of turns is not specified in advance, nor is what people will say during a turn.
6. Repair mechanisms exist for dealing with turn-taking errors and violations (e.g., when two people start talking at exactly the same time, one of them normally stops very quickly).

We can see then that turn-taking is exceptionally orderly and that people are very skilled at recognising when a transition-relevant place is coming up and also how to go about projecting a forthcoming TRP, so as to indicate their turn at talk is about to end. A typical sort of example is shown in Figure 11.1.

Sequence in conversation

An endemic element of interaction and conversation is that one thing always follows another in sequence. As conversationalists, we are very skilled at monitoring

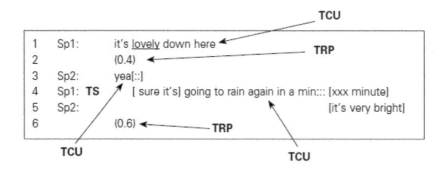

TRP = transition relevant place
TCU = turn construction unit
TS = trouble source

Figure 11.1 **Conversation analytic turn-taking terminology**. A turn is composed of a turn-constructional unit, which can be of any length or form. A transition-relevant pause defines the gap between one speaker and the next speaker. The talk in line 4 contains a self-repair.

our own talk and the talk of others such that we know where we are in the talk, and what is going on. What is more, even though we are very rarely ever aware of this, going about our everyday business in life can be described as 'doing being ordinary'; that is, being accountable to those around you (even if they are strangers), for displaying yourself in such a way so that you appear 'normal, conventional, ordinary'. It is this kind of thing that helps us understand why we feel particularly embarrassed or silly if we accidentally slip when walking along the road, but maybe don't actually fall over, and as we stagger to find our feet, we are keenly aware of whether people around us noticed.

In other words, whenever we are in the presence of other human beings we are forever monitoring, ever so subtly and most of the time unnoticeably, our own and their behaviour. Furthermore, we display ourselves in such a way that our own behaviour can be monitored by whoever happens to be around us. And conversation is probably the most important practice or set of procedures we use for doing all of this – we are keenly sensitive to a continually 'unfolding' sequence of 'what happens next' and 'what's meant to happen next', given what has just been said. Again, this is something we don't consciously think about and only really notice when this implicit attention to sequence seems to go wrong somehow or somebody talking doesn't seem to be paying attention to it.

It is also true that people design their behaviour with some awareness, even minimal, of its accountability. When we are interacting with each other we orient to whatever rules and conventions of conversation are operating at the time. And we choose to follow or ignore such conventions with an awareness of the likely and immediate consequences. In other words, we are always accountable for our actions, verbal and otherwise. Now, given that we are always accountable in some way for what we are doing when in a conversation, we can begin to see why sequence and 'what happens next' is important. In CA this is called *sequential implicativeness*, highlighting the observation that what you do 'next', following something that another person has done, is automatically monitored by both parties. Consider the example in Extract 11.2.

Extract 11.2:   Orientation to questions (adapted from Atkinson & Drew, 1979; p. 52)

```
1   John:  Is there something bothering you or not?
2          (1.0)
3   John:  Yes or no?
4          (1.5)
5   John:  Ehhh↑ ?
6          (0.3)
7   Fred:  No.
```

In this extract John asks Fred a question and according to normal conversational conventions, when you are asked a question, you reply. Now, the 1-second gap between lines 1 and 2 is significant, because it is longer than what you would expect; that is, normally people reply immediately, in less than a second. John displays an understanding or orientation to this normative convention or 'rule' by asking Fred in line 2 to answer either 'yes' or 'no'. He is indicating to Fred his knowledge and understanding that when people are having a conversation and somebody asks a question, then a reply is expected. If you don't get a reply then we might assume something is wrong or not understood – and in fact John provides Fred with the specific answers that might be given to the question he has just asked.

Then, after John's second question, Fred again flouts or ignores the question/ answer rule by allowing an even longer gap or silence. This then leads John in line 3 to say 'Ehhh' accompanied by a very specific rising intonation towards the end of the utterance (this is indicated by the upward arrow). This shows that not only is John asking Fred to act normally and obey the usual rules for turn-taking in conversation, but we also can surmise that he is showing some annoyance at Fred's refusal to answer, which this time eventually elicits a response by Fred in line 4. So, even for something as simple as somebody asking you a question, if you deliberately don't answer them, then this will be seen as somehow flouting the rules or conventions for how questions and answers are meant to work – in sequence. The person asking the question will look for reasons why you didn't answer (e.g., are you ignoring me!). In other words, no matter how small or insignificant a behaviour might be, in the presence of other people, we are always accountable for our actions as a member of the culture.

Structures in conversation

Although we are often not aware of it, we display a sensitivity to various structural elements in talk, such as requests, questions, greetings, compliments, interruptions and many others. Of course, we're also producing such structures ourselves, so that others can recognise we have done so. What does this mean exactly? We need to turn to some of the methods we use for the turn-allocation component of the LMS to get a flavour of how this works. In this section of the chapter we'll look at three: adjacency pairs, endings and formulations.

'Adjacency pairs in conversation': The talk unfolded two-by-two

Many things in conversation come in two parts and they are sequentially organised. A question to somebody normally requires that the recipient provide an answer. A greeting is likely to be followed by a greeting, a summons by an answer, an end of a conversation with two-part farewells, an invitation by an acceptance, an insult by a retort and so on. In CA, these pairings are described as adjacency pairs and come in 'first and second' parts – a first-pair part (FPP) and a second-pair part (SPP).

Consider a typical opening telephone conversation between two friends (Extract 11.3), composed of many pairs of utterances adjacent to each other (thus termed adjacency pairs in CA):

Extract 11.3:   Adjacency pairs in conversation openings (adapted from Forrester, 1996)

1		Telephone rings	SUMMONS	1st PP*
2	Dave:	Yes?	Response to summons	2nd PP to (1)
3	Chris:	Hello, there:	Greeting	1st PP
4		is that Dave?	Question	1st PP
5	Dave:	Yea,	Answer	2nd PP to (4)
6		hi	Greeting	2nd PP to (3)
7	Chris:	How are you?	Question	1st PP
8	Dave:	Not bad,	Answer	2nd PP to (7)
9		how's yourself?	Question	1st PP
10	Chris:	Good	Answer	2nd PP to (9)
11		Look, the reason I'm calling is		Topic

First, we have the ring of the telephone, which is itself a summons (the acoustic analogue of being nudged on the shoulder by someone to get their attention!), and Dave answers it (in the conventional fashion) with a response to the summons. The two parts to this adjacency pair are complete and follow the conventional form. This is then followed by a greeting 'proper' from Chris, (line 3) and then, before Dave answers, a question (line 4) – another first pair part of an adjacency pair. Now note, when Dave replies he not only first provides an SPP for the question just asked, but also responds with his greeting reply in line 6 (an SPP for line 3). What this highlights is the fact that once somebody has produced an FPP, then there is a very strong convention – something we're rarely aware of – that an SPP has to come somewhere later. It doesn't have to come straight away, but it must come.

In our extract we then see a second and a third set of question–answer pairs (lines 7–10) before Chris finally introduces the topic, the reason for the phone call, in the last line above. There are a number of key elements of adjacency pairs of this sort, as listed in the Procedure Highlight box.

11.4 Procedure highlight: Key elements of adjacency pairs

1. They must be normally adjacent
2. They must be produced by different speakers
3. They are always ordered as first-pair part/second-pair part (FPP/SPP)
4. The two pairs are conditionally relevant. The first pair sets up what may occur as a second, and the second will depend on what has occurred as the first (as Psathas, 1995 notes)

This adjacency pair structure follows the *LMS* rule such that, having produced a first pair part of some pair, the current speaker must stop speaking and the next speaker must produce at that point in the interchange a second pair part to the same pair. It is the participants themselves who are very sensitive to the structural form of these interchange formats. These are the 'members methods' that we all produce and orient to when we talk. Let's look in a little more detail at how adjacency pairs are used a resource by people, so as to get to the end of a conversation successfully (overleaf).

11.5 Procedure highlight: Participant orientation and Conversation Analysis

In contrast to other qualitative methods in this book, conversation analysts have a strong commitment to the notion that interpretations, suggestions or claims made about the data being analysed (the actual conversations), must rest upon identifiable evidence in the conversations themselves. Analysis should be *participant-oriented*. When one looks at what people are doing in talk, what they do displays their own recognition that everybody, themselves included, is following certain conventions, regularities and habitual ways of producing conversation. This is not something that people consciously think about – often it is only when somebody doesn't follow a conversational convention that you very quickly see that those around them seek to rectify, change or repair the 'breaking of the rule' that has just occurred.

If it is not possible to identify specific participant-oriented phenomena in the talk which support the analyst's interpretation, then CA is very sceptical about other suggestions that might be being made. Analysis focuses on the conversation itself, where there is no adoption or superimposition of pre-ordained categories during the micro-analysis.

Critical issue **11.6**

Does the suggestion that Conversation Analysis must be 'participant-ori-ented' mean that we should be wary of qualitative methods that rely on the analyst or researcher using a category scheme or method of coding imposed from outside?

Endings: Closing sequences and how to end a conversation

Staying with structures in conversation, turn-taking itself creates a problem for ending a conversation. The sequential nature of talk-in-interaction means that one turn will always follow another (your turn, my turn, your turn, my turn and on … and on... and on). Help, this could go on forever, and we can all remember situations where we seem to find it quite difficult to end a conversation – without being rude, that is. We have to create the possibility of stopping this potentially never-ending process in an accomplished way.

Many of us are familiar with coming to a point in a conversation where you realise that the business at hand is finished, but you're not quite sure how to leave or end the talk. It would be seen as rather unconventional to simply say 'Bye', turn and abruptly walk out of the door. You and the person you are talking to must somehow 'work' towards making the end of the conversation possible in an easy, smooth and acceptable way. So, whoever decides to make the first move towards stopping the conversation must produce an FPP that has a certain kind of special status: one which indicates a move towards possibly finishing the conversation. Where exactly that FPP is produced is important because the orientation of the SPP to this special kind of FPP will show whether the 'next speaker' to the current speaker has taken up this offer (equivalent to: 'do you think we should close the conversation now'?).

Typically, a speaker who wishes to move towards creating the possibility of a 'closing' will initiate a pre-closing phrase or word such as 'Well...' or 'Right...' sometimes accompanied by a change in intonation. Have a look at Extract 11.4.

Extract 11.4:   Moving towards and ending (from Schegloff & Sacks, 1973, p. 307)

1 Dorrinne: Uh, you know, its just like bringing the blood up.
2 Theresa: Yeah, well, THINGS UH ALWAYS WORK OUT FOR THE (.) BEST
3 Dorrinne: Oh certainly. Alright (.) Tess
4 Theresa: Uh, huh,
5 Theresa: Okay
6 Dorrinne: G'bye
7 Theresa: Goodnight

Here, in line 3, Dorrinne uses 'Alright' followed by a pause then 'Tess', and Theresa then takes up the 'offer' of the move towards a close (Uh, huh). What we then see are very typical forms of closing adjacency pairs. In line 6 the speaker initiates a final (terminal) FPP following the pre-closing offering 'Okay' by Theresa in line 5.

Now notice, it may be that following the production of an FPP pre-closing turn, the person spoken to indicates in some way that they don't want to take up the offer. An example of this is given in Extract 11.5.

Extract 11.5: Declining an end move (from Psathas, 1995, p. 20)

```
1   Geri:      Oka:y
2   Shirley:   Alright?
3   Geri:      Mm.h [m:]?
4   Shirley:        [D'yih talk] tih D_ayna this week?
5   Geri:      hhh Yeh...
```

Here, although in line 2 Shirley provides a pre-closing FPP, the offer is not taken up. Instead, in line 3 the response is a rising intonation question sound, and the response to this, in turn, introduces a new topic and the conversation continues. People's sensitivity to this 'closing problem' is often marked, particularly in circumstances where there has been some degree of acceptance of a pre-closing FPP offer, but then again, a change.

The sequential placing of pre-closing parts makes available an opportunity for people to see that the conversation is about to end, and if they want to continue it then the offer or acceptance of this move has to be changed. Schegloff & Sacks (1973) examined numerous conversational endings and noticed that this orientation to the 'problem of how to close' was itself something that participants marked. Having a pre-closing first pair part made a slot for 'previously unmentioned mentionables' possible. And very often it will be marked by such phrases as:

Oh, there was one more thing...

Ehmm, by the way, I just wanted to say...

I just wanted to mention one other thing...

By the way, I meant to say...

What is significant is that here we have an interactional system, which is sensitive to the needs of the participants, where the sequential ordering of adjacency pairs is something that participants themselves orient to.

Activity suggestion 11.7

Next time you are on your mobile or talking to people face-to-face, monitor how you both manage to get to the end of a conversation.

Is it always easy to do? Think of some situations where it seems particularly hard

Formulations in talk

Another commonly occurring structure we find in talk is known as the '*formulation*' – a moment in the ongoing conversation when somebody refers to, or spells out, what they have been saying. Phrases such as 'Look, what I'm getting at…' or 'Oh I see, what you're suggesting is…' or 'The thing I'm saying is…' are very interesting, in that they highlight the reflexive or self-explicating nature of everyday talk. In other words, as people are talking they are making sense of what is going on as it is happening – in the here and now. Formulations remind us that the main business of talking, when it is actually going on, is to demonstrate to each other our understanding of what is being said. But at the same time, these demonstrations or performances of our understanding, once we've done them, become part and parcel of the ongoing conversation. As you are talking you use resources that help display your ongoing understanding of what is being said. At the same time, these 'formulations' themselves can be used and referred to whenever there is a need to 'assemble together' the overall sense of what is taking place. **Reflexivity**, in this sense (which is not to be confused with a process of reflection), is an interdependent element of ordinary action: what this term is getting at is the idea that we are accountable for the things that we do (ordinary everyday actions including talking) and, if necessary, all these things are potentially describable and reportable.

Let's look at a typical example from our data set in Extract 11.6.

Extract 11.6:   An example formulation (Int. 1; lines 2015–2030)

```
1  SHA:   you'll know:: if you feel
2         (0.2)
3  SHA:   you're gonna feel comfortable with them
4         (0.5)
5  TAN:   [mmhh]
```

(Continued)

> ## Extract 11.6: continued
>
> 6 SHA: [and you] won't like have to:: (.) like (.) convince yourself and talk yourself in
> 7   (1.4)
> 8 SHA: it'll just (0.3) it will <u>naturally</u> develop it won't be you::
> 9   (1.2)
> 10 SHA: like (.) making things happen::::
> 11   (0.6)
> 12 SHA: >doing things like that< (.) I think that if it's >gonna be there it'll be there<
> 13   (0.3)
> 14 TAN: [okay::]
> 15 SHA: [and if] it's not then::

Here we see that the interviewee, as she is explaining a particular characteristic of how a friendship develops from lines 1–11, formulates a definition of one element about friendship between people, that is, you can't force it or fake it, culminating with the formulation in line 12, 'if it's gonna be there it'll be there'. This formulation is responded to by the interviewer producing a receipt – that is, confirming the formulation offered.

These formulations also tend to exhibit a two-part structure, as with adjacency pairs:

> **First-pair part = formulation**
> **Second-pair part = either (a) confirmation or (b) dis-confirmation**

So, first a speaker will produce a formulation, and then the person spoken to will produce a response to the formulation that is either a confirmation or a dis-confirmation. CA researchers have established that the preferred response to a formulation is a confirmation or agreement of some kind (e.g., Heritage & Watson, 1979). As we might imagine, if somebody responds by dis-confirming or disagreeing, or even being rather non-committal, then this might be an indication that participants don't have a shared sense of what is going on.

Formulations in conversation typically have four functions as laid out in the Procedure Highlight box.

> # 11.8 Procedure highlight: What formulations do
>
> A. Serve to show the cumulative importance of the talk that has preceded the formulation itself
> B. Act often to make an overall point, a form of 'summing up'
> C. Can be used as a method for moving towards ending a conversation
> D. Serve to indicate the collaborative understandings of what is going on, that is, what is being achieved by both parties.

At this point, it is worth pausing a moment to consider a few points regarding the transcription process. As noted in other chapters, the orthography of CA is very particular – and is that way for specific reasons which we will come on to when we consider our analysis.

The process of transcription in Conversation Analysis

The process of transcription involves playing back small sections of conversation repeatedly, and gradually writing out the words and sounds of the conversation according to the orthographic conventions outlined in Chapter 7. Although this may sound a rather tedious job, the very fact that this is in part true gives the analyst a kind of access to the 'lived reality' of the interaction that is not available in any other way. Harvey Sacks (1996) recommended that recordings should be listened to closely with 'unmotivated attention'. All the things that have been found out about everyday conversation have emerged from an 'unmotivated' examination of naturally occurring talk, from 'an examination not prompted by pre-specified goals [...] but by 'noticings' of initially unremarkable features of talk or other conduct' (Schegloff, 1996, p. 172).

This is a very important point. Analysts have to approach the business of transcription without any pre-conceived ideas about what they think is going on. They have to attend 'without motivation', that is, without some specific theoretical or research focused idea about what they think they will find or how they expect people to behave. At the same time, the repetitive nature of this task needs to be emphasised. Analysts need to listen with unmotivated attention again, and again and again. In other words, until they are as sure as they possibly can be that they have represented as best they can the sounds they hear in a form that allows the process of analysis to begin.

At the same time, it is important to recognise that from the moment you bring to bear your 'unmotivated attention' to the recording in the process of transcription, the very act of attending will help furnish you with the material you need for your analysis and interpretation. Throughout the transcription process it is important to note down separately in a set of field notes whatever aspects of the conversation come to your attention. Throughout, you should always be asking yourself the question, WHY THAT UTTERANCE NOW?; in other words, you should be paying continuous scrupulous, yet unmotivated, attention to the dynamic and sequential nature of the conversation. The process of transcription will draw your attention to subtle and sophisticated aspects of the 'talk-in-interaction' that, as conversationalists ourselves, we rarely notice or pay attention to.

11.8 Want to know more?

There are some very good books and papers on transcription in Conversation Analysis. These include:

Bucholtz, M. (2007) Variation in transcription. *Discourse Studies*, **9**(6), 784–808.

Hutchby, I. & Woofit, R. (2008) *Conversation analysis*. Cambridge: Polity Press.

Mondada, L. (2007) Commentary: transcript variations and the indexicality of transcribing practices. *Discourse Studies*, **9**(6), 809–821.

Ochs, E. (1979) Transcription as theory. In E. Ochs & B. Schiefflein (Eds), *Developmental pragmatics*. London: Academic Press.

Roberts, F. & Robinson, J. D. (2004) Interobserver agreement on first-stage conversation analytic transcription. *Human Communication Research*, **30**(3), 376–410.

Stelma, J. H. & Cameron, L. J. (2007) Intonation units in spoken interaction: Developing transcription skills. *Text and Talk*, **27**(3), 361–393.

Ten Have, P. (1999) *Doing conversation analysis: A practical guide*. London: Sage.

Analysis

Now we can turn our attention to how a conversation analytic study might examine certain aspects of the data set. One of the most important ways to study how people think, feel and behave is through the interview. Whilst there is a body of research that compares talk-in-interaction across formal and informal settings (e.g., home and work settings), relatively few CA studies have focused simply on how people conduct interviews (see Roulston, 2006). Given this background, there are many things that you might want to ask about the 'talk-in-interaction' that occurs in interview settings, such as:

- *What particular procedures do people use so as to have extended turns-at-talk?*
- *Are there any indications in the talk that people recognise that what they are saying is somehow 'on record'?*
- *How exactly does an interviewer indicate that he/she is listening attentively without being overbearing?*
- *What procedures are employed at the beginning of an interview so as to encourage a free-flowing easy conversation?*

The remainder of this chapter demonstrates how CA can be used to study how people manage the business of ending an interview. The aim is to understand the conversational resources participants call upon to reach a conclusion, both of the interview and to close the interaction itself. Let us look at some examples with a view to seeing whether the two structures outlined above (formulations and adjacency pairs) are used by participants in particular ways. The aim of this analysis, then, is to answer the question:

Q: How do people end an interview?

In order to answer this we will ask three subsidiary questions, using each to guide our approach:

Q (a) How do participants produce formulations and what do they look like?
Q (b) Do formulations exhibit an 'adjacency pair' structure?
Q (c) What kinds of adjacency pairs are used to end a conversation?

Let's turn to an example that highlights the subtle nature of how a formulation works and the form it typically exhibits.

Context: The interview has been going on nearly an hour, discussing many different aspects of friendship for the student interviewee. At the beginning of the extract the interviewer (Tanya) encourages the interviewee (Shazia) to produce a summary of her ideas on friendship.

Extract 11.7: First example of a formulation (Int. 1; lines 3606–3661).

```
1   TAN: so:: can you sum up then
2        (0.5)                              (student smiles)
3   TAN: what friendship means to you?
4        (2.2)
5   SHA: uh:: he-he.hhh em:: (1.6) I think (1.3) is something that (1.3) you
6        don't (1.7) it's like a situation where you can (0.8) form like a
7        relationship with somebody you can (0.9) just be fairly comfortable(.)
8        and (0.2) know that no ones gonna judge you and no ones gonna
9        pick at everything you thought ↑>If they do< pick they're not
10       gonna like (0.5) be nasty about it an (2.1) there always gonna be
11       there (.) and (.) they do care about you (0.7) and someone you
12       can trust and stuff bits someone you can laugh with an
13       (1.1)
14  SHA: go out with and stuff and
15  TAN: mmhmm=
16  SHA: =I think you need to have a lot in common
17       (0.6)
18  SHA: cause otherwise (0.6) you're just gonna (0.2) grow apart then
19       (1.4)
```

(Continued)

Extract 11.7:   continued

```
20      SHA:    ↑yea
21              (0.3)
22      SHA:    xx that's it eh he ↑ha-[ha]
23      TAN:                       [okay]=
24      SHA:    =yea=
25      TAN:    =so shall we finish it there=
26      SHA:    ↑yea
27              (0.3)
28      TAN:    okay brilliant
29              (0.2)
30      TAN:    °let me just cance°          (moves towards camera)
31              (0.5)
32      TAN:    °this::: °
33              (0.2)
34      TAN:    .hhhhh
35              (2.6)
36      [recording ends]
```

(a) How do participants produce formulations and what do they look like? Here we see that the interviewee produces a formulation following on from a long description of friendship. The phrase 'Yea, that's it' (lines 20–22) works to formulate what has just been going on ('that' here referring to the immediate preceding conversation between lines 5–18 and 'it' indicating what friendship means to her). The formulation itself is a definitive summary statement. In response, we see Tanya immediately producing a confirmation (line 23) that slightly overlaps the end of Shazia's utterance.

(b) Do formulations exhibit an 'adjacency pair' structure? In this example, we see that the formulation exhibits the 'first-part/second part' structure 'formulation–confirmation' format described above. We can also see the SPP that Tanya produces elicits a 'receipt' from Shazia, which serves to emphasise that her formulation is 'the final word' on friendship (line 24).

(c) What kinds of adjacency pairs are used to end a conversation? At line 25, the interviewer produces a special kind of FPP, one that amounts to a suggestion that offers to the interviewee the possibility of ending the interview (shall we finish it – yes: offer/acceptance). Immediately after this, the interviewer responds to this acceptance with a comment on the nature of the success of the ending of the interview (okay brilliant), and then they move towards ending the interview. Whilst we don't have the recording of exactly the last thing they said, we see the typical move towards a possible ending, again indicating that conversationalists always have to negotiate around the 'turn-taking' problem (see p. 213).

Let's turn to a second example.

Context: Here, the interview has continued for around 45 minutes, and earlier the interviewer (Tanya) had suggested to the interviewee (Amy) that she summarise her views. As the talk proceeds, Tanya asks one additional question about differences between types of friends.

Extract 11.8: Second example of a formulation (taken from an un-transcribed interview in the original data corpus).

```
1   TAN:  and d'you do you feel that you get
2         (1.2)
3   TAN:  different things from your different groups of friends so your
4         university friends and then your
5         (0.7)
6   TAN:  friends from ho::me=
7   AMY:  =a few (.) think so
8         (0.6)
9   AMY:  there's always the old friends at home (0.8) so they come comfort
10        xxxxx so you can go back and you notice (0.7) shall I watch t v
11        or xxx (0.2) little good Chinese at lilk you know (0.7) just little things 1
12        that you take for granted at home but >when your over here<
13        that you really miss (.) °but° (0.2) get to do it all at home with them
14        whereas here
15        (0.5)
16  AMY:  its all about going out and doing ↑new things
17        (0.3)
18  TAN:  mmhmm=
19  AMY:  =so its:: ↑brilliant lets go for it=
20  TAN:  =yea (.)hmm[hm hm hm]
21  AMY:             [°its all good°]
22        (0.5)
23  TAN:  .hh excellent okay
24        (0.4)
25  TAN:  thank you very ↑much:::[I'll have to] stop recording now before it
26        stops itself [anyway ha ha]
27  AMY:               [no problem]          [yea he hey]
28        (0.7)              (both participants move from chairs)
29  TAN:  an I'm sorry about the em
30        (0.7)              (interviewer speaking from other side of the room)
31  TAN:  interruptions with that tap[e I'll make sure] that it (.) it doesn't do
32        that again
33  AMY:                             [that's okay]
34        (0.5)
35  AMY:  it's alright
36        (0.3)
37  TAN:  okay so:::
```

(a) How do participants produce formulations and what do they look like? In this extract we see Amy, first providing a relatively long description of some difference between friendships and then, at line 19, moving to a *formulation*. The first part of the formulation phrase seeks to encapsulate her immediately preceding description 'so it's brilliant'. In the second part, we have a comment on the summary itself along the lines of 'lets go with this one – and even comments on this description' ('it's all good'). In a sense one might say the interviewee is saying 'This is what you have asked for and the one I would like to offer you'. Notice the subtle way the *reflexive* nature of conversation works here –one short utterance serving as a commentary on what she has just said, an indication that what she has just said is the summary offered, and again 'it' itself referring to *what* has just been said – whew!!!

(b) Do formulations exhibit an 'adjacency pair' structure? Again, it would seem that the formulation as an FPP is followed immediately by an SPP, and this response (across lines 19–23) is again positive – *a confirmation*. As before we have *formulation-confirmation* structure.

(c) What kinds of adjacency pairs are used to end a conversation? Notice in this extract, the sophisticated way the confirmation we've just identified is immediately linked (in line 23) with a typical 'pre-closing' okay. However, here – and before the interviewee has an opportunity to respond – the interviewer pre-empts an immediate move towards a two-part closing and instead produces an *offer–acceptance* at line 25. Notice the interviewer producing thanks with considerable emphasis [not just 'thank you' but thank you very much, with rising intonation and stress on 'much'] and as Amy produces an acceptance (no problem) the interviewer continues talking, now indicating quite specifically what the 'thank-you is' designed for (she explicitly refers to the recording). This is the kind of thing conversation analysts are referring to when they say analysis should be 'participant-oriented' – is there evidence in the interaction itself which indicates their orientation as to what the analyst (you) might claim is important? It is this kind of fine-grained analysis on the detail of what happens and when it happens that makes CA stand out from other qualitative methods.

In passing we note that immediately afterwards, we have two adjacency pairs – both times an *apology* followed by an *acceptance* of the apology (lines 29–31). First, 'I'm sorry about the interruptions – that's okay, then 'It won't happen again – it's alright'. You can now begin to get a sense of how endemic structural orderliness is in talk, even though initially conversations might appear rather vague and undifferentiated.

? | # 11.9 Where are we now?

So, up to this point we can say:
1. Conversation Analysis is fundamentally focused on the structures that we find in conversations.
2. The fine-grained analysis reveals how subtle conversational practices are, and that people are very skilled in producing such methodic activities.
3. When we begin to examine extract examples of a particular structure, such as formulations, we can see quite clearly how people orient towards their production and recognition.

Let us turn to one last example from the data set.

Context: The extract begins just following a request by the interviewer for a few summary comments.

Extract 11.9:   Third example of a formulation (Int. 5; lines 2896–2929)

```
1   TAN:   yeah
2          (.)
3   DEB:   you're back like y you know yr || | (0.7) like you're six again
4                 ha h[a ha ha ha xxx xxx s]tupid thi(h)[ngs]
5   TAN:                [ha ha ha ha ha]
6   TAN:                [.hhh] ye(h)ah=
7   DEB:   =ha ha.hhh=
8   TAN:   =feeling comfortable enough to do that with somebod[y]
9   DEB:                                        [de]finit[ely yeah f] that's
10  TAN:                                              [xxx important]
11  DEB:   another one yeah feeling really comfortable in someone's [compan]↑y
12  TAN:                                                        [ye:a:h]
13         (0.2)
14  DEB:   yeah
15         (1.4)
16  DEB:   that would be yeah a °friendship to me°
17         (0.7)
18  TAN:   [okay]
19  DEB:   [°ha ha ha°]
20         (0.3)
21  TAN:   brilliant
22         (0.3)
23  DEB:   °ha ha°=
24  TAN:   =that's [great thank] ↑YOU YEAH that's it=
25  DEB:           [that done?]
26  DEB:   =°ha ha°=
27  TAN:   =is that alri:ght?=
28  DEB:   =↑yeah that's brilliant=
29  TAN:   =we're just gonna stop >sorry I had to look at my<
30         (0.2)
31  TAN:   >phone< I felt really r[u:de] then
32  DEB:             [I feel] dead
33                        *RECORDING ENDS*
```

(a) How do participants produce formulations and what do they look like? After a lengthy summary of what friendship means, Deborah produces a *formulation* at line 16. Notice here, 'that' refers to everything she has just said in response to the interviewer's most recent question. But it might also be noteworthy that part of her

formulation is spoken in a noticeably quiet manner. This might indicate uncertainty about what she has just said.

(b) Do formulations exhibit an 'adjacency pair' structure? Here we see, between lines 18 and 21, that the interviewer *confirms* the formulation – and it would seem very positive (okay, brilliant). However, again we seem to have indications of some kind of interactional trouble. Notice at lines 25 and 27, Deborah seems not to be responding to the interviewer's confirmations in a way that makes clear some orientation to agreement.

(c) What kinds of adjacency pairs are used to end a conversation? This brief analysis above, highlighting potential interactional trouble between participants, may underpin what we observe at line 27, when following an earlier 'pre-closing' offer (line 24 'Yeah, that' it), Tanya now produces a specific *'question–answer'* adjacency pair structure at lines 27–28 asking for clarification over whether it is now 'alright' to move.

Writing up the analysis

You will have noticed that doing the analysis and writing it up really go hand in hand and this would be taken into account when writing up your final report. This example analysis focused simply on the question, 'how do people end an interview'? An essential feature of CA is that it is concerned first and foremost with 'members methods', that is, how people themselves use resources in service of their everyday sense-making practices. The resources people call upon in this instance were of at least two types: formulations and adjacency pair structures. Whilst a more complete analysis would have considered a larger number of examples, our analysis has provided some key information about formulations:

- They can be short or longer utterances and can take many forms.
- They highlight the reflexive nature of conversation as action: we saw that 'doing formulating' is equal to do the formulation of 'this conversation' as what we are doing or have just done, as it is happening.
- The sequential structure they exhibit is the 'adjacency-pair' – people produce and respond to them in two-part formats.

But how do formulations actually help people solve the 'turn-taking' problem implicit in producing a successful ending of a conversation?

Formulations do indeed sum things up. The business of ending a conversation doesn't normally happen smoothly unless participants indicate to each other – well, that's the topic (of the conversation) finished.

Formulations also serve to indicate 'cumulative understandings'. People treat the successful production of formulation–confirmation pairs as indications of understandings. In these extracts, this involves displaying an 'understanding' that now the interview is complete. Notice the way the pre-closing items always followed on from these final-formulations.

Summary points

As with the other methods in this book, Conversation Analysis (CA) is becoming one of the more frequently used qualitative methods in psychology. We need to be aware, however, what form of analysis this is, and why it is slightly different from other methods such as Interpretative Phenomenonological Analysis, Grounded Theory, and Discourse Analysis (particulary Foucauldian Discourse Analysis – see Chapter 8).

1. First and foremost the emphasis is on *structures* and procedures in the conversation. CA does not necessarily focus on the content of the talk. Remember what is central is the methods (these are the ways and means people use to produce 'talk-in-interaction') people use to make sense of their social world *as* they are producing it.
2. CA is both cautious and careful about the dangers of over-interpretation when studying human behaviour. A CA researcher approaches the task of transcription and analysis with 'unmotivated attention'. He/she is simply asking the questions: 'What do we have here and what particular patterns can we identify? What do people themselves do when engaged in talk with one another?'
3. The empirical focus of CA – the attention to the fine-detail of interaction – is analytically sharpened by the complementary notion of 'participant-orientation'. A conversation analyst cannot simply say – oh, look this is what this person is doing/feeling/thinking here. As we saw, whatever suggestions or arguments the analyst develops should be based on a careful 'line-by-line' sequential examination of how participants themselves treat 'what happens next'. If there is no evidence or indication for what the analyst is suggesting – that is, evidence in what people themselves say and do – then we must be very sceptical about what might be said about the interaction.
4. Conversation is not simply talk – this is why the orthography of CA is so detailed – trying to capture as much as possible about the interaction. Remember, a simple shrug of the shoulder could be a 'participant-oriented' second-pair-part to a question from somebody. We need to record, attend to, and describe as much as we can about the talk. It is not the CA researcher's task to second-guess what may or may not turn out to be significant.
5. CA is ethnomethodologically inspired. And because ethnomethodology focuses on providing a rational analysis of the structures, procedures and strategies that people themselves use, there is an enduring focus on the careful examination of *anything* that can or could be 'methodic'. CA is used in many contexts to study everything from the banal, the everyday,

the institutional and the 'extraordinary'. Hopefully, you now have a good idea of what it can bring to psychology.

11.10 Want to know more?

There are a number of more detailed yet accessible introductions to CA including:

Hutchby, I. & Woofit, R. (2008) *Conversation analysis*. Cambridge: Polity.

Ten Have, P. (2007) *Doing conversation analysis* (2nd Edn). London: Sage.

For *ethnomethodology*, there is the excellent:

Francis, D. & Hester, S. (2004). *An invitation to ethnomethodology*. London: Sage.

And not least, interested CA researchers should read the writings of Schegloff and, particularly, Harvey Sacks:

Schegloff, E. A. (2007) *Sequence organization: A primer in conversation analysis*. Cambridge: Cambridge University Press.

Sacks, H. (1992) *Lectures on conversation*. Oxford: Blackwell.

Part 4
Writing Up

12

Writing Up the Qualitative Methods Research Report

Colm Crowley

Introduction

In psychology, the most important way of communicating research findings is, of course, through the journal article and research report. You will quite likely have had a look at some examples of articles on qualitative research by now, as suggested in previous chapters. But the considerable variation in style you see in qualitative journal articles can increase your bewilderment when faced with producing your first qualitative report. In this chapter you will find specific guidance on effectively structuring and focusing your writing for a qualitative lab report.

You have, no doubt, already produced some quantitative lab reports in your research methods course. From your experience of writing up quantitative reports, you will find the modified scientific report style that we recommend here reassuringly familiar. Building on the principles and formats that are relevant to both quantitative and qualitative reports will increase your confidence, by helping you to recognize the essential elements of any research report. The basic principles of writing any scientific report boil down to clearly communicating why and how the research in question was carried out, its findings and conclusions; and conveying all this in a way that would make it possible for the readers themselves to carry out the study again (to *replicate* it), to verify its claims.

But while the overall principles of writing reports for both quantitative and qualitative projects are very similar, there are nevertheless some important differences in what is appropriate for the various sections that structure the report. The following guidelines are best thought of as tried and tested strategies for effective reporting of qualitative research, rather than as rigid prescriptions for how it should be done. Asking 'Is this right or wrong'? is therefore less useful than

'How effectively will this convey what the readers will want to know'? and 'How could it be improved further'?.

Some differences in reporting qualitative research

Elements such as Title, Introduction, Methods and Appendices have important differences in emphasis, and the traditionally separate quantitative 'Results' and 'Discussion' sections are typically replaced in qualitative reports by an *Analysis* section which combines both of these elements, followed by a *Conclusion* section. (In qualitative reports and journal articles the analysis section may be alternatively titled 'Analysis and discussion', 'Findings', or 'Findings and discussion'.)

As with quantitative research, journal articles regarding qualitative research findings vary considerably in format and style, and typically (owing to length restrictions) do not systematically set out all aspects as is expected in a report. Reports, on the other hand, are expected to be more comprehensive than journal articles because, besides being written for academic assessment, they also are often written for the funding agencies of a research project and for policy makers and other interested parties. All such 'stakeholders' will want to have much more detail and evidence.

The *Appendices*, for instance, have a great deal more work to do in a qualitative report, as they are the main source of evidence for the claims made in the *Analysis* section, and this evidence should systematically show how the findings were achieved step by step from the beginning (known as an 'audit trail'). If you are wondering how this emphasis on detail can be reconciled with the typical length restrictions on undergraduate report writing, it will reassure you to know that nothing in the Appendices is included in the word-count.

12.1 Procedure highlight

A note on your writing style: How to break 'the rules'!

In reporting qualitative research, writing using 'I' where appropriate and being reflexive are generally preferred to using the impersonal (indirect) writing style typically (but not invariably) used when reporting quantitative research. Writing in a more personal way using 'I' is congruent with *owning one's position* (see under '*Reflexivity*' below). However, some sections (particularly 'Abstract', 'Literature review' and perhaps 'Method') work better when written in the traditional, indirect style. See under the heading *The Introduction* below for some further guidance.

Include a brief statement of your intention to write in the first person, active voice (i.e., using 'I') as being appropriate for reporting qualitative research (rather than using the impersonal, indirect style of writing that you would in a quantitative research report. Cite a reference in support of this (e.g., Banister, 1994, p. 161). A statement of intention such as this is not included in qualitative journal articles, but is perhaps wise in a research report or dissertation that is being academically assessed, so as this will make it clear that your more personal writing style is deliberate (and that you know why, rather than it just being a lapse in 'accepted' academic writing style!).

The most appropriate place to put in a statement about the writing style you have adopted would be in footnote or endnote. This forewarns any readers unfamiliar with academic writing that adopts a first-person perspective.

Conventions regarding the use of tense (past/present)

All reports, qualitative and quantitative, deal with work that *was* conducted, research that *has already* taken place. Make sure that you write in this style (using the past tense) in the *Introduction* and *Method* sections. However, it is the general practice to write quantitative 'Results' and 'Discussion' sections in the present tense, as Banister (1994) notes, and so it is similarly appropriate for the corresponding *Analysis* and *Conclusion* sections of a qualitative report.

The qualitative research report

The key structure of a qualitative research report taking the form of a modified scientific report, is as follows:

- **Title**
- **Abstract**
- **Introduction**
- **Method**
- **Analysis**
- **Conclusion**
- **References**
- **Appendices**

Useful sub-sections for *Method* are: Design; Participants; Methodological theory; Method of data collection; Procedure; Ethical considerations; Analytic strategy; Reflexivity; (but generally not Materials or Apparatus). For a *Conversation Analysis report*, the Method sub-sections might be: Design; Participants, material and context; Procedure; Reflexive account of selection criteria; Transcription.

12.2 Procedure highlight

How much should I write for each section?

This question is often asked by students writing a qualitative research report. From reading one or more of the previous chapters, it will be clear that about half of the report's word count (or greater) should be given to the *Analysis* and *Conclusion* sections. Your *Introduction* will probably amount to about a quarter of the report, with the remaining words being allocated to the *Method* section. Of course, a great deal of the supporting analysis will be in the *Appendices* (e.g., the memo writing in Grounded Theory (GT) and Interpretative Phenomenological Analysis (IPA), examples of descriptive summaries in IPA, further extract examples of a conversational structure in Conversation Analysis).

The Title

Because it still tends to be an unspoken assumption in much of psychology that methodology will be quantitative, this is not usually mentioned in a title (although it can perhaps be deduced from some titles).

Likewise, it can be apparent from titles that contain words such as 'narratives', 'accounts', 'personal meanings', 'lifeworlds', 'discourses', 'views and experiences', 'social/media representations', 'social construction', 'positioning', etc. that the research reported will be qualitative.

However, it is good practice to explicitly indicate in a title that a qualitative methodology is used, as that might be of particular interest to potential readers. It also makes the task of literature searching by methodology more efficient. Inclusion of phrases such as 'a qualitative'/'a phenomenological'/'a grounded theory'/'a conversation–analytic' investigation/study/inquiry' as a subtitle (or in the main title) is regarded as helpful information. Keeping your title for any report as short as possible (whilst being informative) should be a high priority, of course.

The Abstract

Writing a succinct abstract is a very useful skill to develop. The best journal abstracts are carefully written to have only the essential information, in a format that is as accessible as possible. The abstract needs to summarise the project well. So, include the topic and focus of your research (for instance your aim – however, stating your research question(s) as well would probably be too detailed here), who and how many people participated, what was done (methods of data collection and analysis used), what was found and how it was interpreted (e.g., in a phenomenological analysis, the major themes would be given) and an indication of the conclusions drawn from the analysis, and their implications. It should be quite clear from reading the abstract that you are reporting a qualitative study.

Writing style. Your abstract can be written in the conventional passive, indirect style. There is usually not much to be gained by writing your abstract using 'I'.

The Introduction

The first section of the report should introduce the topic in the usual way recommended: by first briefly setting out its broader context, and progressively focusing more specifically (e.g., close relationships → difference between interactions and relationships → friendship → gender issues in friendship). This background to your research needs to be evidenced by published literature. You therefore need to search for and critically review the most relevant (especially the most recent) literature, so that you can sum up the current theoretical and empirical positions on your topic. Chapter 3 has useful strategies for writing critical review summaries.

Because of the word limits applying to an undergraduate lab report, you will need to be selective in your discussion of the literature (it is usually possible to be more comprehensive in final year undergraduate dissertations and postgraduate literature reviews). In addition to 'funnelling' from the broader context to the particular considerations most relevant to your research, two further principles can guide you in framing your research within the existing literature: constructing an argument (or 'rationale') for your research; and prioritising a discussion of existing qualitative (rather than quantitative) literature on the topic. As each of these principles reinforces the others, you should find yourself interweaving them in your writing.

The rationale entails making it clear why you have selected the particular issue you have chosen for your research – for example, a gap in the literature indicating that the issue remains unstudied, or, if it has been researched, that there are problems with these existing studies. Your rationale should also make a case for the appropriateness of the theoretical approach and methodology you have used. As we have discussed elsewhere, the nature of the question you want to ask will determine the appropriate methodology to use. There are arguments as to the methodological limitations of quantitative research in general for many topics in psychology, so if relevant to your topic, they could be included. For example, see Miell & Dallos (1996) for a discussion of the problems of research on close relationships. In published articles on their qualitative research, psychologists in the past have often included in their introduction section an extensive defence of their use of qualitative (rather than quantitative) methodology. Students often rightly point out that this sort of justification does not appear in articles featuring quantitative methodology. Recently, and as qualitative research has established itself in the discipline, the attitude among qualitative psychologists is changing. Willig & Stainton-Rogers (2008, p. 5) comment that 'there should be no more need to justify the use of qualitative methods than there is to justify the use of quantitative methods'.

Your literature review, while giving some background on the literature relevant to the topic, should ideally identify which studies reviewed are quantitative and which are qualitative. When your review focuses in more depth on qualitative findings in the literature, it will assist you in your subsequent discussion of your analysis (see also the points made in Chapter 3). So you should make an effort to search specifically for relevant qualitative literature. Remember that the PsycINFO database provides a search filter for methodology (qualitative or quantitative). But some caution is needed, as the 'finds' for a qualitative-filtered search will typically display relatively few substantially qualitative studies, mixed in among a majority that are essentially quantitative. For instance, having just one open-ended question in an otherwise highly-structured, quantitatively analysed questionnaire might mean that what appears to be a qualitative study is in large part a quantitative search result.

Summary of rationale, aim and research questions

Your argument throughout your review of the literature should progressively indicate why you were justified in doing your chosen piece of research (including why a qualitative approach was appropriate). This rationale for your research should now be summarised, so as to lead the reader logically to the aim of your research. Your research aim should be explicitly stated – for example, 'the aim of my research was ...' or 'the present research therefore aimed to ...'. Typically, in reporting qualitative research a fairly broad aim is stated (in some way it corresponds to the stated purpose in a quantitative report). For example, '... to gain a greater understanding of the personal meanings of xxx to xxx' or '... to gain a greater understanding of the lifeworlds of xxx'. Tip: the stated aim of a piece of qualitative research could echo the report's title somewhat (in a reworded form), because it is likely that the scope of both (the focus and what is specified) would coincide.

Then add one or more specific research question(s) that would logically follow from this aim. The research questions carry great importance in qualitative investigations, as hypotheses are very rarely used (this is because most qualitative psychology emphasises exploration rather than testing). Indeed, in most qualitative studies, hypotheses would be nonsensical, in view of underlying research design issues. So, in this spirit, care should be taken to frame the research questions in your qualitative study as exploratory, rather than as checking for causal explanations (for a critical discussion of the notion of causality, see Guba & Lincoln, 1985, pp. 129–159).

In qualitative research it is good practice to have a fairly comprehensive, broadly stated *initial research question* to begin with, and to add other, more focused research questions as the research progresses. This is an aspect of having a flexible rather than fixed design. The research questions need to relate well to the research aim. For example 'My initial research question was: What are the views and experiences of the participants regarding xxx? A further research question was: What gender (cultural?) differences are there in the views and experiences of participants'? Note that qualitative research questions should be open rather than closed, asking about processes and explanations rather than answers that could be 'yes' or 'no'. So 'how'? and 'what'? are more useful words in framing qualitative research questions than 'do'?, 'is'? and 'are'? (see 'The research question' in Willig, 2008, pp. 20–22).

Chapter 3 has strategies for ensuring that your research questions are sensible, appropriate and linked to the background literature where possible. The research question/s usually end the introduction most effectively, as they logically lead to the methodological issues presented in the next section.

Writing style. You can write your *Introduction* in a combination of the personal, active style and conventional passive and indirect style. It would be most appropriate to use the traditional indirect style for the literature review, including its associated argument and rationale. However, it is appropriate and entirely sensible to set out your aim and research questions using 'my' and 'I'. As was indicated earlier, it is advisable to write in the past tense, given that you are reporting and summarising already-existing research – for example 'One theme that has emerged from the existing literature is the nature of personal friendships through internet communication'.

The Method

As noted earlier, journal articles are often looser in structure than research reports, and this may be particularly evident when it comes to writing up the methods used. (In some journal articles reporting qualitative findings, the methods are barely explained – perhaps presuming that journal article readers will often be researchers in the same topic, and often therefore familiar with the prevailing methods.) However, there are increasing expectations that methods should be explicit and detailed, and this is especially so with reports, dissertations, etc. In an undergraduate report, having sub-sections in the *Method* section aids clarity and helps to ensure that all the important methodological issues are covered. Strategic use of the *Appendices*, when you need to have additional material about a particular *Method* sub-section, can help you to balance the need for detailed information with the constraints of your overall word limit.

Procedure highlight: Method sub-sections 12.3

We recommend the following sub-sections for a typical lab report: Design; Participants; Methodological theory; Method of data collection; Procedure; Ethical considerations; Analytic strategy; Reflexivity; (but generally *not* Materials or Apparatus).

(Continued)

> # 12.3 continued
>
> However, some designs and methodologies may warrant different sub-sections – for example, in a Conversation Analysis report, Method sub-sections might be: Design; Participants, material and context; Procedure; Extract selection; Transcription.
>
> In research on media representations there would be no participants. In some research designs, certain *materials* might indeed be used (e.g., as a discussion stimulus for an interview or a focus group). The order of your sub-sections can also be varied somewhat. It is therefore advisable to discuss the suitability and order of your sub-sections with your lecturer or supervisor, bearing in mind that readers need to be able to clearly follow what you did throughout the research process.

> # 12.4 Procedure highlight: Appropriate referencing
>
> It is important to support your *Method* section with appropriate referencing. There is an abundance of methodological literature that is highly relevant to the various sub-sections, yet it is often overlooked in undergraduate research reports (only the *Procedure* sub-section can be written without needing supporting references).

Method sub-sections

The *Design* sub-section can be brief. However, just as it would be poor practice to state only that 'a quantitative design was used', it is equally poor practice to write vaguely that 'a qualitative design was used'. The main point to be made is about your design being flexible rather than fixed (see Robson, 2002). The flexible nature of the design (in contrast to the pre-specified characteristic of quantitative designs) means that it is both legitimate and good to revise the focus of the research as it progresses, in the light of emerging findings. This has important implications for the development of research questions: it is considered good practice to develop further research questions during data analysis, for instance. The next point to be made regarding your design is which particular methodology/ies were selected as being appropriate (echoing your rationale in the *Introduction* section). For example, 'a phenomenological methodology using in-depth individual interview methods'.

The *Participants* sub-section should describe the characteristics of the population investigated and the strategy for the recruitment and selection of the research participants. A 'sample of convenience' may well be selected in student research. 'Purposive sampling' (seeking participants with particular characteristics) might be an advantage. Purposive sampling might either have the aim of achieving a homogenous sample (prioritising similarity), a comparative sample (prioritising difference, as in cross-cultural studies), or a diverse sample (maximising differences to gain multiple perspectives). 'Snowball sampling' is a particular purposive sampling strategy where you begin by finding one person to interview for a particular reason, and then continue recruitment by asking them if they would introduce you to somebody else they know with similar circumstances to themselves (the same reason why you interviewed the first person), and so on. This can be useful when recruiting a 'hard to reach' type of population.

The type of sampling should be discussed and agreed with your lecturer or supervisor because of the implications for your analysis and the sorts of conclusions it might (or might not) be possible to draw. It is important that your sample is appropriate for your methodology, aim(s) and research questions.

The number of participants should be given, as well as basic information about their ages and genders and perhaps any culturally distinguishing features relevant to the research. However, it is important to remember the ethical need to preserve anonymity. Giving biographical details (increasingly popular in qualitative articles) can particularly compromise the anonymity of participants recruited among fellow students, as their identities could be more easily recognisable to academic staff and to their peers.

Critical issue: Recruitment of participants 12.5

Who to recruit: Friends, acquaintances or strangers?

In contrast to quantitative research, it is not unusual in qualitative research to recruit acquaintances or even friends as participants; it can be an advantage in gaining the trust needed for the exploration of some topics. There are associated disadvantages too of course. For instance, if your research topic is friendship and you were to interview your own friends, asking them about their best friends or degrees of closeness could become awkward or embarrassing since you would be implicated. Similarly, potential accounts of negative aspects are likely to be somewhat self-censored to avoid offending you. Another disadvantage of interviewing people you know very well relates to how much they assume you already know. If they speak to you as they normally would, much that you should already know will only be alluded to (leaving many gaps in the account). If, instead (perhaps to compensate for this familiarity), your friends respond to you more formally in your role as interviewer (and you are jointly complicit in pretending that

(Continued)

12.5 continued

you are not friends who already know a lot about each other) something else happens: a somewhat unreal game is being enacted – rather like children play 'doctors and nurses'. In balancing these considerations against the barriers to be surmounted when interviewing strangers (particularly on highly personal topics, when gaining their trust and willingness to talk frankly is crucial for the quality of the outcome), the strategy of interviewing people who are acquaintances (perhaps friends of friends) can be an attractive compromise.

Bearing in mind such complications and tricky decisions, you will need to get your lecturer's or supervisor's agreement on the appropriateness of your proposed participants (based on the nature of your relationships with them and your research topic). This will also need to be made clear in order to gain ethical approval.

12.6 Procedure highlight: Referring to your participants

Care should be taken to ensure that appropriate terms are used. It is no longer considered acceptable practice to use the formerly preferred term 'subjects' (which nevertheless still appears in some books and journal articles). The term 'participants' is nowadays preferred and recommended by the British Psychological Society. In some forms of qualitative research (such as co-operative enquiry and participative action research) the participants are considered to be 'co-researchers', so they are referred to as such.

Using existing data

If you use data that you yourself did not collect (e.g., interviews from the data set for this book) then you should make that point clear, and, of course, also include any information about the participants that is available to you (e.g., see Chapter 7).

The *Methodological theory* might be Grounded Theory, Conversation Analysis, Phenomenology, or Discursive Psychology, for example. One of these fairly broad categories of qualitative methodology will have no doubt been mentioned in your *Design* sub-section. However, each tends to have some differing forms, with each form having its advocates and critics in the literature. So the task of this sub-section is to identify which particular form of the overall methodology you are using (and perhaps why you consider this to be more appropriate than alternative forms), and to outline its distinguishing features (supported by referencing). Often the sub-section is best titled with the name of the specific theory selected, for example, 'Interpretative Phenomenological Analysis' (IPA) rather than just 'Methodological theory'. Remember that some methodological theories are concerned primarily with the analysis used (e.g., IPA). On the other hand, many methodological theories have greater implications for the research process as a whole (e.g., Grounded Theory; the ethnomethodological background of Conversation Analysis)

The *Method of data collection* sub-section needs to give explicit details of the type of data collection used (see Chapter 4) and consider its advantages and limitations. For studies that collected interview data (and those using this book's data set), this sub-section could perhaps be more specifically titled 'Interview methods'. In this example, the sub-section would note the different types of interview and make a case for the particular appropriateness of the variety selected for the present research (unstructured? structured? semi-structured? Or, standardised/unstandardised?). If semi-structured or structured/standardised, the procedure for the development of the interview schedule must be described, and the interview schedule must be included (usually as an appendix because of space constraints). Sometimes, in more traditional publications, interview schedules or guidelines might be detailed in a *Materials* sub-section. Whichever method of data collection has been used, it will be important to describe and discuss it clearly in this sub-section, and its title can be varied appropriately.

The *Procedure* sub-section should be succinct and not overly long (a common failing). It needs to describe what you told your participants (verbally and in information sheets) and what you required them to do. For example, if using interview methodology, this sub-section could state the type of location used, the typical length of interviews (or range and average length), whether recorded (on digital audio file, audio tape or video?), how consent was obtained, how the interview schedule was used (prompts and probes, or more formal questions? in fixed or varying order?), how debriefing was done, whether perhaps it was a one-off or a two-stage interview and whether participants were invited to give feedback on the analysis of their material. This is also the place to note any unexpected occurrences, difficulties and perhaps changes you made to the procedures as a consequence. Bearing in mind that the procedure sub-section should be no more than a summary, you might want to strategically place any supplementary details in appendices.

For all psychology students in the UK, the ethical guidelines of the British Psychological Society are a key reference for the *Ethical considerations* sub-section, and an acknowledgement that the research adheres to these guidelines would not be wasted. Crucial aspects to note are your provisions for informed consent, absence of deception, right to withdraw, debriefing and maintaining confidentiality (particularly by means of anonymity ensured by using pseudonyms and, where advisable, changing certain features, such as place names, which might make participants potentially identifiable to those who might know them). It is rare for research not to have any ethical implications (see the points raised in Chapter 6). Even if data has been provided for your project, you should still note what information you have regarding ethics for the data set.

It is important to convey in the *Analytic strategy* sub-section how you carried out a carefully considered analysis, according to procedures and protocols appropriate for the specific methodology you employed. Beginning with the approach taken to transcription and the conventions used for it, for example 'as detailed by Forrester (2010)', go on to briefly explain the steps carried out in data analysis. For example, 'themes were identified in the following way ... using procedures for IPA analysis describe by Shaw (2010)'. This sub-section will necessarily relate to the methodological theory described in the earlier sub-section , but be careful to avoid any overlap.

Reflexivity is increasingly considered to be a criterion for the evaluation of qualitative research. One could say that it is a qualitative parallel to quantitative considerations of validity and reliability, and is seen to be a means of increasing the *transparency* of the research process. Providing a reflexive or personal statement is a means of *owning one's position* as a researcher (in contrast to the positivist ideal of being a non-involved, dispassionate observer). The *Reflexivity* sub-section should therefore demonstrate an understanding of the role of reflexivity in qualitative research (supported with references such as Finlay & Gough, 2003, and Alvesson & Sköldberg, 2009), and explain the procedures for it in your research. For example, your systematic keeping of memos regarding your steps of data collection and analysis should be reflexive and not just descriptive; when offered as evidence in appendices and referred to in appropriate sections of the report these would constitute an important illustration of your reflexivity. Providing a 'personal statement', or 'reflexive account' is also to be recommended and you could indicate here where this can be found in your report (most likely as one of your appendices, bearing in mind your report's word-count restrictions).

Writing style. As with the *Introduction*, you can write your *Method* section in a combination of the personal, active style and conventional passive and indirect style. It would be most appropriate to use the traditional indirect style for most sub-sections. Past tense is expected.

The Analysis

In qualitative research reports, the section following *Method* is more likely to be called *Analysis* (or '*Findings*') than 'Results'. It embodies the most striking presentational differences between quantitative and qualitative research reports. Because this section needs to contain adequate discussion, it will aid structural clarity if the last section of the report is titled *Conclusion,* rather than using the title 'Discussion' more typically used in quantitative reports. The most essential thing about the *Analysis* section is that it needs to be structured to convey clearly to the reader the exact kind of analysis you carried out and what your consequent research findings are. For any readers less familiar with the type of analysis you used, this is particularly important.

If you undertook a Conversation Analysis (CA), then your *Analysis* section could be organised around the structures you decided to compare, as is the reporting convention in CA journals. Chapter 11 illustrates how the analysis focused around how 'formulations' work in conversations. This structure formed the backbone of the analysis.

When conducting a discourse analysis using either Discursive Psychology (DP) or Foucauldian Discourse Analysis (FDA), how you would then organise the analysis would depend in part on the specific questions you had asked – the analysis will reflect the particular focus of the research. Chapter 8 shows how the writing up of the analysis depends very much on the analytic focus of the methodology: in DP it was organised around how accountability about friendship operated, with attention to the detail of the transcript; in FDA, transcript extracts were used to articulate the manner in which friendship relationships themselves constitute a socially constructed friendship discourse.

For thematic forms of analysis such as Grounded Theory and IPA, this section's structure might most usefully be organised according to your categories and codes, or master themes and sub-themes (i.e., the outcome of your coding). Use these meaning clusters to form sub-sections (using sub-headings for clear presentation). The following writing up issues are illustrated by examples of reporting a thematic-type analysis.

The *Analysis* section needs to begin with a summary overview. This could say how many master themes and sub themes etc. were identified in the analysis and name at least the master themes.

Overall length of the Analysis section

When calculating your word-count in a student research report, it is a widespread academic convention to exclude from the final word-count all data excerpts (such as quotations from participant interviews) used in the *Analysis* section,[1] as they are regarded as having a parallel function to that of tables and diagrams in quantitative reports. If this were not allowed, it would be difficult to include adequate evidence from the data and to discuss it sufficiently within the confines of the word limit. One issue to resolve individually, as you see fit, is whether you can realistically hope to include and discuss quotes from every one of your sub-themes, or whether the space constraints of the report suggest that a strategy of showing the structure of your overall analysis in diagram or table form, while noting that you will focus on discussing only selected important themes (and any unexpected themes?). Perhaps your research questions could help to shape a more selective *Analysis* section? An explanation of your strategy for presenting your analysis, and a justification for your approach, would be suitable topics for the summary overview that begins your *Analysis* section.

---

1 Check the regulations regarding this in your own Department with your lecturer or supervisor

=

12.7 Procedure highlight: Where to put figures or tables

As in quantitative report writing, it is not considered good practice to place a an illustrative figure or table at the very start of a section, without at least a paragraph of text preceding it. For more immediate visual impact, some prefer to follow the introductory text with Venn diagrams (e.g., the circle diagrams showing sets of thematic clusters in Chapter 10), or perhaps the tree-and-branch type diagrams of Grounded Theory codes and categories (see Chapter 9). Set diagrams can usefully depict sub-themes that you might want to assign to more than one master theme, by showing such areas of intersection in overlapping diagrams. It might be useful to have a matrix table as well, to display patterns of distribution.

You could go on to introduce each main theme selected for presentation, by describing or defining it and naming the sub-themes that were clustered to form it. Even if you are not presenting some of the main themes (a matter best discussed with your lecturer or supervisor) you might also need to decide whether you have the word count available to present and discuss material for every sub-theme of your featured main themes, or just selected sub-themes that you consider to be the most important or relevant.

Each sub-section could perhaps include a definition or description of the sub-theme, a little about its significance in the research and some interview quotations to illustrate it (labelled by which participant/s and line/s). The inclusion of ample quotations is crucial (see 'Grounding in examples' in Elliott, Fischer & Rennie, 1999, p. 222), and to avoid a fragmentation effect they should be long enough to adequately convey the context (and where possible some element of narrative).

So be confident about including longer quotations. Presenting adequate material in such a way that readers can 'judge it to have represented accurately the subject matter or to have clarified or expanded their appreciation and understanding of it' helps in creating *resonance* (see 'Resonating with readers' in Elliott, Fischer & Rennie, 1999, p. 224).

=

12.8 Procedure highlight: Layout of data quotations

In quoting direct speech from interviews, use paragraph indentation rather than quotation marks. And why not use single line spacing for these data excerpts rather than double? As noted above, do state who is quoted and the line numbers included (e.g., Shazia 454–462). If you are rigorously following the American Psychological Association's report writing style and indenting the first line of each paragraph in the American style, the overall layout will probably look clearer if you then double indent your interview quotation blocks.

When presenting the quotations providing examples of the themes, you will need to introduce and discuss them to some extent. This can be fairly concisely done, and you will be able to consider their meanings comparatively in the light of other views expressed in the same theme, for example, similarities and differences between participants' views and contradictions evident in a particular participant's views. You can also consider them in the light of your research questions or use them to generate further research questions.

As well as this sort of contextual discussion (considered to be an element of the analysis in qualitative research) it is also necessary to consider the analysis in the light of the literature reviewed in the *Introduction* section. It is more efficient to do this as you go along (theme by theme) than to put it in a subsequent 'Discussion' section, which would necessitate considerable repetition of the findings to make sense. The idea is to bring the literature (as reviewed in your *Introduction*) to bear on the specific evidence you are presenting from the collected data, 'weaving' appropriate theory and reported research findings into your analysis of the data (remember, no new literature should be introduced here).

Writing style. A combination of the personal, active style using 'I' and 'my' and the conventional passive and indirect style can be appropriately used. Analysis sections tend to be written more in the present tense.

The Conclusion

More-general issues still need to be discussed by way of conclusion – for example, overall conclusions (interpretation of findings) from your *Analysis* section (drawing out the main points in the light of your aim and research questions). This concluding discussion should relate your *overall* findings to the literature reviewed, whereas in the preceding *Analysis* section you would have discussed more particular issues in the light of the literature.

Other matters for this final *Conclusion* section are strengths and limitations of the research (a critical evaluation), implications of the research, suggested directions for future research and some personal reflection. Base your arguments on evidence however, not speculation. A well-developed and thoughtful *Conclusion* section can make all the difference in gaining the best grade for your report.

Writing style. A combination of the personal, active style using 'I' and 'my' and the conventional passive and indirect style can be used as you see fit. Conclusion sections tend to be written more in the present tense ('the findings suggest') although some elements will be more suitably described using the past tense ('my aim was').

The References

Referencing for a qualitative report should follow the usual American Psychological Association (APA) conventions for any psychology report, dissertation or journal article (or, alternatively, the equivalent conventions specified by your Department, such as the Harvard system). Take care to use the appropriate formats and remember to place your reference list immediately before your appendices in the report.

The Appendices

What to include?

Unlike quantitative reports, when qualitative reports are being academically assessed, the quality, organisation and comprehensiveness of your appendices can play a much greater part in the overall grade achieved, as they provide visible evidence of the analytic process and of how much work you have put into it. The *Appendices* are therefore not just an 'add-on', but a key element of the report. And, not being included in your word count, it makes good sense to make the most of them, as there are normally no size constraints on appendices.

Remember that to profit fully from your appendix material, you need to refer the reader to the relevant parts of it, wherever appropriate throughout your report. Nobody is obliged to look at an appendix item that you have not referred to, and some markers of student work will take that quite literally. Organising the appendices well is very important, so that the reader can navigate quickly from the report, around the appendices, and straight back to reading the report again. It is therefore good practice to include a contents specifying page numbers at the beginning of your appendices.

12.9 Procedure highlight: Checklist for Appendices

1. Ethics paperwork, including example of consent form, etc.
2. Recruiting information, including adverts and recuitment emails
3. Notes about specific material or procedures involved in the research
4. At least one fully coded interview transcript (in GT and IPA)
5. Extract lists (in CA and DA)
6. Comprehensive lists of initial and revised codes, theme or category lists (in GT and IPA)
7. Any theme or category descriptions or definitions not already given in the body of the report
8. Analytic memos
9. Reflective diary (IPA)
10. Any diagrams and tables not included in the body of the report (e.g., diagrams of the progressive stages of theme development)
11. Personal reflexive statement
12. Any further material you consider relevant

While it is sometimes considered sufficient to include just one sample full interview transcript,[2] you are nevertheless normally required to provide electronic copies of all interview transcripts on an approved medium such as a CD. You are generally *not* required to include audio or video recordings of interviews in your appendices; however, you may be required to present them to your supervisor or examiners if requested.

For best presentation, any material originally handwritten should ideally be typed for the appendices (*except for* your initial handwritten coding in the interview transcript margins, which is important evidence for the marker of that stage of your 'work in progress').

Summary points

It will be clear by now that a lab report for a qualitative methods study can, for the most part, be written quite similarly to those you would write for quantitative studies. These summary points will help you with your final write up:

1. The major difference from quantitative reports is with what would traditionally be called the 'Results' section. With qualitative reports this becomes an *Analysis* section that includes discussion, which will summarise and illustrate your analysis and at the same time discusses what it means for the research questions you set out to answer (usually with some reference to the relevant literature).
2. The writing style of a qualitative report is generally the same as that of quantitative reports and other academic work (i.e., written in an indirect style and reporting in the past tense). However, it is advisable to strategically use the first person active voice where appropriate (e.g., using 'I' when discussing reflexivity), and to make your reasons for this explicit to the reader.
3. It is important to describe the particular methodology you used and to indicate that the appropriate procedures for that method were employed.
4. The *Analysis* section of your report will also reflect the kind of qualitative method you used – both in terms of how this section might be structured and how the content is described and discussed.
5. Making good use of the *Appendices* is a major element of a qualitative report. When somebody wishes to check the basis for your arguments and claims concerning your analysis, these need to be supported with detailed evidence from your appendices. So a substantial amount of detail should be included, and the appendices should be clearly organised so that readers can find their way around them easily.

---

2 Check the expectations regarding this in your own Department with your lecturer or supervisor.

12.10 Want to know more?

If you would like to read more about writing up qualitative research and some of the debates underlying it, the following are good sources of further information.

Elliott, R., Fischer, C. T. & Rennie, D. L. (1999) Evolving guidelines for publication of qualitative research studies in psychology and related fields. *British Journal of Clinical Psychology*, **38**, 215–229.

Robson, C. (2007) How to do a research project: A guide for undergraduate students. Oxford: Blackwell.

Willig, C. & Stainton-Rogers, W. (2008) Introduction. In C. Willig & W. Stainton-Rogers (Eds), *The Sage handbook of qualitative research in psychology* (pp. 1–12). London: Sage.

References

Abell, J. & Stokoe, E. (2001) Broadcasting the royal role: Constructing culturally situated identities in the Princess Diana *Panorama* interview. *British Journal of Social Psychology,* **40**, 417–435.

Alvesson, M. & Sköldberg, K. (2009) *Reflexive methodology: New vistas for qualitative research* (2nd edition). London: Sage.

Antaki, C., Ardévol, E., Núñez, F. & Vayreda, A. (2006) 'For she who knows who she is': Managing accountability in online forum messages. *Journal of Computer-Mediated Communication,* **11**, 114–132.

Antaki, C., Billig, M. G., Edwards, D. & Potter, J. A. (2003) Discourse analysis means doing analysis: A critique of six analytic shortcomings', *Discourse Analysis Online,* 1. Available from: Discourse Analysis Online, 2003.

Antaki, C., Finlay, W. M. L. & Walton, C. (2007) The staff are your friends: Intellectually disabled identities in official discourse and interactional practice. *British Journal of Social Psychology,* **46**, 1–18.

Arksey, H. & Knight, P. (1999) *Interviewing for social scientists.* London: Sage.

Arribas-Ayllon M. & Walkerdine V. (2008) Foucauldian discourse analysis. In: C. Willig & W. Stainton-Rogers (Eds), *The Sage handbook of qualitative research in psychology* (pp. 91-108). London: Sage.

Asch, S.E. (1956) Studies of independence and conformity: I. A minority of one against a unanimous majority. *Psychological Monographs 70*(9) (whole issue, no. 416).

Ashmore, M., MacMillan, K. & Brown, S. D. (2004) It's a scream: Professional hearing and tape fetishism. *Journal of Pragmatics,* **36**, 349–374.

Ashworth, P. (2008) Conceptual foundations of qualitative psychology. In J. A. Smith (Ed.), *Qualitative psychology: A practical guide to research methods* (2nd Edn) (pp. 4–25). London: Sage.

Atkinson, J. M. & Drew, P. (1979) *Order in court.* London: Macmillan.

Atkinson, P. & Silverman, D. (1997) Kundera's Immortality: the interview society and the invention of self. *Qualitative Inquiry,* **3**, 304–325.

Bampton, R. & Cowton, C. J. (2002) The e-interview. *Forum: Qualitative Social Research,* **3**. Accessed online 18th June 2008 from http://217.160.35.246/fqs-texte/2-02/2-02bamp-toncowton-e.htm

Banister, P. (1994) Report writing. In P. Banister, E. Burman, I. Parker, M. Taylor & C. Tindall (Eds), *Qualitative psychology: A research guide* (pp. 160–179). Buckingham: Open University Press.

Banks, M. (2007) *Using visual data in qualitative research.* London: Sage.

Barbour, R. S. & Kitzinger, J. (Eds) (1999) *Developing focus group research.* London: Sage.

Beck, L. C., Trombetta, W. L. & Share, S. (1986) Using focus group sessions before decisions are made. *North Carolina Medical Journal,* **47**, pp. 73–74.

Billig, M. (1990) Rhetoric of social psychology. In I. Parker & J. Shotter (Eds), *Deconstructing social psychology.* London: Routledge.

Billig, M. (1995) *Banal nationalism.* London: Sage.

Billig, M. (1998) *Talking of the royal family* (2nd Edn). London: Routledge.

Billig, M. (1999) Whose terms? Whose ordinariness? Rhetoric and ideology in conversation analysis. *Discourse and Society,* **10**, 543–582.

Billig, M. (2001) Humour and hatred: The racist jokes of the Ku Klux Klan. *Discourse and Society,* **12**, 267–289.

Blumer, H. (1969) *Symbolic interactionism.* Englewood Cliffs, NJ: Prentice Hall.

Bowskill, M., Lyons, E. & Coyle, A. (2007) The rhetoric of acculturation: When integration means assimilation. *British Journal of Social Psychology,* **46**, 793–813.

Braun, V. & Clarke, V. (2006) Using thematic analysis in psychology. *Qualitative Research in Psychology,* **3**(2), 77–101.

Brewer, M. B. (2000) Research design and issues of validity. In H. T. Reis & C. M. Judd (Eds) *Handbook of research methods in social and personality psychology.* Cambridge: Cambridge University Press.

British Psychological Society (2006) *Code of ethics and conduct.* Available from: http://www.bps.org.uk/the-society/code-of-conduct/code-of-conduct_home.cfm

British Psychological Society (2007a) Guidelines for psychologists working with animals. Available from: http://www.bps.org.uk/the-society/code-of-conduct/code-of-conduct_home.cfm

British Psychological Society (2007b) *Report of the Working Party on Conducting Research on the Internet: Guidelines for ethical practice in psychological research online.* Available from: http://www.bps.org.uk/the-society/code-of-conduct/code-of-conduct_home.cfm

British Psychological Society (n.d.) *Ethical principles for conducting research with human participants.* Accessed 27th October 2008 from: <http://www.bps.org.uk/the-society/code-of-conduct/ethical-principles-for-conducting-research-with-human-participants.cfm#principles>

Brownlow, C. & O'Dell, L. (2002) Ethical issues for qualitative research in on-line communities. *Disability and Society,* **17**, 685–694.

Bucholtz, M. (2007) Variation in transcription. *Discourse Studies,* **9**(6), 784–808.

Burgoyne, C. B. (1997) Distributive justice and rationing in the NHS: Framing effects in press coverage of a controversial decision. *Journal of Community and Applied Social Psychology,* **7**, 119–136.

Burkitt, I. (1991) *Social selves.* London: Sage.

Burr, V. (2003) *Social constructionism* (2nd Edn). London: Routledge.

Chappell, D., Eatough, V., Davies, M. N. O. & Griffiths, M. (2006) *EverQuest* – it's just a computer game right? An interpretative phenomenological analysis of online gaming addiction. *International Journal of Mental Health and Addiction,* **4**, 205–216.

Charmaz, K. (2006) *Constructing grounded theory: A practical guide through qualitative data analysis.* Thousand Oaks, CA: Sage Publications.

Christians, C. G. (2003) Ethics and politics in qualitative research. In N. Denzin & Y. Lincoln (Eds), *The landscape of qualitative research: Theories and issues.* London: Sage.

Chiu, L. & Knight, D. (1999) How useful are focus groups for obtaining the views of minority groups? In R. S. Barbour & J. Kitzinger (Eds), *Developing focus group research.* London: Sage.

Clare, L., Rowlands, J. M. & Quin, R. (2008) Collective strength: The impact of developing a shared social identity in early-stage dementia. *Dementia,* **7**, 9–30.

Clarke, A. (2005) *Situational analysis: Grounded theory after the postmodern turn.* Thousand Oaks, CA: Sage Publications.

Clayman, S. & Heritage, J. (2002) *The news interview: Journalists and public figures on the air.* Cambridge: Cambridge University Press.

Corbin, J. & Strauss, A. (2008). *Basics of qualitative research: Techniques and procedures for developing grounded theory* (3rd Edn). Thousand Oaks, CA: Sage Publications.

Cromby, J. & Nightingale D. J. (1999) 'What's wrong with social constructionism?' In Nightingale, D. J. & Cromby, J. (Eds), *Social constructionist psychology: A critical analysis of theory and practice* (pp. 1–20). Buckingham: Open University Press.

Cutcliffe, J. R., Stevenson, C., Jackson, S. & Smith, P. (2006). A modified grounded theory study of how psychiatric nurses work with suicidal people. *International Journal of Nursing Studies,* **43**(7), 791–802.

Denzin, N. K. & Lincoln, Y. S (Eds) *Handbook of qualitative research.* London: Sage.

Dickson, A., Knussen, C. & Flowers, P. (2007) Stigma and the de-legitimation experience: An interpretative analysis of people living with chronic fatigue syndrome. *Psychology and Health,* **22**(7), 851–867.

Dingwall, R. (1997) Accounts, interviews and observations. In G. Miller & R. Dingwall (Eds) *Context and method in qualitative research* (pp. 51–65). Thousand Oaks, CA: Sage.

Dixon-Woods, M., Shaw, R.L., Agarwal, S. & Smith, J. A. (2004) The problem of appraising qualitative research. *Quality and Safety in Health Care,* **13**, 223–225.

Doucet, A. & Mauthner, N. (2002) Knowing responsibly: Linking ethics, research practice and epistemology. In M. Mauthner, M. Birch, J. Jessop & T. Miller (Eds), *Ethics in qualitative research.* London: Sage.

Drew, P., Raymond, G. & Weinberg, D. (2006) *Talk and interaction in social research methods.* London: Sage.

Eatough, V. & Smith, J. A. (2006) 'I feel like a scrambled egg in my head': An idiographic case study of meaning making and anger using interpretative phenomenological analysis. *Psychology and Psychotherapy,* **79**, 115–135.

Economic and Social Research Council (2008) *Research Ethics Framework (REF).* Swindon: Environmental and Scientific Research Council.

Edley, N. (2001) Analysing masculinity: Interpretative repertoires, ideological dilemmas and subject positions. In S. Yates, M. Wetherell & S. Taylor (Eds) *Discourse as data.* London: Sage.

Edwards, D. (2005) Discursive psychology. In K. L. Fitch & R. E. Sanders (Eds) *Handbook of language and social interaction* (pp. 257–273). Mahwah, NJ: Lawrence Erlbaum.

Edwards, D. (2006) Discourse, cognition and social practices: The rich surface of language and social interaction. *Discourse Studies,* **8**, 41–49.

Edwards, D. (1997) *Discourse as cognition.* London: Sage.

Edwards, D. (1999) Emotion discourse. *Culture and Psychology,* **5**(3), 271–291.

Edwards, D. & Potter, J. (1992) *Discursive psychology.* London: Sage.

Edwards, D. & Potter, J. (1993). Language and causation: A discursive action model of description and attribution. *Psychological Review,* **100**, 23–41.

Edwards, R. & Mauthner, M. (2002) Ethics and feminist research: Theory and practice. In M. Mauthner, M. Birch, J. Jessop & T. Miller, *Ethics in qualitative research.* London: Sage.

Elliott, R., Fischer, C. T., & Rennie, D. L. (1999) Evolving guidelines for publication of qualitative research studies in psychology and related fields. *British Journal of Clinical Psychology,* **38**, 215–229.

Ess, C. (2002) Ethical decision-making and Internet research. In E.A. Buchanan (Ed). Virtual Research Ethics: Issues and controversies. Information Science Publishing: London.

Ess, C. (2007) Internet research ethics. In A. Joinson, K. McKenna, T. Postmes & U. Reips (Eds), *The Oxford handbook of Internet psychology.* Oxford: Oxford University Press.

Evans, A., Elford, J. & Wiggins, D. (2008) Using the internet for qualitative research. In C. Willig & W. Stainton-Rogers (Eds), *The Sage handbook of qualitative research in psychology* (pp. 315–333). London: Sage.

Figueroa, S. K. (2008) The grounded theory and the analysis of audio-visual texts. *International Journal of Social Research Methodology,* **11**, 1–12.

Finlay, L. & Gough, B. (Eds) (2003) *Reflexivity: A practical guide for researchers in health and social sciences*. Oxford: Blackwell Science.

Finn, G. P. T. (1997) Qualitative analysis of murals in Northern Ireland: Paramilitary justifications for political violence. In N. Hayes (Ed.), *Doing qualitative analysis in psychology* (pp. 143–178). Hove: Psychology Press.

Fleischmann, A. (2005) The hero's story and autism: Grounded theory study of websites for parents of children with autism. *Autism*, **9**, 299–316.

Flowers, P., Smith, J. A., Sheeran, P. & Beail, N. (1997) Health and romance: Understanding unprotected sex in relationships between gay men. *British Journal of Health Psychology*, **2**, 73–86.

Fontana, A. & Frey, J. H. (2000) The interview: From structured questions to negotiated text. In N. K. Denzin & Y. S. Lincoln (Eds), *Handbook of qualitative research* (pp. 645–672). London: Sage.

Forrester, M. A. (1996) *Psychology of language: A critical introduction*. London: Sage.

Forrester, M. A. (2002) *How to do conversation analysis: A brief guide*. Accessed 14th November 2008 from:<http://www.psychology.heacademy.ac.uk/Webdocs_not_nof/CAP/Supplementary_Material/CAguide.doc>

Forrester, M. A. & Koutsopoulou, G. Z. (2008) Providing resources for enhancing the teaching of qualitative methods at the undergraduate level. *Qualitative Research in Psychology*, **5**, 173–178.

Francis, D. & Hester, S. (2004) *An invitation to ethnomethodology*. London: Sage.

Freud, S. (1914) Recommendations for physicians on the psycho-analytic method of treatment. In S. J. Ellman (Ed.), *Freud's technique papers: A contemporary perspective* (Vol. first published in Zeitschrift, Bd. II., 1914. reprinted in Sammlung, Vierte – translated by Joan Riviere). Northvale, New Jersey: Jason Aronson.

Garfinkel, H. (1967) *Studies in ethnomethodology*. Englewood-Cliffs, NJ: Prentice-Hall.

Gibbs, R. (2002) *Qualitative Data Analysis: Explorations with NVivo*. Buckingham. Open University Press.

Gibson, S. (2009) The effortful citizen: Discursive social psychology and welfare reform. *Journal of Community and Applied Social Psychology*, **19**, 393–410.

Giles, D. (2003) *Media psychology*. Mahwah, NJ: Lawrence Erlbaum.

Giles, D. (2006) Constructing identities in cyberspace: The case of eating disorders. *British Journal of Social Psychology*, **45**, 463–477.

Gillies, V., Harden, A., Johnson, K., Reavey, P., Strange, V. & Willig, C. (2005) Painting pictures of embodied experience: The use of nonverbal data production for the study of embodiment. *Qualitative Research in Psychology*, **2**, 199–212.

Glaser, B. G. (1992) *Basics of grounded theory analysis: Emergence vs. forcing*. Mill Valley, CA: Sociology Press.

Glaser, B. G. & Strauss, A. (1967) *The discovery of grounded theory*. Chicago, IL: Aldine.

Glaser, B. G. & Strauss, A. L. (1965) *Awareness of dying*. Chicago, IL: Aldine.

Gleeson, K., Archer, L., Riley, S. & Frith, H. (Eds) (2005) Visual methodologies. Special issue of *Qualitative Research in Psychology*, **2**(3).

Goodings, L., Locke, A. & Brown, S. D. (2007) Social networking technology: Place and identity in mediated communities. *Journal of Community and Applied Social Psychology*, **17**, 463–476.

Gough, B. (2006) Try to be healthy, but don't forgo your masculinity: Deconstructing men's health discourse in the media. *Social Science and Medicine*, **63**, 2476–2488.

Griffin, C. (2007) Being dead and being there: Research interviews, sharing hand cream and the preference for analysing 'naturally occurring data'. *Discourse Studies*, **9**, 246–269.

Guba, E. G. & Lincoln, Y. S. (1985) *Naturalistic inquiry*. Newbury Park, CA: Sage.

Gubrium, J. F & Holstein, J. A. (Eds) (2001) *Handbook of interview research*. London: Sage.

Guimaraes, E. (2007) Feminist research practice: Using conversation analysis to explore the researcher's interaction with participants. *Feminism and Psychology*, **17**, 149–161.

Hansen, S., McHoul, A. & Rapley, M. (2003) *Beyond help: A consumers' guide to psychology*. Ross-on-Wye: PCCS Books.

Harré, R. (2006) *Key thinkers in psychology*. London: Sage.

Heath, C. (1992) The delivery and reception of diagnosis in the general-practice consultation. In P. Drew & J. Heritage (Eds), *Talk at work: Interaction in institutional settings* (pp. 235–267). Cambridge: Cambridge University Press.

Henriques, J., Hollway, W., Urwin, C., Venn, C. & Walkerdine, V. (1998) *Changing the subject: Psychology, social regulation and subjectivity* (2nd Edn). London: Routledge.

Hepburn, A. (2003). *An introduction to critical social psychology*. London: Sage.

Hepburn, A. & Wiggins, S. (2007) *Discursive research in practice: New approaches to psychology and everyday interaction*. Cambridge: Cambridge University Press.

Heritage, J. (2005) Conversation analysis and institutional talk. In K. L. Fitch & R. E. Sanders (Eds), *Handbook of language and social interaction* (pp. 103–147). Mahwah, NJ: Lawrence Erlbaum.

Heritage, J. C. & Watson, D. R. (1979) Formulations as conversational objects. In G. Psathas (Ed.), *Everyday language: Studies in ethnomethodology* (pp. 123–162). New York: Irvington.

Hoffman, E. (2007) Open-ended interviews: Power and emotional labour. *Journal of Contemporary Ethnography*, **36** (3), 318–346.

Holge-Hazelton, B. (2002) The Internet: A new field for qualitative inquiry? *Forum: Qualitative Social Research*, **3**. Accessed online 17th June 2008 from: http://www.qualitative-research.net/fqs-texte/2-02/2-02holgehazelton-e.htm

Holliday, A. (2002) *Doing and writing qualitative research*. London: Sage.

Holstein, J. A & Gubrium, J. (1995) *The active interview*. London: Sage

Hopf, C. (2004) Qualitative Interviews: an overview. In U. Flick, E. von Kardoff & I. Steinke (Eds), *A companion to qualitative research* (pp. 203–208). London: Sage.

Hughes, J. (1990) *The philosophy of social research*. Harlow: Longman.

Hutchby, I. (1996) *Confrontation talk: Arguments, asymmetries, and power on talk radio*. Mahwah, NJ: Lawrence Erlbaum.

Hutchby, I. (2005) Conversation analysis and the study of broadcast talk. In K. L. Fitch & R. E. Sanders (Eds), *Handbook of language and social interaction* (pp. 437–460). Mahwah, NJ: Lawrence Erlbaum.

Hutchby, I. & Barnett, S. (2005) Aspects of the sequential organization of mobile phone conversation. *Discourse Studies*, **7**, 147–171.

Hutchby, I., & Woofit, R. (2008) *Conversation analysis*. Cambridge: Polity Press.

Huws, J. C., Jones, R. S. P. & Ingledew, D. K. (2001) Parents of children with autism using an email group: A grounded theory study. *Journal of Health Psychology*, **6**, 569–584.

Internet Researchers (AoIR). Retrieved January 11, 2009 from: http://www.aoir.org/reports/ethics.pdf

James, N. & Busher, H. (2006) Credibility, authenticity and voice: Dilemmas in online interviewing. *Qualitative Research*, **6**, 403–420.

James, N. & Busher, H. (2007) Ethical issues in online educational research: Protecting privacy, establishing authenticity in email interviewing. *International Journal of Research and Method in Education*, **30**(1), 101–113.

Jefferson, G. (2004) Glossary of transcript symbols with an introduction. In G. Lerner (Ed.), *Conversation analysis: Studies from the first generation* (pp. 13–31). Amsterdam: John Benjamins.

Joinson, A. (2005) Internet behaviour and the design of virtual methods. In C. Hine (Ed.), *Virtual methods: Issues in social research on the Internet* (pp. 21–34). Oxford: Berg.

Joinson, A., McKenna, K., Postmes, Y. & Reips, U. (Eds) (2007) *The Oxford handbook of Internet psychology.* Oxford: Oxford University Press.

King, N. & Horrocks, C. (2010) *Interviews in qualitative research.* London: Sage.

Kitzinger, C. & Kitzinger, S. (2007) Birth trauma: Talking with women and the value of conversation analysis. *British Journal of Midwifery, 15*, 256–264.

Kivits, J. (2005) Online interviewing and the research relationship. In C. Hine (Ed.), *Virtual methods: Issues in social research on the Internet* (pp. 35–50). Oxford: Berg.

Krueger, R. A. & Casey, M. A. (2000) *Focus groups: A practical guide for applied research.* London: Sage.

Kvale, S. (1996) *Interviews: An introduction to qualitative research interviewing.* London: Sage.

Kvale, S. & Brinkmann, S. (2009) *InterViews: Learning the craft of qualitative interviewing.* London: Sage

Ladyman, J. (2002) *Understanding the philosophy of science.* London: Routledge.

Langridge, D. (2007) *Phenomenological psychology: Theory, research and method.* London: Pearson Education.

Lund, T. (2005) The qualitative–quantitative distinction: Some comments. *Scandinavian Journal of Educational Research, 449*(2), 115–132.

Lynn, N. & Lea, S. (2003) 'A phantom menace and the new Apartheid': The social construction of asylum-seekers in the United Kingdom. *Discourse and Society, 14*, 425–452.

Lynn, N. & Lea, S. J. (2005a) Through the looking glass: Considering the challenges visual methodologies raise for qualitative research. *Qualitative Research in Psychology, 2*, 213–225.

Lynn, N. & Lea, S. J. (2005b) 'Racist' graffiti: Text, context and social comment. *Visual Communication, 4*, 39–63.

Lyons, E. & Coyle, A. (2007) *Analysing qualitative data in psychology.* London: Sage.

MacInnes, J., Rosie, M., Petersoo, P., Condor, S. & Kennedy, J. (2007) Where is the British national press? *British Journal of Sociology, 58*, 185–206.

Madill, A., Jordan, A. & Shirley, C. (2000) Objectivity and reliability in qualitative analysis: Realist, contextualist and radical constructionist epistemologies. *British Journal of Psychology, 91*, 1–20.

Mann, C. & Stewart, F. (2000) *Internet communication and qualitative research: A handbook for researching online.* London: Sage.

Martin, S. P. & Robinson, J. P. (2007) The income digital divide: Trends and predictions for levels of internet use. *Social Problems, 54*, 1–22.

Matthews, J. & Cramer, E. P. (2008) Using technology to enhance qualitative research with hidden populations. *The Qualitative Report, 13*, 301–315.

McKie, L. (2002) Engagement and evaluation in qualitative enquiry. In T. May (Ed.), *Qualitative Research in Action.* London: Sage.

Miell, D. & Dallos, R. (1996) Introduction: Exploring interactions and relationships. In D. Miell & R. Dallos (Eds.), *Social interaction and personal relationships* (pp. 1–22). London: Sage.

Mitchell, C., Delange, N., Moletsane, R., Stuart, J. & Buthelezi, T. (2005) Giving a face to HIV and AIDS: On the uses of photo-voice by teachers and community health care workers working with youth in rural South Africa. *Qualitative Research in Psychology, 2*, 257–270.

Mondada, L. (2007). Commentary: Transcript variations and the indexicality of transcribing practices. *Discourse Studies, 9*(6), 809–821.

Morse, J. M., Stern, P. N., Corbin, J., Bowers, B., Charmaz, K. & Clarke, A. E. (2009) *Developing grounded theory: The second generation.* Walnut Creek, CA: Left Coast Press.

Mulveen, R. & Hepworth, J. (2006) An interpretative phenomenological analysis of participation in a pro-anorexia internet site and its relationship with disordered eating. *Journal of Health Psychology,* **11**, 283–296.

Murray, C. D. (2005) The social meanings of prosthesis use. *Journal of Health Psychology,* **10**, 425–441.

Murray, C. D. & Sixsmith, J. (2003) E-mail: A qualitative research medium for interviewing. In N. Fielding (Ed.), *Interviewing* (pp. 128–148). London: Sage.

Neisser, U. (1976) *Cognition and reality.* New York: MIT Press.

Nightingale, D. J. (1999) Bodies: Reading the body. In I. Parker & the Bolton Discourse Network (Eds), *Critical textwork: An introduction to varieties of discourse and analysis* (pp. 167–177). Buckingham: Open University Press.

O'Connor, H. & Madge, C. (2003) 'Focus groups in cyberspace': Using the Internet for qualitative research. *Qualitative Market Research: An International Journal,* **6**, 133–143.

O'Dell, L. & Brownlow, L. (2005) Media reports of links between MMR and autism: A discourse analysis. *British Journal of Learning Disabilities,* **33**, 194–199.

Ochs, E. (1979) Transcription as theory. In E. Ochs & B. B. Schieffelin (Eds), *Developmental pragmatics* (pp. 43–72). London & New York: Academic Press.

Ohara, Y. & Saft, S. (2003) Using conversation analysis to track gender ideologies in social interaction: Toward a feminist analysis of a Japanese phone-in consultation TV program. *Discourse and Society,* **14**, 153–172.

Palmer, R. E. (1969) *Hermeneutics.* Evanston, IL: Northwestern University Press.

Parker (1992) *Discourse dynamics.* London: Routledge.

Parker, I (1998) (Ed.) *Social constructionism, discourse and realism.* London: Sage.

Parker, I. (2005) *Qualitative psychology: Introducing radical research.* Maidenhead: Open University Press.

Parker, I. (1994) Discourse analysis. In P. Banister, E. Bauman, I. Parker, M. Taylor & C. Tindall (Eds), *Qualitative methods in psychology: A research guide.* Buckingham: Open University Press.

Peräkylä, A., Antaki, C., Vehviläinen, S. & Leudar, I. (Eds) (2008) *Conversation analysis and psychotherapy.* Cambridge: Cambridge University Press.

Piaget, J. (1959) *The language and thought of the child [1926].* London: Routledge & Kegan Paul.

Potter, J. (2004) Discourse analysis. In M. Hardy & A. Bryman (Eds), *Handbook of data analysis* (pp. 607–624). London: Sage.

Potter, J. & Hepburn, A. (2003) 'I'm a bit concerned' – Early actions and psychological constructions in a child protection helpline. *Research on Language and Social Interaction,* **36**, 197–240.

Potter, J. & Hepburn, A. (2005) Qualitative interviews in psychology: Problems and possibilities. *Qualitative Research in Psychology,* **2**, 281–307.

Potter, J., & Wetherell, M. (1987) *Discourse and social psychology: Beyond attitudes and behaviour.* London: Sage.

Powell, A. M., Hunt, A. & Irving, A. (1997) Evaluation of courses by whole student cohorts: A case study. *Assessment and evaluation in higher education,* **22**, 397–404.

Psathas, G. (1995) *Conversation analysis: The study of talk-in-interaction.* London & New York: Sage.

Radley, A. & Taylor, D. (2003a) Images of recovery: A photo-elicitation study on the hospital ward. *Qualitative Health Research,* **13**, 77–99.

Radley, A. & Taylor, D. (2003b) Remembering one's stay in hospital: A study in photography, recovery and forgetting. *Health: An Interdisciplinary Journal for the Study of Health, Illness and Medicine*, **7**, 129–159.

Radley, A., Hodgetts, D. & Cullen, A. (2005) Visualizing homelessness: A study in photography and estrangement. *Journal of Community and Applied Social Psychology*, **15**, 273–295.

Ramos. M. C. (1989) Some ethical implications of qualitative research. *Research in Nursing and Health*, **12**, 57–63.

Rapley, T. (2007) *Doing conversation, discourse and document analysis*. London: Sage.

Rasmussen, B., O'Connell, B., Dunning, P. & Cox, H. (2007) Young women with Type 1 Diabetes' management of turning points and transitions. *Qualitative Health Research*, **17**(3), 300–310.

Reavey, P. (Ed.) (2009) *Visual psychologies: Using and interpreting images in qualitative research*. London: Routledge.

Reavey, P. & Johnson, K. (2008) Visual approaches: Using and interpreting images. In C. Willig & W. Stainton-Rogers (Eds), *The Sage handbook of qualitative research in psychology* (pp. 296–314). London: Sage.

Riley, S. C. E. & Blackman, G. (2008) Between prohibitions: Patterns and meanings of magic mushroom use in the UK. *Substance Use and Misuse*, **43**, 55–71.

Roberts, F., & Robinson, J. D. (2004) Interobserver agreement on first-stage conversation analytic transcription. *Human Communication Research*, **30**(3), 376–410.

Robinson, K. M. (2001) Unsolicited narratives form the internet: A rich source of qualitative data. *Qualitative Health Research*, **11**, 706–714.

Robson, C. (2002) *Real world research: A resource for social scientists and practitioner–researchers* (2nd Edn). Oxford: Blackwell.

Robson, C. (2007) *How to do a research project: A guide for undergraduate students*. Oxford: Blackwell.

Rose, D., Fleischmann, P. & Wykes, T. (2004) Consumers' views of electroconvulsive therapy: A qualitative analysis. *Journal of Mental Health*, **13**, 285–293.

Rose, N. (1999). *Governing the soul: The shaping of the private self* (2nd Edn). London: Free Association.

Rosenblatt, P. C. (2000) Ethics in qualitative interviewing in grieving families. In A. Memon & R. Bull (Eds), *Handbook of the psychology of interviewing*. Chichester: Wiley.

Roulston, K. (2006) Close encounters of the 'CA' kind: A review of literature analysing talk in research interviews. *Qualitative Research*, **6**, 515–534.

Sacks, H. (1992) *Lectures on conversation*. Oxford: Blackwell.

Sacks, H., Schegloff, E. & Jefferson, G. (1974) A simplest systematics for the organization of turn-taking in conversation. *Language*, **50**, 696–735.

Sarup, M. (1996) *Identity, culture and the postmodern world*. Athens, GA: University of Georgia Press.

Schafer, R. (1981) *Narrative accounts in psychoanalysis*. Worcester, MA: Clark University Press.

Schegloff, E. A. (1996) 'Confirming allusions: Towards an empirical account of action', *American Journal of Sociology*, **102**, 161–216.

Schegloff, E. A. (1992) Introduction to Harvey Sack's Lectures on conversation. In *Lectures on conversation*. Oxford: Blackwell.

Schegloff, E. A. (2007) *Sequence organization: A primer in conversation analysis* (Vol. 1). Cambridge: Cambridge University Press.

Schegloff, E. A., & Sacks, H. (1973) Opening up closing. *Semiotica*, **8**, 289–327.

Schraw, G., Olafson, L. & Wadkins, T. (2007) Doing the things we do: A grounded theory of academic procrastination. *Journal of Educational Psychology*, **99**(1), 12–25.

Shaw, R. L., Booth, A., Sutton, A. J., Miller, T., Smith, J. A., Young, B. Jones, D. R. & Dixon-Woods, M. (2004) Finding qualitative research: An evaluation of search strategies. *BMC Medical Research Methodology*, 4: article number 5. Available at: http://www.biomedcentral.com/1471-2288-4-5

Sibbald, B. (2008) Regulation has run amok. *British Medical Journal*, **337**, a2916.

Silverman, D. (1998) *Harvey Sacks: Social science and conversation analysis.* Cambridge: Polity.

Silverman, D. (2006) *Interpreting qualitative data* (3rd edn). London: Sage.

Skevington, S. M., MacArthur, P. & Somerset, M. (1997) Developing items for the WHOQOL: A study of contemporary beliefs about quality of life related to health in Britain. *British Journal of Health Psychology*, **2**, 55–72.

Smith, J. A. & Osborn, M. (2008) *Interpretative phenomenological analysis.* In J. A. Smith (Ed.), *Qualitative psychology: A practical guide to research methods* (2nd Edn) (pp. 53–80). London: Sage.

Smith, J. A., Brewer, H., Eatough, V., Stanley, C., Glendinning, N. & Quarrell, O. (2006) The personal experience of Juvenile Huntington's Disease: An interpretative phenomenological analysis of parents' accounts of the primary features of a rare genetic condition. *Clinical Genetics*, **69**, 486–496.

Smith, J. A. & Eatough, V. (2007) Interpretative phenomenological analysis. In E. Lyons & A. Coyle (Eds) *Analysing qualitative data in psychology* (pp. 35–50). London: Sage.

Smith, J. A. & Osborn, M. (2007) Pain as an assault on the self: An interpretative phenomenological analysis of the psychological impact of chronic benign low back pain. *Psychology and Health*, **22**(5), 517–534.

Smith, J. A. & Osborn, M. (2008) 'Interpretative phenomenological analysis'. In J. A. Smith (Ed.), *Qualitative psychology: A practical guide to research methods* (2nd Edn) (pp. 53–80). London: Sage.

Smith, J. A., Flowers, P. & Larkin, M. (2009) *Interpretative phenomenological analysis: Theory, method and research.* London: Sage.

Sneijder, P. & Te Molder, H. F. M. (2004) 'Health should not have to be a problem': Talking health and accountability in an internet forum on veganism. *Journal of Health Psychology*, **9**, 599–616.

Sneijder, P. & Te Molder, H. F. M. (2005) Moral logic and logical morality: Attributions of responsibility and blame in online discourse on veganism. *Discourse and Society*, **16**, 675–696.

Spagnoli, A. & Gamberini, L. (2007) Interacting via SMS: Practices of social closeness and reciprocation. *British Journal of Social Psychology*, **46**, 343–364.

Sparrman, A. (2005) Video recording as interaction: Participant observation of children's everyday life. *Qualitative Research in Psychology*, **2**, 241–255.

Speer, S. A. (2002) 'Natural' and 'contrived' data: A sustainable distinction? *Discourse Studies*, **4**, 511–525.

Speer, S. A. & Hutchby, I. (2003) From ethics to analytics: Aspects of participants' orientations to the presence and relevance of recording devices. *Sociology*, **37**, 315–337.

Stelma, J. H. & Cameron, L. J. (2007) Intonation units in spoken interaction: Developing transcription skills. *Text and Talk*, **27**(3), 361–393.

Stewart, K. & Williams, M. (2005) Researching online populations: The use of online focus groups for social research. *Qualitative Research*, **5**, 395–416.

Stewart, P., Stears, A., Tomlinson, J. & Brown, M. (2008) Regulation – The real threat to clinical research. *British Medical Journal*, **337**: a1732.

Stokoe, E. & Edwards, D. (2008) 'Did you have permission to smash your neighbour's door'? Silly questions and their answers in police–suspect interrogations. *Discourse Studies*, **10**, 89–111.

Strauss, A. & Corbin, J. (1998) *Basics of qualitative research: Techniques and procedures for developing grounded theory* (2nd Edn). Thousand Oaks, CA: Sage Publications.

Strauss, A. L. & Corbin, J. (1990) *Basics of qualitative research: Grounded theory procedures and techniques.* London: Sage.

Suddaby, R. (2006) From the editors: What grounded theory is not. *Academy of Management Journal,* **49**(4), 633–642.

Temple, M. & McVittie, C. (2005) Ethical and practical issues in using visual methodologies: The legacy of research-originating visual products. *Qualitative Research in Psychology,* **2**, 227–239.

Ten Have, P. (1999) *Doing conversation analysis: A practical guide.* London: Sage.

Toerien, M. & Kitzinger, C. (2007) Emotional labour in action: Navigating multiple involvements in the beauty salon. *Sociology,* **41**, 645–662.

Van den Berg, H., Wetherell, M. & Houtkoop-Steenstra, H. (2003) *Analyzing race talk: Multidisciplinary approaches to the interview.* Cambridge: Cambridge University Press.

Van Manen, M. (1990) *Researching lived experience: Human science for an action sensitive pedagogy.* Albany, NY: State University of New York Press.

Voida, A., Mynatt, E. D., Erickson, T., & Kellogg, W. A. (2004) Interviewing over instant messaging. *Extended Abstacts of CHI 2004 Conference on Human Factors in Computing Systems, Vienna, Austria, April 24–29, 2004)* (pp. 1344–1347). New York: ACM.

Wallwork, J. & Dixon, J. A. (2004) Foxes, green fields and Britishness: On the rhetorical construction of place and national identity. *British Journal of Social Psychology,* **43**, 21–39.

Warren, C. A. B. (2002) Qualitative interviewing. In J. F. Gubrium & J. A. Holstein (Eds), *Handbook of interview research: Context and method.* Thousand Oaks, CA: Sage Publications.

Weaver, S. E. & Coleman, M. (2005) A mothering but not a mother role: A grounded theory of the nonresidential stepmother role. *Journal of Social and Personal Relationships,* **22**(4), 477–497.

Wiggins, S. & Potter, J. (2003) Attitudes and evaluative practices: Category vs. item and subjective vs. objective constructions in everyday food assessments. *British Journal of Social Psychology,* **42**, 513–531.

Wilkinson, S. (2000) Women with breast cancer talking causes: Comparing content, biographical and discursive analyses. *Feminism and Psychology,* **10**, 431–460.

Wilkinson, S. (2008) Focus groups. In J. A. Smith, *Qualitative psychology* (2nd Edn) (pp. 186–206). London: Sage.

Willig, C. (2001) *Introducing qualitative research in psychology: Adventures in theory and method.* Buckingham: Open University Press.

Willig, C. (2008a) Discourse analysis. In J. A. Smith (Ed.) *Qualitative psychology: A practical guide to research methods* (2nd Edn) (pp. 160–185). London: Sage.

Willig, C. (2008b) *Introducing qualitative research in psychology: Adventures in theory and method* (2nd Edn). Buckingham: Open University Press.

Willig, C., & Stainton-Rogers, W. (2008) Introduction. In C. Willig & W. Stainton-Rogers (Eds), *The Sage handbook of qualitative research in psychology* (pp. 1–12). London: Sage.

Wood, C. & Finlay, W. M. L. (2008) British National Party representations of Muslims in the month after the London bombings: Homogeneity, threat, and the conspiracy tradition. *British Journal of Social Psychology,* **47**, 707–726.

Wooffitt, R. (2001) A socially organized basis for displays of cognition: Procedural orientation to evidential turns in psychic–sitter interaction. *British Journal of Social Psychology,* **40**, 545–563.

Wootton, A. J. (1997) *Interaction and the development of mind.* Cambridge: Cambridge University Press.

World Medical Association (2008) *Declaration of Helsinki: Ethical principles for research involving human subjects.* Available from: http://www.wma.net/e/policy/b3.htm

Yardley, L. (2008) Demonstrating validity in qualitative psychology. In J. A. Smith (Ed.), *Qualitative research in psychology: A practical guide to research methods* (2nd Edn) (pp. 235–251). London: Sage.

Author Index

Subject Index